W9-BON-812

DEC 2 3 2009

The Power
of
Creative
Dreaming

The Power
of
Creative
Dreaming

Pamela Ball

GRAMERCY BOOKS
NEW YORK

Published by Gramercy Books, an imprint of Random House
Value Publishing, a division of Random House, Inc., New York,
by arrangement with Arcturus Publishing Limited.

Gramercy is a registered trademark and the colophon is a
trademark of Random House, Inc.

Random House
New York • Toronto • London • Sydney • Auckland
www.randomhouse.com

Printed and bound in India

A catalog record for this title is available from the
Library of Congress.

ISBN-13: 978-517-22796-1
ISBN-10: 0-517-22796-7

10 9 8 7 6 5 4 3 2 1

Go confidently in the direction of your dreams. Live the life you've imagined. As you simplify your life, the laws of the universe will be simpler.

Henry David Thoreau

CONTENTS

INTRODUCTION   11

1. PERSPECTIVES ON CREATIVE DREAMING   21

2. DREAM MANAGEMENT   31
Our Dreaming Selves   33
Ways of Controlling Dreams   38
The MILD Technique   47
Prolonging Dreams   52
The Hypnagogic and Hypnopompic States   59
Dream Signs   62
Altered States of Consciousness   66
The Value of Meditation   68
Waking-Induced Lucid Dreaming (WILD)   70
Dream of a Creative Dream   72
How to Keep a Dream Journal   74
Analyzing Dream Structure   78
Errors and Bizarre Elements   82
Increasing Dream Recall   87
Developing Awareness   88
Learning to Wake at Will   89

CONTENTS

Directing Dreams   89
The RISC Technique   90
Balancing Creative and Waking Experiences   92

3. MESSAGES FROM THE GODS   99
Shamanic Societies   104
The Making of a Shaman   105
Following in Shamanism's Footsteps   108
Linking East and West   109
New Age Movement   111

4. THE POWERS THAT BE   113
The *Siddhis*   115
Out-of-body Experiences and Astral Travel   117
Reality States   120
The *Chakras*   127
Creativity in Dreaming   130

5. HEALING THROUGH DREAMS   143
Inner Balance   150
Shamanic Healing   155
Totem and Power Animals   158
Transitional Stages   162
    Puberty   162
    Pregnancy   169
    Death   174
    Illness   183
    Mental disorders   187
    Nightmares   197
The Inner Healer   210

6. THE TOOLS OF THE PSYCHE   213
Archetypes   216
The Tarot   237

Mythological Figures   249
Animals   270
Birds and Flight   278
Astrology   280
Numbers   288

7. CREATING THE WORLD YOU WANT   295
Witnessing   298
Developing your Spiritual Self   304

8. YOUR WORKBOOK   315
Workplan   319
     Gestalt Method   324
Questioning your Dream Characters   325
Daily Audit Plan   327
Incubating the Dream you Want (CARDS Method)   329
Remembering your Dreams   330
Keeping a Dream Journal   332
Recording your Dream   333
How to have a Creative Dream   334
Reality Check   335
Incubating a Specific Creative Dream   337
The MILD Technique   339
Prolonging a Creative Dream   341
Analyzing your Dream   343
Advanced Techniques   344
Refining the Spinning Technique   346
Creating a New Dream Scenario   348
Directing your Dreams   349
The IFE Technique   350
Relaxation Technique   351
Contemplation and Meditation   352
Dealing with Nightmares   353

CONTENTS

Conversations with Dream Characters 354

Addressing Recurrent Nightmares 357

Carrying the Dream Forward 359

Resolving your Dream 360

Tools for Creative Dreaming 361

    Crystals 361

    Archetypal Images 366

    Myths, Astrological Planets, Numbers, etc. 367

Meeting with Spirit 368

Creative Projects 369

9. LIVING WITH CREATIVE DREAMS 371

An Insider's View 376

NOTEBOOK 383

Bibliography 392

INTRODUCTION

The least technical definition that can be found for creative or lucid dreaming is 'dreaming with awareness'. This encompasses a multitude of methods, a multitude of levels and a multitude of experiments. A lucid dream, however, can also be called an altered state of consciousness, and it frequently is. It may also be experienced only occasionally, or, conversely, on a regular basis. Indeed, whether such a phenomenon even exists, except on a subjective level, is debatable. For every person who believes implicitly in it, there is another who thinks such a belief is completely mad and the believer should be locked up! Scientists cannot agree, either, some saying that researching creative dreaming is a waste of time while others are prepared to devote most of their professional lives to the subject. Given this wide divergence of opinion, it is small wonder if the individual who initially takes an interest in lucid dreaming becomes totally confused and decides that the subject is best left alone.

However, as with all things we do not understand, there is fascination and, because we find ourselves fascinating above anything else in life, we persevere. The starting point for an understanding of creative dreaming is acceptance that many layers of consciousness are available to us during sleep, layers of which we have previously chosen not to be aware. Once we have thrown off the straitjacket of previously held belief, we can begin to explore those levels for ourselves.

In this book we have attempted to combine the practical with the theoretical. If we look at creative dreaming in its historical perspective, we discover that people have used dreaming with awareness – another term for the phenomenon – since time immemorial, to help themselves and their communities. Lucid dreaming is not new, although it is only in the 20th century that a methodology has been developed for it, by psychologists. We look at many of these methods and also at the uses to which various cultures have put lucid dreaming, or something very akin to it.

Creative dreaming offers many attractions and opportunities. It can help us to venture beyond the normal boundaries and restrictions which we tend to impose upon ourselves, and develop our ability to fulfil our fantasies. When we dream lucidly we are, in principle, free to do and be whatever we want, restricted only by our ability to imagine and devise a scenario for ourselves. We are bound by no known laws, but can venture forth into our own universe where we can do and be anything and everything.

The experience of lucid dreaming is different for each person, and only you will know whether your dream has been a lucid one or not. This does not matter – even if you cannot definitely prove that your dream has been lucid, if you have gained insight or released tension through it, then it has been of value. Despite the interest of scientists and the establishment of dream laboratories, the many recorded experiences of lucid dreaming have proved impossible to assess fully.

So why should you want to have lucid dreams? What can you do with them? Apart from the pleasure of 'learning to fly', and the ability to ignore the physical boundaries that hamper us in everyday life, we can also reach areas of existence that are beyond us in waking reality. One can become a veritable Peter Pan (or even Tinkerbell) during lucid dreams. Many people have described their first lucid dream as the most wonderful sensation of their lives. Others have discovered lucid dreaming as a result of trying to control unpleasant dreams and at the same time have gained a measure of control over their ordinary, everyday lives.

It is also possible to develop creative responses to the symbols in your dreams and to learn how to express yourself in ways hitherto unimagined in your day-to-day life, through painting, words, sculpture or movement and dance. Creative dreaming may help you come to terms with the 'slings and arrows' of your workaday existence and to understand why certain circumstances have occurred. Finally, through creative dreaming, you may be able to enhance your ability to heal and be healed. All these things are possible once you have moved beyond the initial experimentation stage. Just as a child learns through play, so through creative dreaming you have the chance to learn the art of living fully, provided that you keep your feet firmly on the ground.

The aspect of living more fully is perhaps the most exciting of all. Not only can bad dreams be controlled through dreaming with awareness, but problems can also be solved in an intuitive and innovative way. Lucid dreaming is also flexible in that it enables you to try out or reject different ways of working. It is possible to practise new ways of reacting or responding to others, such as overcoming shyness, becoming more extrovert in company, or changing the emotional tone within a certain situation. For instance, if a member of your family constantly makes you angry, you could ask your dreaming self for assistance in overcoming the problem so that you can control the anger.

As you begin to know yourself better, and gain mastery over your dreams, you will be able to practise new ideas and behaviour within the safe framework of the dream. You decide whether you have got it right. Since a creative dream will often fade when you start to question your actions, you can practise the art of waking up successfully and can give yourself the command to wake up in a good mood, or with enough motivation to complete a task.

When we are in the lucid state, we have access to a great deal of information. Many creative dreamers become conscious of a kind of inner guidance through lucid dreaming. Whether this guidance is accepted as the Higher Self, a guardian angel or a spiritual helper does not really matter. The consensus of opinion is that there is an integral part of us that seems to know better than our conscious self what is right for us. In putting ourselves in touch with this aspect, we are often able to crystallize the type of inner personality that will be most helpful to us as we move through life. The person who consistently uses meditation can manifest a being who becomes a helper, as Jung did with his 'Wise Old Man', whom he named Philomen. Dreamers can also manifest an able inner mentor. When this mentor becomes available to us in both waking and sleeping hours, we are much more able to act with integrity and grace in everyday life. (Techniques for calling upon this aspect are given in Section 8.)

The better able we are to control our dreams, the greater the access we will have to differing options of behaviour, which turn us away from extreme self-interest to care for others and the environment. In lucid dreaming, we are able to make adjustments that would not be possible in everyday life, or would take too long. We are able to experiment with changes which are ours alone. Because they do not take place in the real world, these changes harm no one and yet allow us to perceive what life might be like were they to occur. It has been discovered that at certain stages in the development of control over creative dreaming some very bizarre distortions take place. This quality can be utilized to create an environment in a dream that pleases us and perhaps allows us to release our creativity. We are able to create – or uncreate – whatever we like.

The process of being creative within lucid dreams can involve using their rich imagery to keep us emotionally balanced. We can put our creativity to good use by devising a project portfolio which helps us to remain grounded. How often has an aspect of a dream struck you as particularly weird or beautiful and worthy of note? Often objects in a dream scenario have a particular resonance and these can be preserved for contemplation later. In both the hypnagogic (semi-waking) state and in lucid dreaming, flashes of colour and patterns have especial meaning. Too often, though, these are lost as everyday concerns take over. Maintaining lucidity is one of the biggest challenges for the lucid dreamer. When we become aware that we are using our dreams creatively, then the tendency is for us to wake and lose the lucidity. If you are able to preserve these colours or patterns, or can make a fair representation of them, you are truly putting yourself in touch with real creativity.

Each of us holds within basic archetypal patterns accessible through ordinary dreams. Lucid dreams give us the added bonus of bringing them into conscious memory. If you keep a notebook with you at all times, you can make quick notes or drawings when something strikes you as particularly relevant to objects in your dreams. For example, you might find that in waking life your eye is caught by the formation of windows and arches because of a dream which featured these edifices.

You do not have to be a great artist, sculptor or writer to be creative. All you need are projects which please you. To give a personal example – through a dream in which there was a particular quality of light, a kind of glow, I was able to decorate my home in a way that created peace and tranquillity. Conversely, I was not able to reproduce a certain shade of green of which I was conscious in another dream. In waking life, I have very little sense of colour or tone. The only way I can get such things right is to reproduce the feeling I have of them from the dream. While the inability to do this successfully can be frustrating, the sense of achievement when I do manage it is tremendous.

In our fast-moving world there is not always time to contemplate dreams in the way our ancestors may have done. There will be many who feel that, having assessed their dream for meaning and significance, they do not wish to explore it further. It is not suggested that all dreams should be subjected to every technique covered in this book – some dreams will lend themselves more naturally to one technique than to another. It is suggested that looking at dreams for inspiration and help in living is worthwhile.

One way of using dreams is to take them forward into some kind of resolution through your own creativity. You might try to capture what could happen next through the medium of words, poetry, music or art. Lucid dreaming could even help to enhance your artistic ability in these areas. This actually sounds more difficult than it is in practice. You do not need to share with anyone the results of what you are doing, so once you have got over feeling rather stupid and totally frustrated because your pen/brush/body or whatever you are using will not do what you want it to, you can begin.

Initially the idea is to have fun with your dream and your aim is to be as creative as possible, so finding that you are expecting a character to act in a bizarre way does not really matter. Simply experiment and see what happens. There is a serious intent behind using your dreams in this way. You may find, for example, that an answer to a difficulty or problem pops up spontaneously. You may find your creative projects allowing you to get rid of negative thoughts or feelings. This can be helpful in effecting healing in some way.

Sometimes your dreams will seem to have no relevance at all to your everyday life, nor will their interpretation necessarily reveal great truths. However, using your dreams to initiate creative projects can start a process where blocked energies allow much more freedom of expression within your everyday life.

Another pleasing aspect of creative dreaming is the notion that in this state we are able to effect healing. Able lucid dreamers are convinced that accelerated physical healing is possible. There is no reason to believe that healing of the emotions and of some spiritual ailments – such as the tendency to repeat mistakes without understanding why – could not also be helped through creative dreaming.

It is important here to sound a word of warning over the expectations one might have as regards lucid dreaming and dreaming with awareness. A particular method may work for one person and not another. This does not mean the method is wrong *per se*, but wrong for the person for whom it did not work.

The art of creative dreaming puts one in mind of a scientific study conducted with monkeys. The scientists discovered that the habit of washing potatoes was transferred from one group to another without any apparent interaction between the groups.

The basic behaviour was transmitted and learned in some non-specific way but without being understood. Creative dreaming is similar in that the skill seems to be transferable without necessarily understanding how it was learnt. Everyone has within them the ability to dream lucidly, but how this ability develops is up to them. Those who have found their own way of working with their dreams do not have the right to say that their way is best. Equally, those who practise various methods with little success have no right to cast aspersions on the validity of the method simply because they themselves have failed with it. Keeping an open mind on all counts is a necessary development of your newfound skill and should be rigorously practised.

Open-mindedness is essential to reaching an understanding of the various altered states of consciousness, of how lucid dreaming may be compared with out-of-the-body experiences and astral travel, and of the uses to which it may be put during states of transition – such as puberty, pregnancy and death – and in different types of healing.

The search for knowledge and deeper meaning through lucid dreaming involves understanding the significance of various esoteric symbols, images and ideas. We look at the uses of archetypes, the tarot, myths, astrology and numerology to assist you in reaching your own personal truth. Understanding your personal lucidity and enlightenment will bring you to a state beyond mere lucid dreaming to an experience which is sometimes called 'witnessing'.

In the last two sections of the book, we bring you back to earth with various practical exercises and techniques in lucid dreaming and creative dreamwork. These should enable you to apply what you have learnt and to recognize how these tools provide the means for you to be truly in charge of your own destiny.

It is but a short step from such an awareness to the belief that, through lucid dreaming and using your creativity, you can build a world in which you can take a great deal of pride. Creative dreaming is a state between realities, those of the waking self and the dreaming self. When we are able to harness both realities, we are indeed within reach of a 'Brave New World' of our making.

SECTION

1

SECTION

1

PERSPECTIVES ON CREATIVE DREAMING

Throughout history there have been fascinating glimpses of people's thoughts and beliefs on the art of creative dreaming. Plato said that the faculty of reason was suspended during sleep. Aristotle in his treatise, *On Dreams*, said, 'There is something in the conscious that tells us we are experiencing a dream.' It seems that if we know we are asleep it is a small step to know we are dreaming. Many would put it the other way round; if we know we are dreaming we must be asleep.

Popular belief has it that the first actual lucid dream to be reported in the West is in a letter from Saint Augustine in AD415. He wrote of Gennadius, a physician of Carthage, who had a dream in which he doubted the existence of an afterlife.

He saw a youth who convinced him of the reality of such a thing. Gennadius woke up but realized that he had been dreaming. The next night he dreamt of the same youth and told him the only way he knew him was because of the dream. The youth then asked how he could be seen, even though his (Gennadius') eyes were closed. This Gennadius could not answer. He therefore became convinced that when he was dead, and his eyes were closed, he would still be able to see and that therefore there had to be an afterlife.

Man has always needed reassurance that some part of him will continue to exist after death. By the 5th century AD, it was accepted that seeing was believing and therefore what was seen in a dream really existed. There was an inner state which actually had a reality. It was a short step to the realization that lucid dreaming was a conscious out-of-body experience and therefore a foretaste of the afterlife.

In the 8th century AD, Eastern disciplines, particularly that of Tibetan Buddhist yoga, were aimed at keeping the waking conscious rational state alive during creative dreaming. Indeed the Buddhists were probably the first to understand that dreams were solely the mental creation of the dreamer, but of a different dimension from the ordinary conscious. A state of lucidity would help the practitioner to control his own stray thoughts and the illusions and false conceptions of the untrained mind. In the 12th century, Sufi Ibn-El-Arabi said that the human race would benefit as a whole from controlling thought in a dream. Even today the Sufi tradition holds that 'a phenomenon will occur to the one seeking for knowledge, for a light will occur like a concrete light before his inner vision. This light is the light of all inspiration and wisdom'.

Gassendi, a contemporary of Descartes in the 17th century and much admired, both by contemporary and by later scholars, said, 'If you realize you are dreaming then you can realize you are thinking. The realization that you are dreaming is a function of the brain. Because the brain possesses the power of reflection this is consciousness." Creative dreaming was therefore seen as a product of the brain rather than a journey of the soul or a message from God. At the threshold of the Age of Reason, the perception was one of rationality. The Marquis de Hervey de Saint Dennis described very clearly the development of the abilities needed to control dreaming. These are discussed more fully in the second section of the book.

By the time we meet Frederick van Eeden, who is the first person to actually use the term 'lucid dreams', there is a very clear description of what he believes happens in this state. In a paper presented to the Society for Psychical Research in 1913, he said:

> 'In these lucid dreams the reintegration of the psychic functions is so complete that the sleeper remembers day-life and his own condition, reaches a state of perfect awareness, and is able to direct his attention, and to attempt different acts of free volition. Yet the sleep, as I am able confidently to state, is undisturbed, deep and refreshing. I obtained my first glimpse of this lucidity during sleep in June 1897, in the following way.

> 'I dreamt that I was floating through a landscape with bare trees, knowing that it was April, and I remarked that the perspective of the branches and twigs changed quite naturally. Then I made the reflection, during sleep, that my fancy would never be able to invent or to make an image as intricate as the perspective movement of little twigs seen in floating by.'

Here we have the realization that he is dreaming, the changes in perception, and the sense of wonder. All these are aspects of creative dreaming which have become widely accepted by others as part of their own lucid dreams. Van Eeden also highlights for us the illusory nature of the initial and intermediate stages of lucid dreaming. Elsewhere he says:

'This gave me a very curious impression of being in a fake world, cleverly imitated, but with small failures. I took the broken glass and threw it out of the window, in order to observe whether I could hear the tinkling. I heard the noise all right and I even saw two dogs run away from it quite naturally. I thought what a good imitation this comedy world was.'

Other dream investigators, while not necessarily acknowledging lucid dreaming *per se*, were aware of the presence of consciousness in some dreams. Freud said, 'Consciousness in dreams can provide a positive attitude towards life as well as escapism from it.'

Mary Arnold-Forster learned to deal with her frightening dreams by telling herself they were 'only dreams'. She also seems to have had success in teaching this method to children. It does not appear, however, that Arnold-Forster developed her dream consciousness very extensively, perhaps due to the fact that her only source of information on lucid dreams seems to have been the very few experiences of W. H. Myers.

We cannot do better to introduce creative dreaming and the art of dream manipulation and control than to quote Delarge, who states:

'I say to myself, here I am in a situation which may be troublesome or pleasant, but I know very well that it is completely unreal. From this part of the dream, knowing that I cannot run any risk, I allow scenes to unfold themselves before me. I adopt the attitude of an interested spectator watching an accident or catastrophe which cannot affect him. I think: Over there are waiting for me people who want to kill me; I then try to run away; but suddenly, I realize that I am dreaming and I say to myself since I have nothing to fear I am going to meet my enemies, I will defy them, I will even strike them in order to see what will happen. However, although I am sure enough of the illusory character of the situation to adopt a course of action which would be unwise in real life, I have to overcome an instinctive feeling of fear. Several times I have in this way thrown myself on purpose into some danger in order to see what would come of it.'

Today as then, one discussion which will rage on and on is about why we have dreams and what they mean. There is almost always a huge dichotomy between those who believe that the purpose of dreaming is purely for physiological reasons and those who subscribe to the belief that we dream to ensure psychological health. Some of the former beliefs are discussed elsewhere in the book. This school of thought holds that dreams are primarily mental nonsense with absolutely no meaning whatsoever.

Dreamworkers of the second persuasion are committed to the idea that we dream for psychological reasons. For them, dreams contain important information about the self or some aspect of one's waking life. This type of dream almost always needs to be interpreted (preferably by someone other than the dreamer) though the dreamer has the final say as to what the true interpretation is.

There is a third group who are of the opinion that neither of the two extreme positions are necessarily right or wrong. In their view both ideas may be right, wrong or both and a dream may be of psychological significance but also be physiologically driven. Dreams can therefore be either meaningful or meaningless.

There is a fourth school of thought which would indicate that dreams are, in fact, the knowledge of an inner wisdom. This is expressed in a form which the dreamer is capable of interpreting in many different ways. Such a way of thinking would suggest that the dreamer is given the information so that the dream may be used to make sense of something which is not nonsensical but is 'beyond sense'. We develop this idea further in Creating the World You Want, but it is vital at this point to gain some understanding of the various theories which have developed around dreams over the last one hundred years.

We now know that the nervous system contains two types of nerve cells (excitatory and inhibitory) and that inhibitory neurones play a more important role in the higher functions of the brain – that is, that the nervous system works by inhibiting the grosser functions in favour of the more subtle. Freud knew of the excitatory function and therefore decided that it was possible to discharge nervous energy through 'motor activity'. This is seen nowadays in the management of stress through exercise – a physical release for pent-up energies. Dreams perform a similar function on a mental level, a kind of mental gymnastics.

To understand creative dreaming fully, we must have a basic comprehension of the meaning and function of all types of dreams. We need to have some kind of idea as to what their purpose is for us, from both a psychological and spiritual point of view. How can we use our dreams to help us manage our everyday lives? Can we make a radical shift in our lives and change them for the better and not make use of dreams? Certainly we can ascertain that dreams will often highlight our innermost fears or will warn of impending sickness. Surely we can use them in other ways to learn about ourselves and to maximize the potential within. It is not enough to remark on the fact that something is happening in a dream – we also need to know why. What was the rationale behind the dream? To do this we must be able to remember our dreams.

As people moved away from the theory that dreams 'simply happened', and people became more interested in psychological theory, many came to believe that dreams contained wishes and desires which were unacceptable to the conscious mind and so were somehow repressed. According to Freud and his followers, such dreams were predominantly sexual and quite basic in their content. His theory was that these dreams were deliberately suppressed by that part of ourselves which he named the Ego – the conscious self. This, he believed, explained why dreams are so often easily forgotten. We all apparently have a part of ourselves which acts as monitor and does not allow us access to such material except when the conscious boundaries are removed. Freud's theory was that dreaming exists to permit us to get rid of basic instinctual impulses without harm to ourselves or others. In that way, we are able to preserve our psychological integration.

We remember dreams when the internal balance is disturbed and we do need to make sense of what is going on at the level of these unconscious wishes. All we have to do is to reveal the original impulse, and we can only do that by removing the layers with which we have covered the wish or desire. By learning a technique which Freud called 'free association' and asking the question, 'What does this make me think of?', it is possible to work therapeutically to reveal the hidden content. Initially it would therefore need someone skilled in the art of dream interpretation to assist in working through the problem. Such facilitation is required partly because the technique requires you to work backwards until there is nothing else to be dredged up out of your subconscious. Partly it was felt at that stage of discovery that only someone trained in psychoanalysis would have the knowledge to uncover the hidden meanings. Put more succinctly, it is necessary for us to confront our dreams. Interestingly, this is similar to the idea held in Shamanic cultures that we must confront our demons. As has been remarked later, most religious beliefs hold that a better spiritual state can be attained by working with those aspects of the personality which give problems.

Many psychoanalysts have found themselves unable to go along with Freud's theories. Jung, for example, was of the belief that there was an intrinsic learning process inherent in the dreaming process. Our dreams put us in contact with a source of information which would not be readily available to us in any other way.

SECTION

2

SECTION 2

DREAM MANAGEMENT

OUR DREAMING SELVES

It has been ascertained that dreaming plays a part in the development of the young human being. It is the most helpless of all animals at birth and needs physical parental protection for at least as long again as the period of nine months in the womb – conventionally, of course, much longer. Sleep is a natural way of ensuring that the baby is kept in one place and that growth, learning and the development process continues apace within a secure environment. Rapid Eye Movement (REM) – an indication of a specific type of activity within the brain – has been detected in babies in the womb, and certainly occurs in the sleep patterns of a young child.

The theory then developed that a baby dreams itself into existence. In slightly more technical terms, there is an internal source of excitation during REM sleep which enhances the growth of the child's nervous system. According to one eminent sleep researcher, this allows for the testing and practising of genetically inherited patterns of behaviour without there being any conscious movement. This theory is interesting in that it could account for certain tendencies towards various types of illness – both mental and physical, hitherto thought to be genetically inherited – in families. Examples are heart disease, breast cancer, alcoholism, depression and even what is now called the addictive personality. It can also be seen that this testing and practising is very close to the conscious use of creative dreaming. It has still not been clarified whether we sleep in order to dream or whether dreaming developed as a function of sleep, but we do have some clues in the development of children's waking perceptions of dreams.

Any parent is well aware of the way in which a child can be terrified by his or her own dreams. This is principally because initially a child believes that a dream occurs outside himself – in other words, his dream is actually happening to him – and therefore he has no control over what goes on.

The second stage, the development of the ability to differentiate between an inner reality and one which is external, occurs fairly predictably as the child begins to grow. He realizes that he can exercise a degree of control over circumstances around him, and therefore dreams become partially an external event and partially internal. The child realizes that it is *his* dream and that it will go away if he wakes up.

A third stage of awareness can occur when a child recognizes that the dream is something inside himself and has no reality within the everyday world, while still being very real to him. He can then accept that it is his mind which is producing the images. There is an acceptance that it is 'only a dream'. The inner world is separate from the outer world. Many children develop the ability to recognize within the dream that they are dreaming; this, of course, is the precursor to creative dreaming.

During dreams, the majority of both children and adults tend to remain within the first stage of awareness (i.e. that the dream is an external event). In terms of childhood development, these various realizations take place at relatively predictable stages of growth. An adult dreamer will accept that the second stage is a transition process often recognized by hindsight. The realisation that the dream world has a reality of its own, separate from the material world, is a conscious act and many will not wish to take their knowledge any further than that. The next stage of development occurs only when that recognition is incorporated into the dream scenario itself and then we begin the process of creative dreaming. We have to learn, or rather train ourselves, to lucid dream.

Creative Dream Development

We can assume that lucid dreaming is an extension of the art of dreaming. Taking into account that children often develop the ability to creative dream spontaneously, we can see that, equally, the art of lucid dreaming can easily be forgotten. Therefore, if we are to ensure that everyone can make use of the rich source of information available to us, we first need to relearn how to achieve the altered state of consciousness known as creative dreaming. We then need to ensure that the knowledge and practice are passed on in such a way that they become part of our natural inheritance. Grotesque or strange dreams will no longer seem quite so strange and lucid dreaming will become one of the ways of educating ourselves and ensuring the survival of the most able. Sleep then becomes a natural tool rather than simply a means of regeneration – either physical or mental.

Dreaming sleep is seen as having a distinct advantage over other types of sleep in that there is some merit in there being a mechanism which allows the human being to have a kind of reprogramming function. This prevents the life of the individual from being contaminated by incoming material. Indeed, the brain seems to work in a sort of compare-and-contrast mode. This means that before a piece of knowledge is assimilated, the waking brain runs through its database of material in order to find the closest match it can to the information presented. Only if there is an insufficiently good match does the brain accept the need for an update. It seems that women may be better equipped to assimilate new material, though this may be because they are more able to feel the information through their emotions. A real case of 'feeling it in their waters'!

Dream Function

Dreams also seem to have a part to play in reducing the excitability of the brain. REM sleep – and therefore, presumably, dreaming through the restoration of various neurochemicals – helps us to adjust on an internal level to the environments we have created. It has an effect on mood, memory and other cognitive functions. We have probably all at one time or another been aware of information overload – too much information to take in at one go.

As well as being connected with learning and memory, dreams seem also to play a part in the processing of other material dealt with by the nervous system. This includes handling traumatic experiences and necessary emotional adjustment to various stresses. It is probably for this reason that in Post-Traumatic Stress Syndrome, handling the nightmares that ensue is a valid part of the healing process.

This ties in with the premise that in dreams we have the opportunity to experience – in manageable fashion – those dramas we play out that reflect our true psychological state and the changes that are occurring spontaneously. Dreams are therefore a kind of experimental forum where we can try out changes in our inner psyche before manifesting them in waking life. This clearly aids psychological change and transformation.

Accepting that dreams are a tool for psychological change means that while dreams that we remember are important and of use to us, those that we 'forget' will be equally valid. It would be better to call these dreams 'those we do not retain' rather than 'those we forget', since because dreams are a subjective experience – they happen inside us – we have no proof that we *have* forgotten them except that obtained through scientific exploration. Put simply, dream researchers have discovered that when there is REM activity, the subject is usually dreaming, so the assumption is that when there is REM activity a dream is occurring. (When awakened during this time, the subjects will more often than not remember their dreams.) Under normal sleep conditions, we do not know we have been dreaming unless we remember the dreams.

As the human being develops language he has a tool which enables him to vocalize his concerns, yet at some level there may be no need for him to remember or interpret the dreams he has. The question arises whether, without language, he actually would have needed to differentiate between the inner reality of the dream world and the physical external world. It could be argued that a dream will be remembered only when the sleeping self cannot properly process the material presented. This may be why we consistently forget our dreams on waking up.

However, researchers have argued that there is a process which goes on during dreaming that might be called 'reverse learning' or the opposite of learning. They also stress that it is not the same as forgetting, but is a way of ensuring that the cortex of the brain functions to its maximum efficiency. It is postulated that certain forms of neuronal activity exist which may be monitored and suppressed by a particular activity which is operated only during REM sleep. This gives a scientific twist to Freud's theory of suppression.

According to this theory, any dream is designed to have the individual actively 'unlearning' (clearing the decks of) what is no longer needed. When we do remember our dreams we are retaining exactly what we were trying to unlearn. In theory, remembering several dreams a night would bring about negative responses and reactions and thus lead to the potential for illusions, fantasies and obsessional behaviour. In fact, neither remembering dreams nor deprivation of REM sleep seems to lead to such difficulties. Creative dreaming, where the pattern of REM sleep may be disturbed – and other altered states of consciousness such as meditation – may well lead to changes in perception, but seldom to breakdown.

To reiterate, dreaming may well be an activity developed by some process of natural selection to repair and to test the brain circuits. This occurs according to a particular pattern in order to regulate behaviour and recognition. It has also been proposed that the function of sleep which leads to dreaming is in order to get rid of certain interchanges between networks of cells in the cerebral cortex. In the next section, we will look more closely at the various theories and experiments on the actual activity which takes place within the brain and body during sleeping and dreaming.

WAYS OF CONTROLLING DREAMS

Whenever one looks at creative dreaming, the first thing that strikes one is that there is a degree of control needed over both dreaming and the waking up process. Without this, it is unlikely that we shall have the ability to recall and remember what we have dreamt.

To be able to control dreams, we first have to define what 'control' actually means on an individual level. You may decide that you wish to stop having bad dreams – indeed, later in the book, we devote space to such control. You may wish to use dreams to make something happen in ordinary everyday life; again, this book gives you techniques to help this happen.

For the purposes of this section of the book, the definition of control is simply 'the potential to be able to influence, either voluntarily or involuntarily, what happens'. The suggestion is first of all that you can influence your dreams through dreaming lucidly and by asking for the dream that you want. The second suggestion is that you can have an influence on your everyday life through using your dreams. Your actions will have an effect on what occurs. You do at the same time need to differentiate between voluntary and involuntary control. Voluntary control means that you decide you want something in particular to happen and take steps to cause it – involuntary control refers to unintended consequences of your actions. An example of voluntary control in a dream is to confront a figure within a nightmare and to bring it into submission. Involuntary control is to wake up from the nightmare, not dealing with the issue in hand.

It is possible to begin to control dreams even before you enter into the dream state. The simplest way to learn control is to try to choose the topic of the dream. This is a type of dream incubation in which a person works to induce a dream to answer a question or resolve a conflict. It does not necessarily require lucidity. It is, however, a creative use of dreaming.

Often, attempts to choose a topic are initially woefully abortive and it seems that the subject of the dream has little relevance to the chosen topic. With practice, however, you will begin to see that it is what the unconscious has understood of the topic that has been processed. Supposing you have set the topic as 'the way forward.' In your dream, you become aware that you may have the image of playing a ball game with a dictionary instead of a ball. The dreaming self has interpreted forward as 'for word'.

When, after some practice, you are confident of your ability to dream lucidly, you can either accept the image for what it is or, by choice, change it into something more appropriate. For instance, you may decide that the way forward is a game of words and that you need to use your knowledge of words to help you. Then again, by recognizing that you are dreaming and deciding that you are subconsciously using the wrong technique, a need to change becomes obvious. In a creative dream, you will tell yourself that you are dreaming and change the image of the dictionary into a ball.

Another aspect of dream control is to try to influence the setting of the dream. Normally such attempts have had little success – it is almost as though the dreaming self needs to choose its own scenario to put its message across. It is actually a complete mystery as to what determines the original setting and situation where one finds oneself in a dream, unless it is the search for information and psychological balance. Some dream enthusiasts contend that dream control can only occur within the framework of the original dream setting – any actions within the dream are only appropriate within that original setting. That is, any inappropriate action we may attempt to force is blocked within that particular framework.

This line of thought does not allow for the inexplicable and sudden changes which may occur in the ordinary dream scenario. Often these spontaneous changes alert the dreamer to the fact that he or she is dreaming and open up the possibility of dream manipulation. We do have the ability to exercise what has been called concurrent control – the ability to decide on, or change, the course of a dream as it happens. We can choose to change a dream setting at will and exactly how to do this is dealt with more fully in the section on nightmares.

As one becomes more proficient at becoming – and staying – lucid, it becomes easier to change small details and then more important aspects of the dream scenario. This type of control is not exercised only in creative dreams, however. Whenever we make a choice or act in a dream we are exercising an element of control. Trained lucid dreamers are simply able to make coherent choices and actions in the knowledge that they are dreaming, and are therefore able to observe their effects on the dream scenario. The ability to control a dream setting comes from the manipulation of something which is formed from our own inner reality. When we are able to accept that that construct can be adjusted, we are able to manipulate the various parts of our dreams.

Being successful in creating a dream scenario does not necessarily mean that one has the ability to control the developing story of events in a dream. It is only with fairly comprehensive training that we are able to make adjustments to more than one component of a dream. It is the observer part of the dreamer, the self-awareness, which experiences and assesses the events happening in a dream. There is some evidence that highly motivated people can consciously choose to dream about their chosen subjects. Post-hypnotic suggestions have also been used to bring about particular dream goals. In controlling dreams there are inevitably certain questions which arise:

• Do we have more control over our experiences in dreaming than in waking?

• Can we programme or control our dreams?

• Does controlling dreams affect our waking life?

The answer to the first question is 'No, not consciously.' It is only when we choose to work consciously with our dreams and to impose an element of control on them, that we can allow ourselves to make comparisons between our waking and sleeping selves. In the waking state we are often consciously imposing controls and inhibitions, which means that we make decisions in the light of what we 'know' to be real; in the dreaming state, the subconscious rationalizes its decisions only in the light of the unfolding events of the dream story.

To the question of programming, the answer is 'Yes, with practice and belief in the ability.' As shown above, it is possible to choose, in our waking state, the topic of the dream although not necessarily the course of dream events or the actual dream scenario. Because dreams are entirely created by the inner self, it should be possible to experience anything imaginable. However, it may be that we fail because we are not being able to summon up enough creativity. We may not have enough emotional investment in the process to enable us to create suitable images or energy patterns. Some dream workers also argue that there are physiological limitations on the ability to control dream imagery.

We would suggest that in answer to the third question there is an interrelationship between the dream state and waking life. There is, in fact, a two-way traffic. Just as our waking life affects our dream time (day residue), so also we can use the information and images that we receive from dreams in various creative ways. Imposing control on our dreams allows us to move with purpose in a particular direction on a voyage of discovery. We are able to 'explore' the huge creative database of what has been, what is, and what is to come – sometimes known as the Akashic

Records. From a spiritual point of view, we are able to put ourselves in touch with the part we might call the Higher Self and make use of its ability to guide and monitor our behaviour. How well we can influence dreams will depend on our perception of our own abilities.

If perhaps we subscribe to the Buddhist belief that all life is illusion, then we will believe that we can manipulate all aspects of the dream process. We will believe that anything is possible and that without losing consciousness we can pass from one state of reality to the next without difficulty and without harm. The ultimate aim is to achieve union with the Absolute, whether we do this through dreams or through death. It is through manipulation and passing through the various states of illusion that we finally reach a state of bliss. Dreams are just one stage of this unreality, and creative dreams are a realization of that state of illusion.

Masters of Tibetan dream yoga have perfected the art of passing in and out of sleep without losing consciousness. The Tibetan Buddhists, creators of the dream yoga, teach that it is possible to control every aspect of dream imagery. They use dream control as a method of understanding the illusory nature of all experience. They have as their goal the transcending of the relative state and the embracing of the Absolute. In the 'Doctrine of the Dream State' from *Tibetan Yoga and Secret Doctrines*, we find the following instructions:

'At the outset, in the process of realizing [the dream] to be *maya*, abandon all feeling of fear;
And, if the dream be of fire, transform the fire into water, the antidote of fire.
And if the dream be of minute objects, transform them into large objects;

Or if the dream be of large objects, transform them into
small objects:
Thereby one comprehendeth the nature of dimensions.
And if the dream be of a single thing, transform it into
many things;
Or if the dream be of many things, transform them into a
single thing.'

There are, of course, many dream workers and researchers who
disagree with the principle that dreams should be controlled in
any way whatsoever. However, because you as dreamer are not
in a laboratory setting, you may want to experiment and to try
out various ways of controlling aspects of your dreams. It is
worth remembering that even now opinions vary as to why we
dream, so it is more than probable that your own beliefs will play
a significant part in how much control or what sort of control
you will impose. If you believe that dreaming helps to balance
your psychological makeup in some way, you will not wish to
impose too much control on the dreaming process. If, however,
you believe that the lucidity reached in dreams can help you gain
a measure of peace and tranquillity and eventually bliss, then you
may choose to experiment with more control. Equally, if you
believe that the dreaming self holds within itself answers which
are not consciously available, then you will wish to access this
material through dreams.

Many people would find it extremely difficult to produce creative
dreams under laboratory conditions. We are perhaps fortunate
that people such as Alan Worsley have been able to give us the
benefit of both their own personal research and that done in
co-operation with others. Worsley found that ordinary dreams
use a number of principles that can be utilized in the art of
creative dreaming. It is more than possible in lucid dreaming to
deliberately search for information on a chosen subject by

'selecting' the correct material, for instance from a particular book. The selection in ordinary dreaming is much more random. Some actions are easier than others in lucid dreams – reading is hard but is one of the best ways of testing whether a dream is creative or not. Reading single words or short phrases is relatively easy, but reading long sentences is more difficult.

Apparently, Worsley was never able suddenly to turn on a light in a dark room, although he was able to do so easily in a light room. This brings us to some interesting experimentation carried out by LaBerge and associates into the ability to manipulate light and mirror images within a lucid dream.

In this experiment, dreamers were asked, while dreaming of an indoor scenario, to find a light switch. They were then asked to try to turn it on and see what happened, then to turn it off and again see what went on. They were then additionally asked to turn the lights on and off by willing it to happen and then to observe the results. In the actual experiment these two tasks were varied, so that some people tried the act of will first and some second. One interesting finding was that people found it easier to 'use' a dimmer switch to alter the intensity of the light rather than a conventional on/off switch.

The instructions for this particular experiment asked the individuals to practise the task while they were awake before attempting it in the lucid state, so that they would know exactly what they were doing. Then they were asked to attempt each action at least once in a creative dream, using the state of lucidity as often as necessary. As soon as they woke up, they were to report what had happened.

A second part of this experiment entailed working with mirror images. The dreamers were asked to find a mirror in their dreams. Then the instruction was to observe their reflection in the mirror and, watching the image carefully, move their hand to their face. They were to note how the image behaved, finally trying to pass through the mirror into a different scenario on the other side. You may like to experiment with these tasks yourself in order to find out exactly how much control can be imposed, since it varies considerably from individual to individual.

The success of such experiments does depend on both practice and belief. This 'mirror' task is very similar to the experiments which can be done when first attempting to learn out-of-the-body techniques and astral travel by passing through barriers. Worsley found that flying close to the ground was easy, progressively getting harder the higher he rose. Ullman and Zimmerman in their own study also found that a complete change of scene would be difficult to achieve.

Creative dreams are also closely related to the act of meditation. Studies at the Maharishi International University (MIU) by Suzi Gackenbach and her colleagues discovered that trained meditators consistently reported more lucid dreams than did control subjects. Traditional Tibetan Buddhist monks believe in accordance with their teaching that meditation – and therefore creative dreams – should be virtuous and not self-promoting in nature. Tibetan thought also says you should use a form of reality-testing by trying, when you are awake, to convince yourself that you are dreaming; that is, thinking to yourself, 'This is a dream'. As mentioned elsewhere, it is advisable to be careful how you differentiate between fantasy and reality. This method helps you enhance perceptual awareness and therefore increase the frequency of lucid dreams. Physical form – size and shape – can become subject to the will when the mental powers have been properly developed by the use of yoga.

It would seem that such practices teach the practitioner of yoga to appreciate the part that his own mental powers play in the manipulation of matter. The practitioner learns by his own experience and experimentation that he can alter the character of his dreams through the use of his own will. In the dream state he learns to manipulate the images and proves they are constructs of the mind and therefore unstable. It is but a short step to the point where he realizes that form and perception are closely linked to one another in the 'real' world as much as in the world of dream and fantasy – he has discovered the power to create. Modern exponents of creative dreaming have developed a technique, based in part on ancient belief, to help them towards efficient lucid dreaming.

THE MILD TECHNIQUE

The MILD (Mnemonic Induction of Lucid Dreams) technique was developed by Dr Stephen LaBerge and his colleagues during their investigations into creative dreaming. Most people who are interested in any type of dreamwork will have developed their own version of the technique, since the recall of dreams is a tremendous aid to personal growth. The steps as they were set up are as follows:

1. Set up dream recall

Learn to wake up from dreams and to recall them. Initially, you may need to use an alarm clock, soft music or diffused light. Eventually you will be able to wake up at will by giving yourself the instruction to do so. When you do wake from a dream, try to recall it as fully as possible and, if necessary, write it down.

2. Focus your intent

As you go back to sleep, concentrate intensely on the fact that you intend to remember to recognize that you are dreaming. Use an expression to fix this idea in your mind such as: 'Next time I'm dreaming, I intend to remember I'm dreaming.' Keep focused on this idea alone and don't allow yourself to be distracted by stray thoughts.

3. See yourself become creative

Perceive through your imagination that you are back in a dream you have had, whether it is the last one or another one that you clearly remember. Tell yourself you recognize it as a dream. Look for something odd or out of place that demonstrates plainly that it is a dream. Tell yourself 'I'm dreaming' and, knowing what it feels like to be dreaming, continue to remember your chosen dream.

Then imagine what your next lucid dream will feel like. See yourself carrying out your chosen plan. For example, note when you would 'realize' you are dreaming. See yourself carrying out a dream action such as flying or spinning around.

4. Repeat until your intention is fixed

Repeat steps 2 and 3 until your intention is fixed; then drift off into sleep. Sometimes while falling asleep your mind may wander. If so, repeat the steps so that the last thing in your mind before falling asleep is the thought that you will remember to appreciate the next time you are dreaming.

This technique is a method or process designed to allow a dreamer to induce creative dreams at will at any stage during a night's sleep. Many people find that waking early and then dozing for another hour or so induces the best types of lucid dreaming, while others find that deliberately taking a nap at other times of the day has the maximum effect. The condition of the brain and body at the time of day when naps are to be taken needs to be just right to bring about lucidity – relaxed and aware. It has been established that probably the best time for creative dreaming is during the final period of sleep. In a full night's sleep it seems that lucid dreams tend to be grouped towards the end of the night – or rather the early morning – and become more likely with each REM period of the night.

Experiments and dream diaries show that creative dreams are not evenly distributed throughout the night. It seems that a period of wakefulness just before an attempt to become lucid might help to focus the dreamer's attention on the matter in hand. Thus the *intention* to dream lucidly also plays a part in the process.

In a study to discover whether short naps were better than full nights for creative dreaming, those who took part agreed to maintain the same number of total hours of sleep. They agreed to change their pattern of sleep to waking up for two hours before going back to sleep for two, or waking for four and going back to sleep again for two. This meant that the brain would have got back into its waking rhythm before being deliberately switched off again and presupposed that all the participants could easily fall asleep again.

During this study, which admittedly was very small and therefore inconclusive, there was some indication that the nap delayed by two hours was better for creative dreaming than one delayed for four hours. Lucid dreams seemed to happen more often in the nap periods than in the nights and the number of dreams per hour in the nap periods was also higher. When one looks objectively at such findings it is easy to see that creative dreams are more easily incubated in the nap periods, presumably because the hypnopompic and hypnagogic states – explained a little later in this section – are more easily accessible. The dreamer is in a relaxed state, having already slept, and is of a mind to pay more attention to his dreams and to deciding whether he is dreaming or not. It may be that dreams being more common in the later hours of sleep are more accessible and easily remembered after short naps in the morning. The results did show that such short periods of sleep were worth considering as a potentially very powerful creative dream-induction technique.

In a second study – which also unfortunately did not have many participants and therefore should probably not be considered statistically viable – the time at which people took the last one and a half hour's sleep of their night's sleep was experimented with. This was compared with what happened when people simply stayed in bed for an extra 90 minutes. The three variables considered were:

• To get up 90 minutes early, stay awake for an hour and a half, then doze for 90 minutes.
• To have the usual amount of sleep but wake up one and a half hours early and practise MILD for five minutes before completing the last 90 minute period of sleep.
• To sleep as normal, then wake up to do MILD for five minutes before sleeping an extra one and a half hours.

When the data from prolonged sleep periods were studied it became obvious that simply staying in bed for an extra one-and-a-half hours did not cause lucidity by itself. Deliberate techniques had to be used as well for any significant lucidity to be present. An analysis of the number of creative dream incidents occurring in each dream recalled showed that the 'delayed nap' lucid dream frequency was six times higher. It appears that this delay does contribute in quite a major way to success with creative dreaming. There does not seem to be a 'best' time to take a nap. It would depend a great deal on the dreamer's own routines and how he or she managed their own sleep patterns.

In a further study, participants were asked to note the times they woke up during the night and whether they had just awakened from a dream or a creative dream. This was an attempt to find out what the relationship between lucid dreaming and the cycles of the biological clock was, if any.

It is not clear whether the 64 subjects who took part expected to have creative dreams or not. If they were practising the MILD technique, one would assume that they were. In 79 per cent of the recorded awakenings, people had just had a dream; 7.6 per cent of those were lucid dreams.

In this study, creative dreams occurred later in the night on average than non-lucid dreams. When people awoke during the night without having recalled a dream, non-creative dreams then tended to happen later on during the sleep period. Most lucid dreams in this study occurred after four hours of sleep, and about half after 6.5 hours of sleep. It would appear from this study that going to sleep with the express intention of being aware of what happens during the night is enough stimulus to promote lucidity for a number of people. It would be interesting to discover whether creative dreams occur according to the rhythms of the principles of the regeneration of *chi* (essential energy). Chinese medicine dictates that organs and cellular structure are regenerated or rested according to quite stringent rules of rhythmic activity dependent on the time of day.

Yet another study attempted to find out whether creative dreaming could be stimulated by brief periods of intense focusing. Creative dream-induction techniques do require one to remember to attend to the task in hand. This particular study aimed to find out whether fifteen minutes of intense focusing had any validity as an induction technique. Again, quantifiable results were very thin on the ground. This meant that, once again, the results could not be said to be statistically significant. However, periods of focusing for fifteen minutes at nighttime (rather than in the morning) did seem to have more of an effect on an individual's chances of becoming lucid the following night.

Such experiments are very useful in the study of creative dreams, but it is worth remembering that lucid dreaming is such an individual pursuit that many people may not wish to become part of an experiment for fear of losing their hard won ability.

PROLONGING DREAMS

One of the problems which occurs as we learn to have creative dreams is that we tend to wake up within a very short interval of realizing that we have become lucid. This problem does disappear the more adept we become, but it takes time and patience to overcome the initial hurdle. Most people develop their own methods of holding on to the awareness of lucidity, but there are also some tried and tested techniques which will work.

It was Harold von Moers-Messmer who, in 1938, first described a technique for stabilizing creative dreams. He proposed the technique of looking at the ground in order to stabilize the dream image and stay lucid at the same time. Such methods of focusing on an aspect of a dream, in order to stop oneself from waking up, have also been tried by several other researchers.

As with mediumship and channelling, one's own body offers the easiest way of checking reality in dreams. When there is a change of consciousness, one's perception of the body changes and as one leaves that state and becomes more aware of the everyday world, the body can seem larger or smaller, heavier or lighter, more twisted or straighter than is usual. By looking at your hands or feet, becoming aware of them and recognizing whether they feel 'right', you can assess whether you are in the everyday world or not, and can return to normal.

This is the case in assessing whether you are awake or dreaming or indeed in a state of lucidity. If the hands or feet seem anything other than normal, then you are probably dreaming. It seems to be the act of concentration which stabilizes the surroundings; the more you make use of such techniques the easier it becomes to remain lucid or even to deepen the state of lucidity. Being conscious of your extremities, and whether they are the way they should be, allows you a measure of control over your own process.

However, one of the biggest problems in using vision to stabilize a creative dream, particularly for the novice, is that the visual sense tends to destabilize and disperse first when a dream comes to an end. Other senses can also diminish, touch usually being the last to go. Often the first sign that a lucid dream is about to come to an end is the loss of colour and clarity. It therefore becomes necessary to find some way of prolonging the state of changed consciousness in order to experience further lucidity. One of the methods favoured by experienced creative dreamers is a technique called Dream Spinning. This technique was first put on record by Stephen LaBerge after his own experiments in December 1978. In common with other methods of working with changes of consciousness, this procedure requires, for the Western mind, a certain degree of suspension of disbelief.

While the yogins and dervishes of Eastern religions had long been aware that sound and movement could influence the mind, they knew it was also an inner state of being. This concept is less acceptable to Westerners. Anyone with an interest in the inner personality does need to experiment with ways of controlling the mind with its varying states of consciousness. LaBerge correctly identified – as did others who were experimenting at the time – that it was the sensation of movement within the body rather than relaxation which allowed lucidity to be maintained, thus preventing the dreamer from properly awakening. Initially it seemed as though less muscle tension – and therefore greater relaxation – might hold the key to not waking up.

In fact for LaBerge himself it seemed that this simply led to what he termed a 'false awakening'. Further experimentation suggested that both falling backward and spinning were effective in producing creative dreams of awakening and therefore deepening the dream state. Once he had perfected the technique, he discovered he could spin himself successfully into new dream scenarios most of the time. Lucid consciousness was present in the majority of these new scenarios. His results suggest that spinning could be utilized to produce transitions to match any expectations the dreamer might have. Some of the methods used both by Laberge and others are outlined below.

Spinning

This method could be used when you have recognized that you are in the middle of a creative dream. As the dream begins to fade, but before you become properly awake, try spinning on the spot. You should do this as rapidly as possible and begin from an upright position. This should happen while you are still aware that the 'essential you' is still in the dreambody. Sometimes it will work with your arms outstretched and sometimes with your arms folded or crossed on your chest. Do experiment until you find what is best for you. Try not to have too many expectations to begin with, for as we continually point out, these techniques do take time, patience and practice. One of two things should happen next:

1. You may wake up, in which case for your own records you should first of all note the time, then lie as still as possible and finally compose yourself for sleep again. It is possible that you may go back into the same dream.

2. You may find that you have spun yourself into another vivid dream scenario, in which case, remembering that you are dreaming, continue with that particular dream.

While spinning keep repeating to yourself that the next scene will be a dream. (It is important that you experience a strong sense of movement in this for reasons which are explained elsewhere.) Experienced dreamers may also wish to instruct themselves that the dream will be a meaningful one.

During the day, if you wish, you may actually practise spinning. Try to imagine that you are in a creative dream and that it is fading. Then actually spin around as you would in the dream. Allow yourself to re-orientate within the physical world before going about your normal duties. With a little practice, you may be able to induce the feeling of spinning without actually spinning. Do treat this exercise with caution if you have, or think you have, a health condition which may make it difficult for you.

Going with the flow

A second way of prolonging lucid dreams is to use the technique of 'going with the flow'. In this method, when you find yourself in the middle of a creative dream and it is beginning to fade, the idea is that you carry on with what you were doing in the dream, but ignore the fact that the dream is losing clarity. Some people find this process somewhat difficult. Initially, this method was devised as a control experiment rather than an actual technique. Again, if it works for you then it is worth using. As you continue with whatever activity you were doing, repeat constantly to yourself, 'The next scene will be a dream.'

As a variation on both the ideas of spinning and flying, going with the flow can consist of the sensation of riding a large wave, much as one would at sea. When you become aware of instability, switch to riding the wave; the dream will either stabilize or you will find yourself in a different scenario. The up and down motion seems to have the same effect as spinning, probably because it has an effect on the very delicate structure of the inner ear which monitors balance within the body.

On a personal level, I find this method preferable. I discovered this some years ago without the benefit of other people's experience when experimenting with creative dreams. In actual fact, in waking life I detest such a movement, which is usually found on fairground rides.

Once again, it is perfectly permissible to practise during the day for these dream activities. In the first case, imagine you are in a lucid dream and that it is beginning to lose colour or becoming unstable. Then continue to do what you were already doing while remaining aware that you would be dreaming. In the second case, experience the feeling of riding the wave for a few moments, not forgetting to reorientate yourself in the everyday world when you have done so.

Rubbing your hands together
A third method of prolonging lucid dreams is to rub your (dream) hands together. For some people, this may take a little more practice, but in some ways it is an extension of the method given above of concentrating on your extremities. When you are aware that your dream is lucid and that dream begins to fade, try rubbing your hands together very hard. You do need to experience the movement and friction, because your physical body then reacts as though it was really happening. Continue to rub your hands either until you wake up or move into a different

dream scenario. Keep repeating to yourself a phrase which reminds you to remain in the dream, such as 'I am continuing to dream'.

Again take the time to practise during the waking day. Perceive yourself as being in a creative dream that is fading. Rub your hands briskly together, as you will in the dream, so that you can replicate that feeling within your dream.

Flying

Flying is not strictly a way of prolonging dreams, but it has so much in common with spinning that it is worthwhile including it among techniques to be used. It is fun to do, and once you learn how to do it, is worth doing for the sheer joy and escapism that the sense of movement and freedom gives. You can fly in just about any way you please, inhibited only by your imagination. Some people may fly with arms extended in front of them, to be aerodynamically correct. Others may find themselves with arms held by their sides. Yet others may find themselves using a kind of swimming movement, or using a paddling movement of their hands. There will also be others who quite logically grow wings in their dreams.

Trying to fly is often a good way to do a reality check. If you are flying without assistance, then you can assume that you are dreaming. The technique for dream-flying is very easy. First, push off against some kind of resistance and see if you are capable of floating in the air. Next, concentrate and see if you can move through the air towards a dream object. Lastly, see if you can pass through a barrier in your dream without rationality superimposing itself. Remind yourself that you are dreaming, but stay focused on the act of flying. You might continue the experience by repeating an affirmation which reinforces the feeling. You might, for instance, say 'If I am flying I am dreaming'. Initially, you may find that you are waking up but gradually you will find that you can hold the state of flying.

Sensory manipulation

We have already mentioned that the visual sense is often the first to fade, followed closely by the other senses. One way of prolonging your dream is to use the senses to help you to stay with the dream. Some people have used the hearing sense, by listening to voices, music, or their own breathing – a technique well known to yoga practitioners. Others have used the faculty of speech, by initiating or continuing a dream conversation with your dream characters. Touch also can play a part in anchoring a lucid dream, such as by rubbing or opening your eyes in the dream; touching your dream hands and face; touching objects or being touched.

It is fascinating to discover that apparently your senses continue to operate in dreams as they do in real life. Within the dream scenario, all of the senses tend to be enhanced when one finally achieves the art of creative dreaming. Everything seems brighter, more colourful and in greater detail than before. Those who have used mind-enhancing substances comment that lucid dreams are similar in effect to hallucinogenic drugs.

There can be great pleasure in achieving such intensity within the dream state without any other assistance. It is worthwhile experimenting and playing with these effects to find out just exactly what your own limitations are. We tend, in waking life, to block out a great deal of both sensory input and output. In creative dreaming, we are able to concentrate on what is happening with the 'inner' being and to achieve a kind of personal pleasure that is not possible in any other way. So when you have the time and the inclination, try playing in dreams with each sense in turn, to your own satisfaction. Gradually you should find that it is almost as though someone has turned on a light switch in your workaday life. The intensity spreads to ordinary everyday occurrences, allowing you to use each of the senses with more of the pure joy which is inherent in everything.

These techniques allow you to prolong your lucid dreams. You will find that as you experiment with other people's favourite methods, you will develop your own unique versions. Part of developing your own system does mean that you have to have some control over the process of waking up, and for that we must go back to basics. This requires an understanding of the hypnopompic and hypnagogic states.

THE HYPNAGOGIC AND HYPNOPOMPIC STATES

The hypnagogic and hypnopompic states can be thought of as the entrances to the 'bridge' between waking and sleeping. At one time it was thought that hypnagogic activity was more common in women and subjects of lower social class – yet at the same time others thought that those who were able to achieve an imagery closer to proper dream symbolism were more creative and less conformist in their attitude. It does seem that the more an individual's creativity is recognized and developed, the more potential there is both for hypnagogic images and later for creative dreaming. While there may be distinct differences between the hypnagogic state and lucid dreaming, many researchers feel that the boundaries between the two states are blurred.

The rich imagery which is available to us in dreams, both lucid and otherwise, means that we must learn to make use of two states of awareness. These are of prime importance in the management and understanding of dreams. Many people feel that the states of alertness which occur just before (hypnagogic) and just after (hypnopompic) sleep are akin to – or may even be – creative dreaming.

To some extent this is true, in that they are both times in which the material available to the dreaming self is presented for review. In the state of lucidity, one is aware that one is dreaming, while in the hypnagogic state one is aware that one is not. Some dream interpreters tend to feel that the hypnagogic state particularly is very similar to the creative dreaming one; it is certainly worthwhile comparing them.

In the hustle and bustle of everyday life, it is very easy to lose the images which manifest in dreams. The hypnopompic state occurs between going to sleep and waking up and is one in which we are often able to retain the images of the dream state, to remember the 'great' dreams or anything which we consider to be important. In this state, the images are not necessarily connected with one another but pop up at random, and very quickly disappear. Only if we train ourselves to remember and work with the images do we make use of this state. It is often in this condition that the dreamer hears their name called – the voice is often accepted as that of a relative who has passed over, or by some as that of the Spirit Guide or the Higher Self. When people cannot accept that this is feasible, they will often disregard this highly creative time and lose a great deal of information. With practice, it can be a time when wishes and desires can be given substance and brought into reality.

The hypnagogic state is one which occurs between being awake and going to sleep. As the untrained dreamer settles into the sleep state, images occur apparently without any particular order. Such images might be of tranquil scenes or beautiful landscapes. Archetypal images representing such things as the four elements, shamanistic animals and spirit faces – familiar or otherwise can also occur. This is akin to the random scanning which goes on when a graphic artist selects pictures to illustrate a particular theme. It is doubtful if the dreamer necessarily knows or recognizes any of the images.

As the dreamer begins to accept more responsibility for his dreams, perhaps incubating lucid ones, the images become more pertinent. The more the dreamer becomes 'open' to such images, the quicker the mind responds to the inner images which are 'the stuff of which dreams are made'. The images become more meaningful and detailed, tending to appear more rapidly when their validity is accepted by the dreamer. When the dreamer accepts the images as part of the subconscious, lucidity becomes more attainable.

It is sometimes worthwhile to use straightforward dream symbolism to make sense of the figures and shapes which can appear in the hypnagogic state. During the semi-dream state and the fluctuation of awareness of the hypnagogic period, images may be transient but nevertheless offer food for thought and a way of getting rid of the remaining traces of everyday existence (known as day residue). This leaves the mind free to deal with the more meaningful images which can then be released through either creative or conventional dreaming. It seems that the mind is more receptive to 'programming' for lucid dreaming in both the hypnagogic and hypnopompic states.

This idea of the mind needing to be programmed gives a great deal of validity to the techniques used in creative dreaming to confirm lucidity, such as affirmations and reality-testing. During the dream itself, spinning and flying and expectations of success can be enhanced by work in the hypnagogic state, because the usual filters which operate within the conscious mind are no longer operative.

The faculties of clairvoyance, clairaudience and precognition can all begin to become apparent during the hypnagogic period. During this time images often become very well-defined, auditory fragments are heard and the individual 'knows' something which was previously unknown. This awareness becomes the basis for lucidity in dreams and the dreamer learns to look for what have been called 'dream signs'.

DREAM SIGNS

These help the dreamer to recognize that he or she is in the middle of a creative dream. Not all of them occur at one time and sometimes only one triggers the awareness of the beginning of lucidity. These differences can be:

1. In the dream ego state.
2. In the characters within a dream.
3. In objects.
4. In the setting.

The ego state

In the ego state, the perception of one's self is changed. These changes are perceived mainly in the following ways:

Action

The actions taken by the dreamer are unlikely or impossible in waking life. The most extreme example of this is 'flying', although such an act seems very simple in the dream state.

Body Sense

In this state, the individual becomes conscious of an unusual sensation or sensations on or in his or her physical body. For instance, it may feel as though the skin of the body is too tight or too loose.

Emotion

During the dream, the individual experiences unusually intense emotions. As an example there may be extreme terror, or the recognition of being in love with one of their own dream characters.

Form

When there are changes in form, the dreamer becomes aware that the physique is distorted or that they are in a body that is somehow different from the way it should be (e.g. a limb may seem to be larger or smaller than it actually is in waking life).

Out of Body

Here, the dreamer becomes aware of sensations as if he or she were out of their body. This seems like an altered state of consciousness within the dream state.

Paralysis

In this state, the dreamer finds himself or herself totally unable to move, often feeling completely trapped. This awareness is recognized by meditators and spiritualists as part of changes in consciousness.

Role

Here, the dreamer is playing a role completely different from that of his or her normal waking self – perhaps one that in waking circumstances would be odd or strange (e.g. being a parent when in waking life the dreamer is childless).

Senses

The senses may be considerably sharper or duller within the dream and the individual is able to see, hear or feel things differently. Colours, for instance, may have a different tone or hue from normal.

Sexual

In this state, the dreamer may feel sexually aroused or become aware of different sensations in the erogenous area. This may occur as a result of the dream, or other sensations may be translated as being primarily sexual.

Thought

The dreamer becomes aware within the dream that they are actually thinking, or recognizes that they have altered the dream through power of thought. An example of this is changing the ending of a bad dream for a better outcome.

Characters

The characters in dreams can also show changes which can alert the dreamer to the fact that he is dreaming. As with the ego state, these are more particularly:

Action

A dream character takes an action which is either unlikely or impossible in waking life (e.g. walking through a wall).

Form

A character in a dream is in some way different from what could be expected. For instance, oddly formed or dressed inappropriately.

Place

The background of the dream seems inappropriate for a dream character and not what the dreamer would expect.

Role

The role that a dream character plays is totally different from the one known by the dreamer.

Bizarre objects

Another way in which the dreamer can become aware that they are in fact dreaming is when objects seem bizarre or inappropriate. This tends to happen in three ways:

Action

An object in a dream moves or acts in a way that would normally be impossible in waking life. For instance, a live fish moving on dry land.

Form

The dreamer becomes conscious that something is constructed in a very strange way or doesn't even exist in waking life (e.g. a composite animal which is neither one thing nor the other, perhaps with the head of a horse and the body of a cow).

Place

An object in a dream is positioned where it is not likely to be in waking life – the combination may be somewhat bizarre – for example, a penguin on a tropical island.

Setting

Finally, a dreamer may be alerted to the fact that they are not in the real world but are dreaming because the setting or environment is weird or strange. Again, this can be recognized in three ways:

Form

It may be that the environment of the dream is out of place, wrongly built or impossible. An example of this might be the dream taking place under water.

Place

Here the dream happens in a place where the dreamer is not

likely to be or want to be in waking life (e.g. being in a brothel when it is highly unlikely and indeed would seem improper).

Time
Often dreams happen where the dreamer recognizes that they are either in the past or in some future place of which they have no knowledge. This is sufficient to alert them to other bizarre elements in the dream.

As you begin to record your dreams, it is worthwhile noting anything which may constitute a dream sign, since it is then possible to build up a personal 'file' of occurrences which will alert you to the beginnings of a state of lucidity. These occurrences also alert you to the need for the development of ways in which to control your dreams and other altered states of consciousness.

ALTERED STATES OF CONSCIOUSNESS

Dreams and altered states of consciousness seem to open up channels of communication with the supernatural. Hallowell, working specifically with the Saulteaux tribe, has shown that their dreams enhance everyday life, confirming or verifying the belief system by which they live. This helps them to make various adjustments to their day-to-day experiences.

Where altered states of consciousness are accepted as normal (generally in 'primitive' cultures), dreams and creative dreams form an integral part of the development of the individual. Bourguignon, Hallowell and Wallace in their various researches have discovered the point that lucid dreams are used to expand experiences and enhance the development of the self. By studying primitive cultures and their use of dreams and/or drugs, we gain fresh insight into the workings of our own subconscious.

This is backed up by research into hallucinogenic drugs by people such as Timothy Leary and La Bere in the late 1960s.

There has developed a cultural patterning within the community of modern-day drug takers which offers well set out shared expectations and a degree of social support for the individual both during and after the experience. The development of 'positive' ritualization, such as the communal use of drug-taking equipment – whether right or wrong – approaches very closely that which is seen in primitive cultures. Such rituals seem to provide comfort, support and security in the introduction to altered states of consciousness achieved through the use of drugs.

Lucid dreams, hallucinations and spirit visitation represent only three aspects of a whole series of altered states of consciousness where certain steps and changes can be acknowledged. In most human societies, the handling of these three aspects has been culturally accepted. It is only in 'sophisticated' Western society that widespread acceptance of the requirements of the inner self has not been manifested. Ways of understanding these altered states can develop as follows:

1. Perception and cognition
The way different people manage altered states of consciousness and the expectations they have can make a contribution to the building of behavioural patterns and rituals. Such patterns can provide outlets for the various belief systems to function properly, religious or otherwise.

2. The psychobiological
The actual inductions of the varying states of consciousness do have similarities – they often depend on the usual environment and the learnt experiences of the individual. For instance,

someone who has learnt to induce lucidity through yogic practices will naturally find it easier to stay with those techniques than to use dream techniques.

3. Interpersonal and 'other-worldly' aspects

Alterations in personal perception and contact with the spirit world can dramatically change individual behaviour when they are permitted to do so. Also, there can occur some modifying of group action, through the use of altered states of consciousness, whether through the individual or group leadership. The growth in cult activity in the lead-up to the new millennium is one such example.

4. Social structure

Just as the individual can have an effect on group behaviour, so a group with common aims and ambitions can affect the society of which it is part. The setting up of women's consciousness groups in the 1960s (of which dreams and expectations of the future played a major part) has gradually led to women believing that they can not only survive in a hitherto mainly male environment, such as the business world, but also maximize their own potential.

As a means of influencing society in a wider sense, altered states of consciousness such as meditation, creative dreaming or a combination of both have a profound effect.

THE VALUE OF MEDITATION

Meditation is and always has been a tool for entering an altered state of consciousness during which it is possible to experience other realities and different states of being. It requires the development of several sorts of discipline.

- Firstly, there is the physical discipline which teaches the participant to be able to sit or lie still without difficulty.
- Secondly, there is the ability to quiet one's mind and empty it of all distractions, both internal and external.
- Thirdly, there is the ability to accept the imagery and symbolism that such a mind produces when left to 'idle' and scan the databanks of all awareness.
- Fourthly, the state of perfect peace which is the final aim of all meditative practices.

One of the instructions most often given to the creative dreamer is designed to have him remain as still as he can and maintain his position once he realizes and appreciates that he is dreaming. This is to enable him or her mentally to hold onto the images which appear, and not to wake up, thus driving the dream away. Looking at physical control, it is possible to see that to enhance lucid dreaming, the ability to control and relax the physical body is an important attribute. Those techniques such as *hatha* yoga, *qi gung*, *t'ai chi* and so on which are often considered to be moving – or more correctly standing – forms of meditation, enable the individual to remain in contact with his or her inner being without undue strain on the physical. The natural changes that occur in diet and exercise as you become more proficient in such techniques also make the achievement of lucid dreams more probable, since you are less likely to be clogged up by toxins and 'dis-ease'.

In the normal run of things when one puts oneself in a learning situation, the mind takes over and seems to create, of its own volition, all kinds of distractions which take our attention away from the matter in hand. Meditation is a tool which can be used to help to focus the mind and prevent the intrusion of unwanted thoughts. Many of the exercises, such as concentration, contemplation and creative visualization, which form the basis of meditation, can be applied to the art of lucid dreaming. Concentration on an external object initially, then on an internal image, trains the mind not to be distracted by external sounds or stray ideas – that is, not to go off on some wild-goose chase, but keep the mind on the matter in hand.

Contemplation enhances this ability, but also gives the ability to remain within your own space, continually observing what appears to be going on without any particular input from you and without trying to affect the outcome. It gives the ability to choose consciously a particular thought or idea for consideration. Visualization, on the other hand, helps to train you to accept that you can call images to mind or 'make things happen' on an inner level. Having this ability increases the potential for a state of lucidity.

As one progresses further in learning about and understanding meditation, much of the symbolism and imagery which develops is similar to dream imagery. Creative dreams are, it is thought by some, a development of hypnagogic imagery. Meditation helps to stabilize the fleeting images which first appear as one begins to explore the edges of the mind. It is these images which appear as the facility of creative dreaming develops. There is a shorthand form of symbolism, as well as a fund of archetypal images, which can be harnessed in meditation and then cross-referenced into lucid dreams.

WAKING-INDUCED LUCID DREAMING (WILD)

The close similarities between meditation and creative dreaming, particularly Waking-Induced Lucid Dreaming (WILD), have been noted by many. A variety of methods have been developed using and combining both techniques to achieve maximum lucidity. These can be divided into three categories:

1. Meditating on your chosen subject and then using the altered state of consciousness to instruct yourself to become lucid during a dream later on.
2. Meditating early in the morning, with the intention of going back to sleep afterwards. A brief period of meditation can be the equivalent of several hours' sleep; a period of meditation puts the mind into a state which is more conducive to creative dreaming.
3. Meditating and shifting consciousness into a state of waking awareness. That is, entering the creative dreaming state directly.

These categories obviously require a degree of experience and practice, but for the more experienced lucid dreamers it is possible to enter directly into a lucid dream straight from the waking state. Obviously this requires a high degree of control, both of the self and of the dreaming process. It also requires an understanding of the actual process of dreaming. We have already spoken of the hypnagogic state between waking and sleeping. What is now popularly called WILD actually begins when the dreamer enters directly into REM sleep and into dreaming from the waking state. This kind of dream has many similarities with the out-of-the-body experiences which we explore in greater depth elsewhere in the book – the main difference being that in the latter the individual does not believe that he or she is dreaming, but is truly experiencing something completely different.

The experience of weird vibrations, strange noises, electrical sensations, such as pins and needles, feelings of pressure on the chest, difficulty in breathing and floating – sometimes away from the body – are, it is true, common to both states of awareness – out-of-body experiences and WILD. This may be put down to purely physiological factors as the body passes into the REM sleep state. In primitive cultures, though, these states may be the ones in which the individual faces his 'demons'.

What we are really concerned with is how to induce a WILD, and there are a couple of ways in which you can do this. The first method is counting oneself to sleep. Rather similar to the idea of counting sheep until one falls asleep, this method consists of recognizing that when you wake up, you repeat, 'One, I'm dreaming; two, I'm dreaming, etc.', until you fall asleep again. This helps you to be fully aware of your own state, and makes the transition from waking to sleeping considerably easier. The second method uses the technique of allowing your attention to focus on various points of the body in a particular order. Those familiar with acupressure points may like to use those as their reference points, while others may like to use more anatomical references. For instance, become aware of your hands and arms, feet and legs and so on. This ties in with the idea of doing a 'reality check', using your own body as a guide, and enables you to re-enter the REM state directly.

DREAM OF A CREATIVE DREAM

There is another aspect of lucid dreaming that needs to be considered. We have already defined a creative dream as one in which you become aware that you are dreaming and, with practice, maintain that lucidity. There are various states of awareness, just as there are various states of consciousness. One of these awarenesses is to dream of having a lucid dream. One of the biggest difficulties that anyone trying to explain lucid dreams has, is that each person is so highly individual that no one can quite classify the various stages of consciousness which occur. This is where you do actually dream of being *aware* of dreaming. It is this that probably demonstrates better than anything else the multi-levelled aspects of the dreaming self.

We have spoken elsewhere of the hypnopompic and hypnagogic states as being the bridge between waking and sleeping. During those states, the dreamer has choices as to whether he or she is going to move into a state of lucidity or – voluntarily or otherwise – move into dreaming proper. An analogy – or visual image – might be that in his dream he has come through a single doorway into a passageway.

Close to the entrance, our dreamer is able to perceive two doors at the far end of the passage, through either of which he may choose to pass. One is labelled 'Dreams Proper' and the other 'Dreams Lucid'. As he moves closer to the doors, however, he perceives that they are both ajar and he becomes confused as to which to go through. There is information coming from both and it depends where he stands as to how he picks up the information. On one side of the passage he is clearly dreaming, whilst on the other he is searching for lucidity. In the middle area there is some doubt as to whether he is either dreaming or lucid – it in this state that he dreams of creative dreaming. It is worth noting that if the dreamer is capable of asking the question 'Am I dreaming?' then he is probably lucid.

Creative dreams and dreams of lucid dreams actually feel very different – both need to be experienced to be clear which each individual dream is. Dreams of creative dreams are remembered as dreams, while lucid dreams somehow seem more real – in the here and now. Thought processes after lucid dreams are stronger – it is easier to come back through the 'doorway' into a normal state of consciousness.

In order to sort out which dreams are which, it is necessary to keep a record of all your dreams – of whatever sort – and for this you need to learn how to keep a dream journal.

HOW TO KEEP A DREAM JOURNAL

Keeping a dream journal – i.e. documenting all of our remembered dreams – can provide a remarkable insight into our dreams. However, it can also be somewhat taxing. Over time, it can provide material for us to work on from hitherto hidden places. It may be that over a period of time most of our dreams appear to be connected with a specific subject. Having thought that we understand the sequence of dreams, we establish the theme and can shelve it and return to it later. The same theme may come about months or even years in the future, with greater vision and more dream material to work on. Keeping a dream journal enables us to observe and to map our improvement in learning about ourselves and comprehending everyday life.

Each dream has its own individual interpretation at the time of being dreamt, although it may need reassessing when recognized as being as part of a series. The dreaming brain is highly effective in that it will offer material for consideration in as many different ways as possible until such times as we understand. That same dreaming self can obscure the information in non-essential material which needs removing before the dream can be worked with. Even creative dreaming can lose clarity in this way, and what has started out as an easy process becomes cluttered and difficult. Lucid dreaming particularly does not necessarily need interpretation through symbols in the same way as 'ordinary dreams'. Dreams have so many elements that they can be interpreted in many different ways and usually need multiple explanations.

Using a dream journal helps us to take note of both the material of our dreams and also the way in which our dreams are put together. The more we learn to remember our dreams, the better at dreaming we become. So many individuals who claim not to be very good at dreaming are amazed at both the quality and quantity of their dreams when they do start recording them.

People who are learning to experiment with creative dreaming will, by and large, have learnt how to keep a dream journal. For those who have not here are some brief instructions:

1. Any paper and writing implements can be used – whatever is most pleasing for the individual.
2. Always keep your recording implements at hand.
3. Write the account of the dream as soon as possible after waking.
4. Use as much detail as possible.
5. Note at which point in your dream you consider you 'went lucid'.
6. Be consistent in the way that you record your dreams. One simple scheme is given below.

Name
Age
Gender
Date of dream
Where were you when you recalled the dream?
State the content of your dream.
Write down anything odd about the dream (e.g. animals, bizarre situations, dream signs, etc.).
What were your feelings in/about the dream?

Writing down the dream has a particular kind of satisfaction. However, just as many people now like to use a computer and any available software to make their records easier, there those who would rather use a recording device in order to secure the uninterrupted flow from sleep to the waking state. Using a tape recorder and 'speaking' the dream fixes it in your mind and requires less concentration than writing it down. You are therefore much more in touch with the feelings and emotions of the dream. Try clarifying the dream as though it is still happening to you. For instance, 'I am walking through a forest' rather than 'I was walking through a forest'. This allows you to get hold of what was happening to you as a participant as well as an observer.

When you make your preparations for sleep into a habit or ritual you will concentrate your mind on the activity of dreaming. This also includes the preparation of your journal, perhaps recording the date and time you went to bed, the subject you hope to dream about and so on. Using affirmations to achieve creative dreaming or to dream about a certain subject helps to train the subconscious to respond to your needs rather than introducing material at random. Impressing on your mind that you will have a dream to record in your journal is all part of that training.

Remember when you are recording dreams to make a note of times when you wake up during the night, or the approximate time into your dream that you think you have become lucid. Initially you will find that this is quite difficult but gradually you will discover that you are fairly accurate at estimating the time – it is as though your body clock recognizes what is being attempted. You should then be able to highlight your most prolific dreaming period. Holistically, once one takes care of the inner workings, one can dream more efficiently and be in touch with the physical body.

Those with a mathematical or scientific frame of mind will prefer to look at their dreams analytically and find instances of statistical relevance to make it easier to trace dreams with similar themes, energies and objects. These can also be recorded in your journal. Particularly when experimenting with creative dreaming it helps to carry your journal with you during the day. One reason is to note down instances of synchronicity – occasions when you see something which approximates to a dream image, whether bizarre or otherwise – and the other to note down possible subjects which might be worth while exploring lucidly, or as subjects for creative dreaming.

In the beginning, don't try too hard to obtain results. Being laid back will enhance your chances of success rather than getting completely stressed out because the dreams are not appearing to order or are not what you thought they should be.

We have spoken elsewhere about the importance of not 'chasing away' the dream. Suffice to say that when you wake up, preferably gently, remember to lie still and recall your dream – whether lucid or otherwise – before moving quietly and gently to record it in your chosen way. Your recall will be better and you may find more significance in the dream and your handling of it than if you have shocked yourself awake.

When experimenting with creative dreaming, you are not looking for meaning in the dream – you may wish to explore that later. You are instead looking to appreciate the sensations and feelings that your lucid dream has given you and the insights that you might gain into your everyday life or your personality. It is just as important to record these latter aspects as it is to record the content of the dream itself. Note particularly if there are other aspects in the dream which might bear exploration from a lucid standpoint. For instance, you might find that you are not landing up in your chosen situation more times than are coincidental. You might then wish to experiment with becoming more focused and therefore more accurate in your targeting. Your journal will help you to become more aware of the whole of your own dreaming process and you will be able to experiment with whatever controls are important to you.

ANALYZING DREAM STRUCTURE

Whether your dream is lucid or otherwise, you will always need to analyze its structure. There are several ways in which you can do this. The more proficient you become, the more your dreams will begin to make sense. As time goes on, you will begin to see certain themes and ideas repeated over and over. These will begin to fall into place until you have internalized what you need to know. By keeping a dream journal, you will find that certain parts of one dream – and the way that they have been structured – may well relate to segments of another dream and the answer is hidden therein.

Firstly, write out the dream in your own words. The best way to analyze the structure of a dream is to split it into its component parts exactly as written it in your journal. You will need to decide how your dream may be split into segments – it is, after all, your dream. The way that you choose to divide it up may be very different from the way that someone else would. Try to look for natural breaks that divide it into two or three distinct parts – each with their own story. Take as an example the dream below, which we received via the Internet and have partially edited without changing any of the main components.

'I was in a big building with a group of people and didn't know anyone. Somebody had been murdered by a member of the group I was with. We decided the murderer was the boy who was sat in the corner on his own. We had to kill him as he killed someone in the group. We all decided that he had to be stoned to death and all joined in. A large cat appeared that ate everyone one at a time, as slowly and 'curly' as possible. But he had taken a liking to me so he didn't kill me. Then I found out that the cat was really my best friend.'

Here the dream may be divided into four main parts: **1**, Where the dreamer was and how she felt. **2**, The action of the dream and the dreamer's inclusion in the group. **3**, What was happening to the group. **4**, The dreamer's realizations.

1. I was in a big building with a group of people and didn't know anyone.
2. Somebody had been murdered by a member of the group I was with. We decided the murderer was the boy who was sat in the corner on his own. We had to kill him as he killed someone in the group. We all decided that he had to be stoned to death and all joined in.
3. A large cat appeared that ate everyone one at a time, slowly and curly as possible. But he had taken a liking to me so he didn't kill me.
4. Then I found out that the cat was really my best friend.

This dream can also be divided into only two acts or parts – the one dealing with the group and its actions and the one dealing with the cat:

1. I was in a big building with a group of people and didn't know anyone. Somebody had been murdered by a member of the group I was with. We decided the murderer was the boy who was sat in the corner on his own. We had to kill him as he killed someone in the group. We all decided that he had to be stoned to death and all joined in.
2. A large cat appeared that ate everyone one at a time, slowly and curly as possible. But he had taken a liking to me so he didn't kill me. Then I found out that the cat was really my best friend.

The next part of analyzing the dream structure is to find out which is the most important segment. Here, when we look at the first way of partitioning the dream, the part that is most important is the killing of the boy and the violence involved. We might give this part a title and call it 'Murder' or 'The Killing'. Giving each part a title helps to fix the section in your mind, and helps to give quicker recall. Also, should you wish at a later date to use this dream for creative work, it gives you a starting point from which to work.

Using the second method of dividing up the dream, both parts are equally important since they are both to do with death. It is the difference between the two ways of killing which is of note – the fact that the cat is discovered to be the dreamer's best friend is the resolution of the dream.

You should also name the other segments of the dream. Using the first method of dividing the dream up, section one could be called 'The Building' or 'Setting the Scene' – it is important that the name resonates with you. You might call the second section 'The Stoning' or 'An Eye for an Eye', depending on which aspect of the section has most meaning for you. Often, naming the part helps you to recall your reactions in the dream.

It is also necessary to discover within each section whether you, the dreamer, are active (taking action) or passive (inert). In the first section in our example, the dreamer is passive and is conscious of her lack of friends. In the second, she is aware of herself participating in the group decision-making but is also aware of the boy on his own. In the third, she becomes aware that she is somewhat passive since her survival is dependent on the cat, and she is again on her own. In the final section there is a partial resolution since she has her 'best friend' – the cat – and is neither active nor passive.

Looking closely at the dream in this way begins to uncover the similarities and differences between each segment. Each section, except the first and last, has an element of aloneness in it. In the first, the dreamer knows nobody; in the second, the boy is alone; finally, in the third, the dreamer is again set apart. There is also killing, violence and death in the main parts of the dream. Someone has been murdered and as a subplot the murderer must himself be violently killed by virtue of a group decision. At this point, however, the cat becomes an agent of death in that he (an individual) begins to eat (absorb) members of the group. The dreamer, also an individual, is saved by the fact that she realizes that the cat is actually her best friend. Thus one theme of the dream is uncovered – that of needing to belong, contrasting with the need to be an individual.

The differences in the segments are also recognizable. In the first section, the dreamer is alone, and knows no one. In the second, she is a member of a group, and in the third, she is watching a lone cat absorb the rest of the group. In the last segment, it is her relationship with the cat which is important. Thus another theme which is revealed is that of meaningful relationship.

A further similarity/difference comparison reveals that while each section is indeed to do with death, the methods by which death comes are different. In the section to do with murder, a particularly primitive method is chosen by the group: that of stoning. In the segment to do with the cat, the method is at one and the same time natural (a cat eats its prey) and also bizarre. The cat eats the members of the group in a slow and 'curly' way, one after the other. This would tend to suggest that the dreamer has to be conscious of her need to face some kind of ending – which may possibly be violent – in order to achieve a different standing with someone who has the potential to be destructive. The general theme therefore seems to be the need for change in the dreamer.

Once the dream has been worked on in this way the various

themes can be listed and further work done on the symbols in each section which pick up these themes. As an example we have already seen that in the first section our dreamer is aware of not knowing anyone. She also does not seem to know the boy accused of murder, nor initially does she know either the cat or the fact that he seems to be her best friend. Some useful consideration might be given through dreamwork as to whether the dreamer is something of a loner and how she reacts to the world she lives in.

There is an element of the absurd or bizarre in this dream, in that the dreamer unexpectedly recognizes that the cat is her best friend. It is at this point that she might have become lucid.

ERRORS AND BIZARRE ELEMENTS

There is a fascinating aspect to creative dreaming, particularly as we first begin to learn how to handle the preliminaries. This is the presence of the absurd. Often it is the presence of the unusual which alerts us to the fact that we are in the middle of a lucid dream. We still do not fully understand how the dreaming brain works, though we do know that dreaming is associated with REM.

There is a theory that the dreaming brain is less intelligent than the waking brain, although this would have to depend on the definition of intelligence. Certainly the sleeping brain works with a degree of irrationality which follows no known logic. In normal dreaming, REM signals tremendous variations in electrical activity and it is this activity which governs lucidity and, apparently, irrationality. Cultivating the art of creative dreaming means that we have to discover how our dreams work and which boundaries are self-imposed and which not. Most bizarre episodes are errors of perception or errors of context.

Errors of perception occur when we 'forget' that anything is feasible in dreams and begin to impose the inhibitions and strictures that apply in everyday life. For instance, instead of accepting unquestioningly that we can pass through barriers or do quite naturally things which we would not do in ordinary life, we may become afraid of physical harm or impose a rational thought that something is dangerous. We then would not continue with the action. In ordinary dreams, we would complete the action without thinking about it; at the beginning of learning how to lucid dream, we would find that we have stopped the action – or have been stopped – while the practised creative dreamer will continue with the action anyway.

Being able to suspend disbelief is perhaps easier for people who have already practised out-of-the-body work, altering the perception of their personal boundaries or who have attempted astral travel. These techniques are given elsewhere in the book.

By the time we have consciously decided to become lucid dreamers, we will have picked up a number of inhibitions about our social behaviour. Just as in waking life we have to learn how to bypass those inhibitions, this must also be done in lucid dreaming. When we dream of characters, we recognize these dream figures are our own *perception* of them and not necessarily how they really are. However, the way that we have understood their effect on us can have a direct influence on how we dream about them. We might, for instance, expect a mother to act in a nurturing way and become somewhat confused when she appears as a highly charged sexual being. Lucidity dictates that rather than being shocked awake at this apparently bizarre behaviour, we are able to accept it and recognize that we are dreaming – the dream can then continue and unfold as we wish.

For creative dreaming to be successful, one further step needs to be taken. As children, before we have internalized social consequences, we are entirely innocent. It is to this innocent approach and purity that we must return if we are to understand the errors that the dreaming self can make. A dream can be so 'real' that objects and people seem to be truly present. It is as the level of lucidity changes in a dream that it is possible to correct the error of thinking that a dream character is real. We realise that we are dreaming.

When we remember that there is an internal reality which exists, we can become aware that the dream character or object – however bizarre – has a valid existence within the dream. It is our perception which, for the purpose of the dream, is flawed. This gives rise to the necessity of accepting, with a degree of innocence, that creative dreaming helps us to differentiate between an inner and outer reality. The crossover between inner and outer reality is when we allow our dreams to help us to understand the way in which we unconsciously react to other people and to our environment. Irrational thought tends to follow patterns set up in childhood. There are those, however, who would still subscribe to the belief that, in the dream state, the brain is dysfunctional.

Researchers Hobson and McCarley have put forward an argument dealing with the bizarre elements and erroneous thought in the content of dreams. These aspects have been attributed to the suppression of unacceptable drives and urges, although they probably have a much simpler explanation when approached from a neurophysiological perspective. When the dreamer experiences oddities, such as the forming of dream symbols, inappropriate scene changes or two characters merging into one or becoming grotesque, these events may directly reflect the state of the dreaming brain. Hobson and McCarley have discovered that there is a strong possibility that the link between the brain stem and the fore brain may not be fully efficient: it is simply doing its best to create some kind of coherence.

Both arguments are well demonstrated in the mirror task mentioned previously given to dreamers being tested for creative dreaming in laboratories. Here, those who undertook the task discovered that there was a high degree of instability in the images of self as perceived in the dream mirror. There was also a tendency to not show normal images. This may be because the self-image is a very personal construct, heavily affected by experience. On the other hand, it may also be because in REM sleep the brain is in a particular state not conducive to tying the images down mentally in a logical way. The dreaming brain is apparently both capable of producing and of accepting the weird or bizarre.

Most of us are not fully familiar with the concept of creative dreaming, although we are aware that such a dream requires an element of control which is not apparent in 'ordinary' dreaming. Briefly, although we may be aware that we are dreaming while still apparently asleep, when something totally absurd happens in the middle of such a condition, we assume that we are not in control and therefore the dream is not lucid. This may not necessarily be so.

The apparently nonsensical may have a validity of its own which must be built into our understanding of the dream. Creative dreams show a pattern of abnormality that non-lucid dreams don't. There is a belief in some circles that the presence of the apparently bizarre in lucid dreams is associated with the pre-lucid state. The absurd tends to vanish as beginners become better at creative dreaming, returning as the dreamer becomes even more adept. It would seem, therefore, that absurdity triggers lucid dreaming.

There are several levels of lucidity. The most elementary is the one that the majority of the uninitiated would accept – becoming aware of dreaming without understanding how dreaming is different from being awake. At the highest level, the dreamer is not only conscious of the fact that he or she is dreaming, but needs also to have total grasp of the ramifications of this knowledge, thus being able to make whatever adjustments are feasible within both the dream state and everyday life.

The absurd, irrational or bizarre in dreams, particularly in creative dreams, could be a result of not fully appreciating how dreams can, with practice, be manipulated. Perhaps the best analogy is that of aiming for a dartboard and just glancing off the outer rim as we throw our dart. We have hit something which is vaguely associated with our target, but which could deflect us from what we are trying to accomplish.

With practice we can either reject that part which does not belong within the framework of our dream, or 'store' it for further consideration. Technically, such cross currents may occur because of the different intensity of brainwave activity during REM sleep; this has been found to vary considerably at different times. It is possible that our inner perceptions and experiences change according to those brainwave rhythms. Only when we have patiently collected enough data about our own dreams are we able to test our individual dream reality. Hopefully this then gives us the courage to explore the anomaly we have thrown up, allowing us to use dreams creatively.

The Marquis de Hervey de Saint Dennis in his book, *Dreams and the Means to Direct Them*, describes very clearly the development of the abilities needed to control dreaming:

• Increase dream recall

- Become aware you are dreaming
- Learn to wake at will
- Be able to direct dreams.

If we look at these four things in more detail, we have the framework necessary to be able to work towards a more coherent way of understanding – and using – our own dreams. Although there has been much research and experimentation done over the years and various methods have been developed to assist in this process of understanding, they are really all extensions of his very simple technique. Throughout the book, and particularly in 'Working with Dreams', there are various suggestions and exercises to try, but to begin with it is vital that you do not try too hard to get results. Time spent now on the basics will give a good grounding when you find that suddenly and almost without effort you are dreaming lucidly at will.

INCREASING DREAM RECALL

Earlier in this section there are detailed instructions on how to keep a dream journal, but before actually doing that, you need to train yourself to remember your dreams. As a first step when you wake up in the morning, lie still and try to recall your dream. It does not matter if you can only catch hold of a small fragment. Ask yourself the question, 'What was I dreaming about?' Gradually, with practice, you will remember more and more of your dream. As a reality test, check that you really are awake – taking a note of the exact time for future reference.

Incidentally, the reason you should lie still is because movement seems to chase away the dream, whereas remaining still helps to 'set' it so that it is more easily recalled. Learning such a habit will also enable you to go back more easily into the dream state as you become more proficient at creative dreaming.

An extension of this technique will help to train you to remember more of your dreams. We now know that we dream more prolifically in those periods of REM which take place at approximately 90-minute periods after we have first fallen asleep. If you wish, you can train yourself to wake up at appropriate intervals, firstly by using your alarm clock or some such device, later by simply telling yourself that you will wake up. Use the same technique of lying quite still until you have recalled some aspect of a dream. Again, it does not matter if initially this process seems difficult – it does get easier with practice! Only when you have recalled as much as you can should you then move and use your dream journal to record as much of the detail as you can. Do remember that often the details of one dream can appear in another – nothing is too trivial to record. If you have remembered it, it has relevance. It is suggested, however, that you practise at weekends – or those days when you are not running to a tight schedule – at first.

DEVELOPING AWARENESS

Previously you have only been concerned with remembering the dreams that you have had. The next stage is to become aware that you are dreaming while still remaining asleep. Eventually this will give you a degree of control over the dreaming process; for now it is sufficient to be certain that you are actually dreaming. Various ways of testing reality are given elsewhere, but as a start, ask yourself a simple question such as, 'Am I dreaming?' or 'Is this a dream?' You will soon develop you own shorthand or dream signs which will tell you whether you are awake or asleep. These are explained more fully earlier in this section. There may, for instance, be some kind of distortion in what should be a perfectly ordinary object or perhaps an unexpected visual clue.

LEARNING TO WAKE AT WILL

In some ways, learning to wake at will is an extension of both dream recall and becoming aware that you are dreaming. The first step to learning to wake up at times predetermined by you will already have been mastered as you learn to recall your dreams. Recognizing that you are dreaming then gives you a choice as to whether to remain asleep and lucid or not. Initially, as you come to an understanding that you are dreaming, you will wake up spontaneously, the dream will disappear and you will have had a frustratingly brief awareness of what lucidity feels like. As time progresses the more bizarre elements of the dream can help you to anchor yourself in the dream reality, rather than in the waking self.

You can remind yourself that you are dreaming but aware – perhaps using an affirmation such as, 'This is bizarre or not the way it should be, therefore I know that I am dreaming' – and can allow yourself to 'hold onto' the dream. There are various techniques which have been developed by experienced creative dreamers for staying with the dream such as 'spinning' and 'going with the flow', as explained earlier, under 'Prolonging Dreams'. As a beginner, all you need to do is to establish some control over sleeping, waking, ordinary dreaming and creative dreaming. For many, the changes are so subtle that the dreamer can only quantify them himself. The transition between sleeping and waking is known as the hypnopompic state, which we explained earlier in this section.

DIRECTING DREAMS

It is now well known, since the RISC technique was developed as a therapeutic tool, that one can learn to direct dreams. Many people first begin to use lucid dreams as a way of controlling bad ones – questioning and assessing your own state of consciousness is a proven technique in handling nightmares and night terrors. If you are prone to such disturbances, it is worthwhile pre-programming yourself several times during the day by repeating to yourself a phrase which will alert you to the fact that at those times you are not awake. You could use an affirmation such as, 'Next time I'm dreaming, I will remember I'm dreaming' or 'When I dream, I want to be aware that that is so'. Develop your own reminder that is a positive statement and has meaning for you. It will work for you because you really mean it. Keep your thoughts focused on this phrase for short intervals during the day. When you find your mind wandering, remind yourself once more that you will recognise when you are dreaming, then let it go and return to your everyday concerns.

The next stage is to direct the dream itself. After having pre-programmed yourself, you can incubate a dream, but the easiest part – once you have worked out how you do this – is to manipulate your own dream. Further instructions appear elsewhere in the book but, using the RISC technique below, which is, after all, very close to the Saint-Dennis way, it is possible to make small changes which can be very pleasing, simply by willing those changes to be so.

THE RISC TECHNIQUE

The assumption of dream therapy (using dreams as a therapeutic tool) is simple: if you have bad dreams which make you wake up in a bad mood, reframe your dreams. You can change the scripts. Improving the outcome makes everything seem better, and should lead to better moods. There are four steps that you can learn in the privacy of your own home.

Recognition When you are having a dream which you feel is a bad one, recognize that you do not need the feelings that it leaves you with, whether that is anger, fear, guilt or any other negative feeling.

Identification You need to be able to identify what it is about the dream that makes you feel bad. Look at the dream carefully and find out exactly what it is that disturbs you.

Stopping a bad dream You must always remember that you are in charge. You do not have to let a bad dream continue. You can either wake up or, recognizing that you are dreaming, become lucid.

Changing the dream Each negativity in your dream can be changed for the positive. Initially, you may have to wake yourself up to work out a better conclusion, but eventually you will be able to do it while you are still asleep.

To begin with, you might try to make the changes you need on your own; it is amazing how quickly you will begin to feel the benefits even if you are not consciously aware of having made any changes. Working with a therapist sometimes facilitates the result, but it is not always necessary.

In using this method in a therapeutic setting, it is usually fairly easy for the dreamers to pinpoint for themselves the issues which need to be dealt with, though the therapist's experience may help. By starting with a change of attitude (to the dream itself), other such changes to deeper realizations which make themselves felt are made much easier. As a result, it becomes much simpler to change everyday behaviour. Using creative dreaming then allows the individual to practise different and more appropriate behaviour before actively making use of it.

One of the side-effects of using this particular method is that it enables the dreamer to handle difficult feelings or memories which surface from the past. By being gentle with yourself you are much more able to deal with traumatic events in a more objective way, building images which trigger feelings of strength and power and thus enabling you to decide how secure you feel in addressing the issues. Not only can you work through the interpretation of dreams, but also through dream manipulation to create more positive feelings about the past, cope with mechanisms in the present and lay the foundation for a more positive future.

BALANCING CREATIVE AND WAKING EXPERIENCES

It is extremely important when working with lucid dreams to keep a strong hold on the reality of your present everyday world (the here and now). You must understand that while it is perfectly feasible to function in both realities, you do need to appreciate that the world of lucid dreaming can be very seductive and can take you away from the true appreciation of the world you live in.

There is a danger in the initial stages of exploration of becoming obsessed with the idea of having a lucid dream and allowing this to take over your waking life. We have talked of the various methods of altering your sleep patterns by napping and waking yourself from sleep in the search for lucidity, and this is fine if you have a lifestyle which supports such activities. Questioning yourself periodically during the day as to whether you are awake or dreaming is also fine. The demands of everyday life can, however, conflict with the needs of the inner self and – as always when working with changes of consciousness and awareness – a sense of balance and discipline should be established early on.

There is also the possibility of getting caught up in the intricacies of the techniques themselves which are used to induce creative dreaming. It can be fun to learn to spin, fly and alter size and shape, but this is a little like having only a starter at an important meal, then leaving before the dessert. To appreciate a meal properly, one needs the whole experience, and so it is with lucidity – meaning 'of the light'. Many of today's spiritual traditions have, as an integral part of their beliefs, the experiencing of light, which ultimately suggests a perception of true reality. However, this light is initially an interior light and, when accessed through creative dreaming, should be treated with the dignity and respect it deserves.

From a practical point of view, the suggestion is that initially you attempt lucid dreaming only when you know you have time the next day to process what has happened, quietly and sensibly. As part of your initial preparation, you will have already taught yourself how to incubate the dream you want (or need), to record your dreams and interpret them. Now a further stage is necessary to learn how to deal with the effects of creative dreaming. Almost inevitably your perceptions will change, but gradually, you will learn how to incorporate the higher vibration of lucidity into your everyday life. Then creative dreaming will become an integral part of your way of life. You will quite literally see and feel things more clearly. Indeed, as in the words of the song by The Waterboys, you will see 'the whole of the moon'.

Kelzer suggests 'the close tutelage of an experienced guide' when working with lucidity. As with meditation, talking through your experiences with someone more knowledgeable can help to deal with problems and put things into perspective. It has continually been stressed that each individual's experience is different but, as mentioned elsewhere, there are certain stages which are gone through quite naturally. It does help to obtain someone else's reaction to what is occurring.

There is the danger for some people of an attack of the 'Messiahs'. In this, because the experience is so mind-blowing, it can seem as though one has been destined to 'save the world'. One wishes to share such an experience with anyone who will listen, and quite a few who do not. Those who have not been through any of the preparatory stages or have not achieved either voluntarily or involuntarily the same stage of lucidity, cannot have a full comprehension of the emotions associated with the event and may not enjoy being told that they are living inappropriate lives! This is truly a time to learn when to speak and when to remain silent.

Conversely, the experience can give such a sense of vastness and boundless energy that the individual is left feeling at the same time both humbled and vulnerable. A period of quiet contemplation and the careful management of everyday tasks can have a balancing and grounding effect, so that the dreamer has a better concept of living life in a mindful way – or of prayer through action.

There may be the distinct feeling that one should withdraw altogether from the world, and a strong sense of unworthiness. It is easy to begin to understand why monks and nuns of all denominations are required to undertake mundane and ordinary tasks as part of their discipline, as a way of belonging to the real world. A wise mentor will not allow the pupil to become unworldly in his explorations, and a healthy burst of normal activity such as cleaning or gardening can restore the mental balance. Such tasks undertaken with a degree of joy seem to be accomplished in half the time anyway.

Talking about your experiences with someone else often means that you are able to see and assess the quality and intensity of your own awareness. Just as there are various levels of perception, there are more and less intense experiences within the framework of creative dreaming. If every dream were of the same intensity we would become totally unbalanced, so it is right that we learn to use this new tool with circumspection and to learn from others what is possible and what is not. Your first experiences will tend to be spontaneous, containing a fair percentage of the 'wow' factor – a strong sense of awe and wonder.

New sensations and perceptions occur, possibly never to return with the same power, yet most lucid dreamers have discovered that each new perception brings its own delights within the physical world. Accept each occasion on its own merits. It is said that comparisons are odious, so no one dream is better or of more use than another. If you have 'gone lucid' or, rather, achieved lucidity it will be for a purpose often only understood after level-headed consideration.

One thing to be continually borne in mind is that it does not matter if you have not had a creative dream for some time even if you have diligently practised all the techniques, and set about to incubate such a dream. Creative dreaming is only one level of consciousness, and it is more than possible that your mind is benefiting from the practice in other ways. This apparently unproductive time may simply be a period where there is a great deal of internal adjustment going on. The more you gain mastery over your mind, the more focused your living becomes.

For this reason alone it is wise not to try to force lucidity. As discussed throughout this book, each change of awareness occurs naturally and of its own accord. Trying to force it is like using a

Pandora's box

crowbar to open a box. Pandora's box ultimately contained Hope, but not before a great deal of sorrow was released into the world. You will wish to release your own inner joy and tranquillity, not things you cannot easily handle. Be gentle with yourself and work to achieve a sense of balance within.

SECTION

3

SECTION

3

MESSAGES FROM THE GODS

Dreaming and lucid dreaming also have a place in the religious and social frameworks of many cultures.

It is known that in ancient Babylon the dream played an extremely important part in religion and everyday life. The gods were held to reveal themselves through dreams, to declare the Will of Heaven and foretell the future. One of the titles of their Sun god was Baru-Tereti – the seer of the revealed law – whose seers or 'Baru' consisted of a special class of priest. Answers to prayers were obtained by sleeping in a temple and invoking Makhir, the androgynous god of dreams.

Modern researchers into dreams and dreaming in primitive societies have largely taken clarification of the following as their goals:

1. The classification of the two classes of primitive dreams. These are i) important visions which are mainly of cultural significance and therefore available to all; ii) dreams by the individual which are of meaning only to him.

2. The understanding of the part that the dream plays in primitive society and the beliefs and theories about it.
3. The relationship of the individual to his culture and his perception of the relevance of dreaming, lucid or otherwise.
4. An understanding of the symbolic language of the culture being studied.
5. To discover whether there is a universal language of dreams applicable to *all* societies.

One of the most interesting findings of this research has been the persistence of ancient beliefs in these societies despite the encroachment of Western ideas and ways of living. To many primitive peoples, 'real' dreams include hypnopompic hallucinations (false perception on waking), incidences of sleep paralysis and other types of nightmare experience. The Kagwhaiv tribe of Brazil, for instance, believed that nightmares were caused by the ghosts of ancestors. Native Newfoundlanders appear to hold a similar belief. It has also been discovered that Zulu men regard nightmares of suffocation with particular horror and can often be hospitalized because of such dreams. Whereas we in the West tend to dismiss such experiences, many native peoples treat them as relevant and interpret them.

Typical nightmarish dreams of the Sambia tribe have similar images and storylines as those seen in more sophisticated societies. These may consist of images such as being swept away by floods while crossing a river, being engulfed by fire or fog and waking up at the point of no return. In that culture, these dreams are discussed quite openly, though personally troubling dreams are only shared privately with close companions. 'Wet' dreams and virtually all sexual dreams are only shared on an intimate level.

When comparing the Zunis and the Quiche tribes, it has been discovered that for Zunis dreaming is more intimate and personal, while for the Quiche dreaming is a more social activity, purely because dreams are seen as a message for the soul and become verbalized into stories. Zunis are passive in the dreaming process, while the Quiche are active and open. For the Quiche the benchmark of their humanity is to be able to speak articulately – their greatest anxiety is how to control dreaming in order to create meaning. The Zuni define their humanity by the fact that they eat cooked food, since no animal has this ability.

When we look at the Huichol Indians, a Native American tribe, we find that they actually make a physical representation of their pleas to the Sun gods, an action thought to be based on dream symbolism. Fearing a drought, they will take a clay disc and paint the face of the sun on one side. This is a circular figure which is surrounded by rays of three different colours – red, blue and yellow – which they call his arrows. On the back of the disc they paint the progress of the sun through the four different quarters of the sky. These are represented by a large cross-like figure with a circle in the centre; also represented pictorially are the hills of the Earth and cornfields. Wealth and money are designated as crosses. Also shown are curved lines (meaning rain).

These discs are physical representations of the Indians' inner thoughts, desires and dreams. Through them, he communicates with the gods. The discs show pictorially all that the individual perhaps fears but longs to express for himself and act as a constant reminder of his needs. They are therefore both a form of art and part of a ritual.

When a people are accustomed to picturing certain aspects of their beliefs in such a way, they also become used to the symbolism of their dream lives. They therefore accept much more readily that their dreams may reflect their waking reality, and vice versa.

So-called 'primitive' people generally gain much from their practical experience in order to retain knowledge of their rites and rituals. These become tangible expressions of the carefully monitored thoughts and dreams of their ancestors, and then become fixed, in turn giving rise to further dreams and thoughts. Oral tradition requires that all knowledge that becomes superfluous at the time is apparently lost, perhaps only to return through dreams at a later date. Often that recall seems to have been aided by the use of 'sacred' substances.

The Huichol Indians, mentioned above, even today make extensive use of the psychoactive cactus, peyote; it is at the heart of their religion and culture. 'God's Flesh', the name given to sacred mushrooms by their forebears, is still consumed by the Mazatecs of Mexico in their rituals. In North America, there is the renowned example of the Native American church whose members consume peyote as a religious sacrament during their all-night ceremony or prayer meeting, although this is strictly outside the law.

SHAMANIC SOCIETIES

The cultures we have been looking at are inherently shamanic in their nature. Mircea Eliade, one of the most famous researchers of shamanism, suggests that shamanism is an 'archaic magico-religious phenomenon'. The shaman is the force behind the ecstasy of the people; they make use of his or her own spirit helpers (in modern-day shamanism, more and more women are becoming shamans), in order to invoke the guidance of the said spirits. Present-day work with creative dreams reflects most of the rules and guidelines that have been used for thousands of years in shamanic cultures.

Shamanic practices set out to enhance altered states of awareness in order to make contact with the various energies present. The premise is that everything is alive and has its own specific vibration. Most traditional cultures totally accept that the very subtle spirit energies of both animals and apparently inanimate objects can only be reached through dreams, trance and ritual. These spiritual energies are encountered most often as archetypes (basic models of being) and are accessed most readily through the dream state.

The more primitive societies also accept as perfectly natural the idea that an animal spirit will become their guide and guardian – something which more sophisticated peoples must relearn to do. It is not unusual for native Indians to refuse to kill or maim a member of a particular animal species and they will often try to prevent others from doing the same. When an animal spirit has revealed itself through dreams, whole families will pay due deference to that spirit and will elect to be guided by their relative's hidden ally. They will not necessarily receive inner guidance from that guardian animal themselves. Often it is the particular quality of the animal that is most required. It is perhaps interesting that in modern dream interpretation the qualities of the animal are often most important within the individual's understanding of the dream.

THE MAKING OF A SHAMAN

Shamanic peoples have usually cultivated the wisdom to be awake rather than asleep within the dream world. This actually encourages and enhances dream encounters with spirits. Each shaman's training is geared towards inducing an extremely inward looking state of being which means he is able to be all of three things – participant in the experience, observer and controller of what is occurring. Creative dreaming therefore is recognized as an integral part of the shaman's training.

In both dreams and shamanic visions, the spirit entities are seen to confer gifts but also to create challenges – sometimes in a teasing fashion, but also in a frightening way – to allow the individual to overcome his own doubts and fears and to grow spiritually in wisdom and courage. In addition, spirits often appear in disguise; part of the training is being able to recognize illusion when it appears. When such illusions are recognized, the practitioner senses that he is in the presence of something which transcends day to day reality. In most shamanic cultures, initiation consists of various stages. These are:

1. The participant confronts his personal demons, cleanses himself of emotional baggage and then, perhaps the most difficult of all, accepts what his life task will be (i.e. serving the good of his people).
2. The initiate must confront some form of possession. During this stage, he may appear insane to others, being prone to rambling speech, inappropriate laughter and other signs of madness.
3. After considerable purification and ritual practices, the initiate gains control, both over himself and his deities.

In some cultures, such as the Tamang, this third stage is seen as a light located between the eyes. This corresponds to the Third Eye in yogic practice, being both the 'light' of consciousness and the soul from within. It is this stage in which the shaman is able to travel within his soul between the heavens and the underworlds, and where magical flight is possible. Shamanic flight at this stage is not an experience of an inner reality, but is a journey beyond physical limitations. The shaman is now able to see 'clear' visions rather than the more crude which he has previously seen.

The simple *experience* of shamanic practices and techniques does not ensure that one becomes a shaman. There are degrees of training into which the individual must become fully initiated. The true shaman must master shamanic journeying and recognize that his calling is a sacred trust and that throughout everything he must serve his community, whether large or small.

There are three ways in which the individual can become a shaman, and these still apply today to people who wish to become initiates.

- The first is through having been born to it. This is hereditary transmission, and often this is somewhat sporadic. Not every descendant of a shaman is naturally a shaman themselves.
- The second is through a call or selection, and is usually entirely spontaneous.
- The third is perhaps the most difficult, and is through personal choice and seeking.

While this last way is the way of most modern-day shamans, traditionally this path is not as complete as the others and means that the initiate must become proficient in the art of trance management and dreaming. He must also undergo a traditional type of training where he becomes well versed in the shamanic techniques, identification of spirit, the secret language of the art, and the myths and culture of his calling. This is usually given through the master shamans and through spirit. This way is often achieved in part or wholly through dreams, both lucid and otherwise. Creative dream experiences at this time in which the candidate dies or has some organs consumed and replaced and is thus reborn, can be terrifying. Survival of these kinds of dreams concerning the death of the individual, however, does give the shaman those personal constructs which maximize his or her ability to work and heal others.

FOLLOWING IN SHAMANISM'S FOOTSTEPS

Traditionally shamanism has been a rich source of material for people new to lucid dreaming. Apart from the numbers of investigations, scientific, pseudo-scientific and academic which have already taken place, there are many 'ordinary' people who have expressed an interest in the practice of shamanism. There is a type of circularity here, in that the exploration of dreams, whether lucid or otherwise, often leads to the desire to understand a more esoteric way of being. Conversely, a search for the meaning of life often calls for an understanding of dreams and particularly changes of consciousness such as lucidity.

Investigators have discovered that shamanism tended to occur in hunter-gatherer societies. It has proved more difficult to identify shamanism in today's highly structured societies. However, a society is post-shamanic when its inherent myths and legends have strong traditions of movement between two worlds, whether that is *ascent* into heaven or some 'upper region', or *descent* into the underworld. In such a society some aspects of mysticism, traditional or otherwise, can combine with prophetic practices leading to the said society becoming 'post-shamanic'. Shamanism then develops into more specialized, focused practices.

By and large, as a society changes from the primitive to the shamanic, and later progresses to the post-shamanic, there are several criteria which need to be met:
1. Economic change has taken place resulting in more formalized agriculture and perhaps manufacturing or crafts, rather than simple hunting and gathering.
2. There is a more structured social system and more specialization of occupation.
3. Ceremonies and rituals, combined with techniques for achieving

altered states, are no longer solely the province of the shaman – the systems of belief and access to spiritual knowledge are more sophisticated.

4. Trance techniques are used to achieve altered states of consciousness, particularly in regard to access to other realms, though shamanic ecstasy is still used.

5. Other forms of ecstasy become just as important as shamanic ecstasy which go beyond a feeling or perception of the sacred, the demonic or of natural spirits in other realities.

6. The religious life of the society is regulated by a priesthood or clergy that is more structured and 'professional'.

7. The role of guide to the souls of the dead to the afterlife is no longer the duty of the shaman. Various other guides, such as angels and journeys into light, become more apparent.

8. The shaman is no longer solely in charge of counselling, divination and healing within the society.

LINKING EAST AND WEST

The experiences of shamans during their initiations are very much mirrored in what Indian yogis and Tibetan lamas go through as they move towards enlightenment. In Tibet the lama is a priest who, although born into his calling, has undergone a long period of training before initiation.

Of prime importance to yogis is the process of understanding and preparing for death. Central to this belief is the idea that dreaming itself is a preparation for death. It is only through understanding illusion that the soul can prevent its return and rebirth within the physical realm. It must experience various levels of existence and prove all of them to be illusion. This physical world is only one of those levels, as is the dreaming state. This knowledge must be assimilated before the soul can reach the state of bliss known as *satori*.

Both Hindus and Buddhists perceive creative dreaming as a training geared to the above understanding and also as a preparation for death and the afterlife. By changing one's perception and the way that dreams are accepted as a natural part of the learning process, the fear of death is not quite so prevalent. Death then becomes merely a change of state where the individual enters a dream and does not awaken within the physical world. The 'nobly born' one – that is, the newly dead – must traverse the planes of illusion called *bardos*.

The individual's perception of the upper realms, spirit world – or whatever name it is given – varies from culture to culture. In Tibetan belief, the spiritual task of each transitional soul is to remain calm and emotionally stable throughout its experiences of the bardo states. If he is able to do this, these states begin to disappear after about forty days. The *Bardo Thodol* (*Tibetan Book of the Dead*) is a course of instruction deliberately used to remind the dead person that he must experience and transcend the 'reality' of the *bardo* dream. This follows the Tibetan belief that the soul can still hear when addressed by a living companion.

In this state, which is akin to limbo in the Christian religion, the lives of the dead are reviewed. According to the soul's acceptance and understanding of both the life last lived and the illusory states, the soul may need to return and reincarnate to achieve a better way of existence. Most souls, unless they are highly evolved, are not able to remain calm in such a situation. The Tibetan is aware that the demons are created by the soul's own negative expectations. The first reaction, as in nightmares, is to try to escape from the demons which are thus manifested. If, however, the soul remembers – or is reminded – that all is illusion, it creates the opportunity for itself to escape from the wheel of life. This means that it is free from the necessity to incarnate again, though it may *choose* to do so in order to assist the progress of mankind. The point of being able to dream lucidly in this life is to try to achieve a complete 'oneness' with everything that is not clouded by illusion. The belief is that waking life, like the dream, will ultimately dissolve into nothing and is therefore not real. Awareness of one's correct state brings one ever closer to a perception of true being as a state of bliss, known by many different names.

For those who choose to reincarnate in order to help the world's progress, there has to be an act of extreme dedication. These enlightened beings swear to renounce *nirvana* (their concept of the state of bliss) over and over again until all sentient beings are themselves enlightened. Their vision of oneness fades and dies if it is not consistently reinforced by effort. The art of creative dreaming is part of that continuous process. This concept has been adopted by many in the modern Western world.

NEW AGE MOVEMENT

In modern cultures, many people are exploring and enhancing aspects of self-development which were previously the sole province of priests and mystics. The New Age Movement which they embody – a term coined in the 1960s – is a highly diverse system of beliefs, a synthesis of Eastern and Western thought which emerged out of the pursuit of alternative realities.

Communities based on beliefs in spiritual values have grown up alongside the new way of thought which the movement propounded. These spiritual communities, although not necessarily identifying themselves as New Age, are fully aware of – and make use of – techniques such as creative dreaming to achieve a higher plane. Synthesizing shamanic practices, the use of psychedelics and wisdom culled from various ancient world religions, participants are achieving a 'new' mysticism. People such as Timothy White, one of the foremost present-day authorities on the philosophy of world religions, and Jeremy Taylor are prepared to give credence to the fact that many of the old religions owed their insights to the use of psychoactive substances.

Combining our modern understanding of the psychological changes which occur in altered states of consciousness with ancient knowledge and practices means that ordinary people now have at their disposal the ability to transcend everyday reality. Even physicists are accepting that their perceptions may not necessarily be final. It would seem that scientific theory and philosophy are becoming more and more closely linked. Creative dreaming, along with other altered states of consciousness, seems to act as an effective bridge between the two.

Many of the techniques which were part and parcel of primitive and shamanic practices have been rediscovered within the New Age context. Astral travel and projection quickly became part of the Spiritualist movement in the latter part of the 19th century and have found their way into modern-day practices. Out-of-the-body and near-death experiences have also achieved a certain respectability. This has happened even more so as anaesthesia improved and more sophisticated healing methods developed. Gradually people have realized that techniques such as lucid dreaming can be of assistance in achieving these states. A comparison of these different states of consciousness is offered in the next section.

SECTION

4

THE POWERS THAT BE

We referred in the last section to the New Age Movement, which has played a huge part in reviving interest in old techniques and altered states of consciousness. When modern practitioners first began to experiment with these techniques, there was an apprehensive reaction without a true understanding of what the development of these energies really meant. Instinctively people recognized that pilgrimages to holy places, such as India, and inner journeys were important and a huge movement towards self development began.

THE *SIDDHIS*

The *Siddhis* are held by the yogis to be powers that develop as one learns the art of self-development. They are the powers of clairvoyance, healing and predetermination, which become apparent the more comfortable you are with a wider viewpoint which takes in your responsibility for yourself and the community in which you live.

It has always been accepted that dreams have a meaning peculiarly their own. They arise from a hidden part of ourselves and filter through to consciousness, sometimes in a way that is easy to interpret and sometimes in a way that needs some kind of additional knowledge that cannot be quantified in the normal fashion. In the past, priests and wise men (and women) were called upon to interpret the straightforward symbolic content of others' dreams. When a dream could not be accepted as valid by the dreamer, it usually meant that it was not supposed to be looked at from an individual viewpoint but in the light of the message it held for the community. This meant that dreams were common property and it was understood that there were certain people who were more prolific dreamers than others. Priests and shamans would be required to develop certain rituals and esoteric awareness to help them interpret the dreams they were told.

Ancient dream interpreters were markedly down to earth in the way they tackled dreams. There was little mysticism and superstition: they were logical and neither overly scientific nor esoteric. It was accepted that the dream was a movement of the soul that created images which had to be interpreted by reason. In sleep the soul would move in one of two ways, either in sympathy with the Ultimate or through its own power.

Such an idea is comforting for us in the modern day since it allows us to accept the idea of predetermination, precognition and dreams about the future with equanimity. We become aware of the future because at some level we already know about it and our dreaming self is prepared to give us the information in a useable form so that we can act appropriately. So, the more conscious we are of other aspects of life, the more aware we become that the boundaries between time and space are the confines of illusion, and we can work to transcend those parameters through dreams. Creative dreaming allows us a much wider aspect to knowledge if we so desire.

Elsewhere in the book we will show how to dream of the past in a lucid fashion and the same technique can be used to put you more in touch with the future. In creative dreaming, it is possible to suspend disbelief and accept that the information that you are receiving may or may not be valid. When you have practised the technique enough you will learn to trust the process and then to accept that you are able to connect with the future. Whether you care to call it clairvoyance or something else, it really does not matter. What does happen is that in a situation where you need to decide on a course of action, you are able to predict with a fair degree of accuracy what is going to happen.

In waking life, you can often find yourself in a situation where you are fairly certain that it has happened before. This is known as the phenomenon of déja-vu. With this you may like to experiment to find out whether in fact this is true. You may well be able to travel back in time to discover whether such a thing is a 'soul memory' which has imprinted itself upon your psyche. The recognition is a spontaneous breakthrough from a different part of your being.

OUT-OF-BODY EXPERIENCES AND ASTRAL TRAVEL

One of the old-style *siddhis* was the ability to 'fly', which was accepted as an extremely powerful state. This is today recognized as an out-of-the-body experience and astral travel and projection. There is so much confusion over the various altered states of consciousness that it is worthwhile spending some time in understanding the similarities and differences.

Lucidity is simply conscious awareness of the dream state. As we have seen elsewhere, it is probable that without a great deal of practice the creative dream is not always controllable as fully as the dreamer would have expected. Various components of the dream can be controlled, but by and large, it is not possible to control the scenario, the action, the characters and everything else at the same time. While one aspect is being controlled, the others tend to slip out of kilter. The dreamer sometimes has control over their own actions, but not over anything else. Often a stray thought will have the effect of changing the lucidity of the dream. It is quite likely that at this point there will be a loss of lucidity due to the emotional charge of the frustration; it is very easy to become reabsorbed into the old (non-lucid) dream again and lose objectivity.

In an out-of-the-body experience, the participant is also fully aware, but this time beginning from an 'awake' state. There is usually an awareness of when the out-of-body experience is coming to an end, and a sense of re-entering the physical body, which has been separate from the travelling self. If properly trained, the individual will have a degree of control over his surroundings and his actions, which usually are fairly passive and non-invasive of others' privacy. Often part of such training has consisted of the idea of remaining connected to the physical body by a silver cord or other similar type of connection, so the idea of slipping back into the physical body is considered to be quite normal.

Spontaneous out-of-body experiences, such as those which occur during great trauma or near death, often mean that the person is fully aware of another dimension other than the one in which he normally exists. Creative dreamers, however, tend to initially believe that this other dimension is a construct of their own mind. During out-of-body experiences the individual is often aware of his or her own physical body as a separate reality, whereas the lucid dreamer tends not to experience the physical body as a separate reality. There is, of course, some blurring of the boundaries of these states. The novice out-of-body experiencer, on becoming aware of that state, will automatically and spontaneously slip back into the inert physical body. This is akin to what happens in the creative dreaming state, where on becoming aware that one is dreaming, one wakes up.

Perhaps before comparing out-of-body experiences with lucid dreaming it is necessary to compare out-of-body experience with astral travel and projection. Many people would not differentiate between these states, but if we make one simple differentiation between them it is simpler to understand. Out-of-body experiences are simply that. There is the sense that the physical body has been left behind and that the subtler astral body has lifted away from the physical body into a new perception. Astral travel and projection occur when one voluntarily projects the astral body and moves away from the physical body for a greater or lesser distance.

The techniques are quite simple and consist initially of being aware that you can will such a thing to happen. The more relaxed you are, the looser is the connection between the two bodies and there is the subjective experience that the astral body can be free from the physical body. It is often sensible to think of the process as though you were removing an outer garment that you will come back to later and pick up when you are ready.

Astral projection is therefore the second stage of the process where you set yourself a target and push yourself towards it. You become aware in the process that the normal constraints of not being able to pass through walls and other obstacles do not apply, nor is there a perception of time or distance. Astral travel is the way of carrying out these actions, of moving from place to place or from dimension to dimension. Some people would say that they simply 'think' themselves there, others choose to fly there (similarly to creative dreaming), whereas yet others will perform some other action such as rolling themselves into position.

What is important is that the process requires two acts – one to get out of the body and one to move into position. It is a matter of personal preference as to how you achieve this state. In most training methods you will experiment first of all by moving through the denser physical plane with ease and actively practising such things as seeing your astral hand passing through a wall. You might then try transporting yourself to the roof of your house or other nearby building and experiencing the world from that position. Only when you feel ready to do so, will you move on to travelling into other dimensions and experimenting with the perceptions that that brings.

In lucid dreaming, you will generally find that you are required to undertake one action, whether that be spinning or repetition of your trigger phrase or statement of intent. To achieve your objective requires focus and stability. For most people the lucid dream is seen as a totally personal construct of the dreamer's mind seen from a subjective viewpoint whereas an out-of-body experiencer does not see his way of achieving his aim as subjective at all, but rather as an objective reality. One can only reiterate that the two states 'feel' different.

It might be suggested, too, that both states depend upon the expectation of the end result. One would not necessarily expect to achieve a mystical state directly from a lucid dream, though, as we shall see in Section 7, this may well be possible, whereas that expectation might be present in an out-of-the-body experience, particularly a spontaneous one.

REALITY STATES
In the process of learning to dream lucidly, you learn how to test

reality and to be able to state, 'This is a dream'. An out-of-body experience can take place from a waking state and is often simply accepted as a non-waking reality. It does seem that people will accept that the creative dream is unreal after waking up, though there is often some doubt after returning from an out-of-the-body experience.

The two states can be brought more closely together if both are thought of in terms of non-waking realities, perhaps state (a) for lucid dreams and state (b) for out-of-the-body experiences. In this way, the individuals can differentiate for themselves which one they are having and which one they prefer. Often that will depend on which of the two they were introduced to or discovered first. Both are equally valid and both worth investigating. The deciding factor may well be for some the relative ease with which they can move around in the two states or how easily they can make things happen.

Inevitably, it is at this point that the question arises as to how many realities there actually are and the answer is of course 'as many as can be created'. The only way to deal with such a question is philosophically and to accept that each state is created by us with whatever constraints and ideas that we have at our disposal. If in a lucid dream we decide we can pass through walls, then that becomes possible when we have suspended disbelief to the point where we can do it. During an out-of-body experience, we can transport ourselves with little difficulty to another place if we believe we can. The waking state has a reality of its own which does not allow us to pass physically through walls or transport ourselves from place to place. However, that belief only works for the waking reality because there is an innate sense that these things are not possible and we have not yet overcome the conditioning of many many generations. So it is with the statement 'This is a dream'.

We define a dream as a mental occurrence arising from a sleep state – that being the important aspect. A dream arises from a sleep state. What we call an out-of-the-body experience does not usually arise from a sleep state, whereas a lucid dream does. Each state arises from a different point of origin and can be differentiated only in that way. The content of each experience is very similar.

It is only really when we come to compare a Wake-Induced Lucid Dream with an out-of-body experience that the lines become somewhat blurred. The methods of bringing each about are different and, for those who wish to experiment with inducing out-of-the-body experience, one of the accepted methods is as follows. To leave the body you might try the 'lift-out' method. To do this you simply visualise yourself becoming lighter and lighter and eventually floating out of your body, whether you are lying down or standing upright. You will probably experience a strong sense of freedom and be much more aware of those things that are happening to you. In Near-Death Experience (NDE), which is very similar to an out-of-body experience, but often caused by trauma, one becomes aware of what is happening to the physical body, which has been left behind.

It is interesting to compare the realities as they are experienced. By and large, people who have experienced out-of-the-body episodes have said that the latter state is that of entering a more spiritual environment, whereas creative dreamers say their experience is more 'real'. Both states raise questions which require answers as to the true nature of reality. Most people come to the conclusion that reality is based on our own mental models of the world. This is not so far from the Tibetan concept which views the physical realm as our own construct and this life as but a preparation for death. People experiencing out-of-body states take as their prime reality the spiritual realm, whereas lucid dreamers start from the perspective that the everyday world is reality and their dreams are separate from it. This difference in perspective is immaterial: the result from either state is capable of creating profound changes in the individual's world.

Speaking of the effect that both experiences have, it is believed by many that lucid dreams are not remembered except with training, but out-of-body experiences are. To be fair, this will depend on you, the individual. Both will have what might be called the 'wow' factor, since both states are beyond the norm, but once they are accepted and are acclimatized to neither will have more validity than the other. One way of giving them both validity is to use them for different purposes. You might, for instance, use one to explore philosophical and spiritual questions and the other the more mundane aspects of your existence. The triggers and starting points that are given in Section 6 through the Archetypes and so on, can be used for either purpose and allow a complete reassessment of the way you think of the world you inhabit.

There are those who seem to infer that out-of-body experience is a poor-quality creative dream and vice versa. This is obviously one of those arguments that can never be properly resolved. It is pointless to try to evaluate which state is better or more complete – both are types of altered consciousness and both therefore deserve further exploration.

Those readers who are content to keep an open mind may like to spend some time looking at the table on the next page which provides a comparison of creative dreams and out-of-body experiences. We hope the information will help to resolve any confusion.

A Comparison of Lucid Dreams and OBB Experiences

LUCID DREAMS	OUT-OF-BODY EXPERIENCES
Experienced by 50–70 per cent of the general population.	Experienced by 14–25 per cent of the general population.
Occur only during sleep.	Occur usually when awake.
The dreamer can with practice consciously influence the dream.	The out-of-body experiences are more objective and tranquil.
The dreamer and the physical body are not visually experienced as a duality. The physical body is not often seen.	Give a strong sense of separation between the physical and non-physical (astral) bodies. The physical body is often seen.
Vivid perception of all aspects of the dream, but always with a dream-like quality.	Perception is more akin to the waking state, but vivid with training.
The dream is experienced as a subjective reality produced by the dreamer's inner self. 'This is my dream.'	The out-of-body experience is seen as objective and 'beyond self'. 'This experience was given to me.'
EEG traces show REM dream type.	EEG findings not well researched.
Remembered and accepted as dreams, the positive impact is greater only when highly trained.	Often a highly positive impact on the individual, whether the experience is spontaneous or otherwise.

With an understanding of the various states of consciousness, you are ready to set out on an intriguing exploration of where creative dreaming and its attendant states can take you.

Consciously to access these different parts of the personality, many New Age people have learnt to use updated versions of the ancient techniques. Through these it is possible to make use of natural occurrences to help one to enhance events that happen during creative dreaming. Usually as one relaxes naturally into sleep, there is something which is called the myoclonic jerk. What actually happens is the body – or various muscles – let go suddenly. In a state of half-sleep this is translated by the mind into a sensation of falling. Normally this causes the individual to wake up; when he or she is training for lucid dreaming, however, it is possible to hold on to this sensation of falling and continue to do so without waking up. This helps eventually to make the physical body less open to the rather odd feelings which may occur, or be induced, during spinning or flying when creative dreaming. These can occasionally give rise to a fear reaction which can awaken the dreamer. Working with the myoclonic jerk and extending the feeling of falling into one of flying can also give the dreamer a sense of control which they might not otherwise have.

If, in waking life, you have a fear of heights or of sudden movements, you can use this same method of continuing to fall to retrain yourself to overcome that fear. (Many people believe that such fears arise from difficulties experienced by the baby during the birth process.)

Also, breathing techniques can be used, firstly to help you to become even more relaxed, and secondly to begin to overcome the restrictions of the physical world. For instance – after using the technique given below – on breathing out, the command can be given to lift yourself slightly off the bed. At first nothing is likely to happen, but gradually the sensation of 'lifting' will become apparent and a state akin to being 'out of the body' will ensue. You could also reverse this process and feel yourself gradually sinking through the bed in progressive stages. Do remember, too, that this is a mental process and it is therefore the mental part of you which is responding to the command and not your actual physical being. Success will depend on your beliefs and the amount of caution exercised.

Yogic breathing practices actually teach one particular exercise which is designed to induce calmness and tranquillity. The exercise follows, below. In fact, it has now been proved that this exercise alters the rhythm within the brain. Ancient texts also advise the seeker of truth to sleep on the right side, presumably because this stimulates the body rhythms in a particular way; empirical evidence suggests that creative dreaming is indeed stimulated in this position. You may like to experiment for yourself as to the various positions and postures which achieve maximum lucidity.

1. Place the first two fingers of the right hand on your forehead so that the tips of your fingers are between your eyebrows. This brings the thumb into position against the right nostril and the fourth and fifth finger against the left.
2. Close your eyes and concentrate on the point at which your first two fingers touch your face. This will help to focus your mind.
3. Press the right nostril closed with the thumb, and inhale gently and quietly through the left nostril to a count of eight.
4. Close both nostrils and hold the breath for a further count of eight.
5. Release the right nostril, holding the left one closed and exhale gently and quietly through the right nostril to a count of eight.
6. Keeping the left nostril closed inhale gently and quietly through the right nostril to a count of eight.
7. Repeat step three, then release the left nostril, keeping the right one closed.
8. Exhale gently and quietly through the left nostril to a count of eight.

This exercise should be repeated at least seven times, and as many times as is felt necessary. Such breathing helps one to clear the breathing passages, relieves headaches and acts as a natural relaxant.

THE *CHAKRAS*

From this state of relaxation, working with an ancient method of perception, it is possible to understand the subtle energy centres of the human being. These centres are known as the *chakras* (the Sanskrit word for 'wheel') and can be worked with to enhance the facility of creative dreaming.

The major *chakras*, their positions and generally accepted colours are (also see the illustration on the next page):

Base or Root *chakra* (located at the base of the spine)	Red
Spleen *chakra* (slightly below the navel)	Orange
Solar-plexus *chakra* (approximately six inches above the navel)	Yellow
Heart *chakra* (in the centre of the chest)	Green or pink
Throat *chakra* (at the base of the throat)	Blue
Third-eye or Brow *chakra* (in the middle of the forehead)	Purple/violet
Crown *chakra* (at the top of the head)	White

There are other minor *chakras* in the hands and feet.

For the purposes of creative dreaming, the *chakras* can be used as a way of changing consciousness in a very controlled manner. Each *chakra* rules different parts of the physical body and has an effect on the mental abilities. They are principally a gateway between the physical being and the spiritual – the very subtle energies that have given people the opportunity to understand their inner selves and the meaning of life. In order to work with these spiritual centres, the dreamer will need to create for himself some kind of structure to enable him to visualize the energy moving around the body. He needs to make sense of all of those things that he must learn and remember. Perhaps the easiest visualization to use is the one illustrated overleaf, which shows the position on the body of each *chakra*.

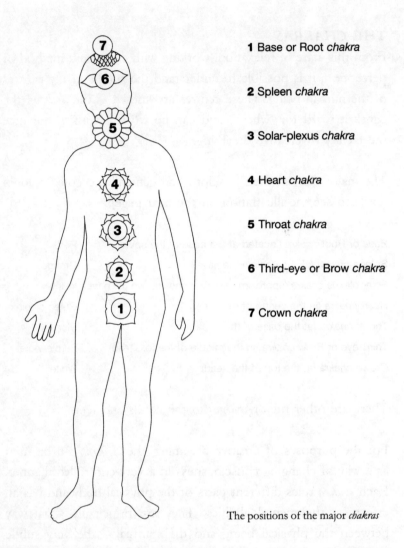

1 Base or Root *chakra*

2 Spleen *chakra*

3 Solar-plexus *chakra*

4 Heart *chakra*

5 Throat *chakra*

6 Third-eye or Brow *chakra*

7 Crown *chakra*

The positions of the major *chakras*

The more the dreamer understands, the more they are able to deal with increasingly complex ideas. So it is with lucid dreaming – the more proficient one becomes, the more one is able to deal with complex ideas in dreaming. Each intricate spiritual centre should become activated as the nervous system matures.

The activation of the spiritual centres should really follow a set pattern, very similar to the growth in understanding that a child goes through in the passage to maturity. From the time when a child becomes aware that he is a physical being with individual features, he needs to be nurtured through to a greater understanding and philosophical appreciation of the external world. This should happen during adolescence and is expressed through different emotions. Along with the discovery of the need to answer questions about his being, he constantly learns and stores knowledge. As each *chakra* becomes activated, the child becomes better equipped to deal with what life may have in store. This is such a natural process that the subtlety of the energies is rarely noticed.

To go through the process of relearning the art of becoming a fully functioning human being, there are certain visualizations and exercises which can be done, thereby giving better access to the information that we all hold within on a spiritual level. Initially, it is easier to deal with the *chakras* from the base up and to perceive the energy moving upwards to the crown of the head. When we are able to access this information and retain it on a conscious level through the use of creative dreaming, we have a tool fit for living life in a new way.

A suggested visualization is to see each *chakra* as a revolving wheel about the size of a tennis ball and 'play' with each *chakra* in turn, sensing it becoming first larger then smaller in turn. (This may take some practice but it is worth persevering.) The *chakras* can also be visualized as spheres of light or colour or, as many people prefer, something in the shape of a diabolo, below.

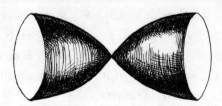

Such a visualization helps to give a sense of the spiritual energies which play such an important part in all our lives. While it starts off as a visualization, before long we do actually begin to sense the energies themselves.

When you have become proficient at moving the energy from feet to head, try moving it in the opposite direction, finally circulating it around the body from foot to head and back again. Initially such a practice may make you feel too energized and therefore unready for sleep. However, diligent practice will help you to differentiate between the various stages of lucid dreaming.

If you have difficulty in moving the energy up and down, try circulating it from left to right and right to left. Take time to find what works for you and visualize yourself surrounded by a cocoon of – preferably – white light. Other higher vibrational colours, such as purple and blue, may also be used. This is a protective device which means that you can make further use of other subtle energies that become available. It is useful when working with changes of consciousness to have developed such a routine so that you feel secure during any experimentation – creative dreaming can sometimes give you a more creative experience of this aura.

CREATIVITY IN DREAMING

Your dreams are the way in which that truly creative part of you, the unconscious, makes itself both heard and felt. There are two ways of looking at ordinary dreams. Either they are a message from that part of you with which you are not easily in contact – the subtle energies – or are a series of symbols which are presented for intelligent interpretation. Whichever way, you have at your disposal a vast library of information which can help you to express your inherent creativity.

Lucid dreaming takes access to this library to even greater depths, unlocking parts of our psyche that we did not know previously existed. Working on the principle that the answer to any question lies within yourself through dreaming lucidly, you are able to give a degree of structure to the creative process. Examples of the above are legion throughout literature, science and the arts. Robert Louis Stevenson paid homage to the help his 'little people' gave him. From his description, these helpers appeared in his creative dreams. Henri Fabre in *Souvenirs Entomologiques* says:

'A brilliant beacon flares up in my brain and then I jump from my bed, light my lamp and write down the solution the memory of which would otherwise be lost; like flashes of lightning these gleams vanish as suddenly as they appear.'

Most creative people seem to be lateral thinkers; that is, they are able to make a quantum leap in their understanding, able to make connections within their thought processes that are not apparent to most people. This process seems to be enhanced by lucid dreaming. By contrast, scientists and engineers are by nature logical and more linear in their thought processes. For them, it is important to be able to prove their reality in waking life. This type of person will often not accept their dreams until they have proof of their dreamt reality.

During the process of learning how to control creative dreaming, you are always required to check your reality. This is usually by asking the question, 'Am I dreaming?' The second stage of learning is to tell yourself during the day that you will have a lucid dream. The third stage is to decide on the subject of your creative dream. All of these processes are explored more fully in other parts of the book.

It is important to realize that, unless you have undergone a degree of training in not only remembering and annotating but also structuring your dreams, it is difficult to access the full content of your inner 'database'. It is therefore important that you successfully do all of these things. In this way the mind opens up to possibilities far beyond those of waking consciousness. Often a few notes of music, some verse or a particularly beautiful tone or colour will appear in your dream. On consideration it may not be as beautiful or relevant as it seemed initially, but often contains the beginning of an idea or project. With the ability to dream lucidly, you are able to select what appeals to you and build on it.

One of the tasks that we must do in learning to dream creatively is to ensure that we remove the restrictions placed on us by the community in which we live. From the time we are quite small, we learn to listen to the supposed wisdom of our 'elders and betters'. It is then far too easy to lose touch with the inner voice which, if allowed, guides us into correct action. Just as a computer must delete a programme which is malfunctioning, so humans must learn to eradicate false presumptions. This can only be done by continually questioning oneself by asking, 'What makes me unique?' By understanding our strengths and weaknesses it is possible to tap unfathomed depths of awareness that need to be addressed.

It is not until we accept that the dreaming process is perhaps of prime importance within our framework of work tools, that we are able to understand ourselves and what we need to do to bring out the best in us. The way that a child grows in understanding as it matures is a good matrix for spiritual and creative growth. Creatively, one tends to go through a similar sort of growth process when developing one's own especial projects and can learn to harness this energy. This theme of growth is often developed in dreams as we become more proficient in understanding and taking control of our lives.

By referring back to the *chakra* system, you will be able to develop creative dreaming to the point where you are deliberately using it to develop your creativity. Once you have decided what makes you unique, you can look at yourself in different ways and develop an appreciation of the meanings of each *chakra*. These are shown below:

CHAKRA	MEANING
Base or Root (located at the base of the spine)	Self-image
Spleen (slightly below the navel)	Relationship
Solar-plexus (approximately six inches above the navel)	Emotion
Heart (in the centre of the chest)	Self-knowledge
Throat (at the base of the throat)	Self-expression
Third-eye or Brow (in the middle of the forehead)	Objective Spirituality
Crown (at the top of the head)	Creative Spirituality (the Future)

Self-image

It may be that you have never thought of yourself as being particularly creative. Take some time to look first of all at what you do best. Try to get some feedback from close family and friends as to their opinion, but remember that it is only their opinion about you, it is not a judgement. Look also at what you like doing and also what you would like to do. Make a few notes to help you remember, but again remind yourself to be flexible in what you are doing.

Now set yourself a period, say a long weekend, when you will instruct yourself to practice lucid dreaming to make changes. It is always a good idea to do some preparation beforehand, such as making certain that your diet has been light but nutritious, that you have not overloaded your system with toxins, and that you have previously slept well.

During the day, tell yourself that you will be working with your self-image and making changes in the way that you think of yourself. List any changes that you would like to make, such as 'I would like to be (more outgoing/positive/less aggressive about myself etc.)' and repeat the affirmation whenever you think about it during the day. Interestingly, a good time to repeat your affirmation is when you are carrying out a totally mundane task such as using the toilet or washing your hands.

Finally, before you go to sleep, use the method shown in Section 8 to induce creative dreaming using your chosen affirmation. This way you have both instructed yourself to have a lucid dream and opened yourself to change.

Relationships

When you feel ready to tackle the questions surrounding your relationships, whether they are work-related or personal, you can adapt the above technique to help you. Again, take time to prepare yourself, looking at the relationships around you and whether you feel you function well or badly within them. Do they support you in the process of creativity? Is there something that you wish to change? Are you happy or miserable? What action do you wish to take? Remember always to make notes to enhance your memory (this also gives you a record for future projects or work and can often give you encouragement to continue with the process at a later date). There is no time limit on working with yourself.

Once again, take the opportunity to choose carefully the time when you will carry out this technique. It is wise to make time when you are successful in creative dreaming to clarify your thoughts and feelings without interruption afterwards. Lucid dreaming does not always take place immediately after giving ourselves the instruction and can sometimes surprise us by its spontaneity.

Choose an affirmation which expresses what you are trying to achieve, always expressing it in positive terms. Such an affirmation of intent might be 'I would like to understand my relationship with...better' or 'How can I improve my relationship?' Remember that these are only suggestions and your own affirmation will express your needs more fully.

State your intention during the day and also just before you go to sleep in the same way as you did with self-image, reminding yourself to have a lucid dream. Again write down and tabulate the results.

Emotions

You will have appreciated by now that the process of self-development and the enhancement of creativity cannot be hurried and that it sometimes seems to have its own agenda. Sometimes you think you have dealt with a particular stage of development only to have it return with more ferocity at a later date. When we are dealing with our emotional baggage, creative dreaming allows us to be more objective in our assessment of ourselves. At this stage you are able to step into the role of observer and often work through and reject some of that baggage.

The technique of harnessing lucid dreaming at this level of consideration is similar to that which we have used previously.

Again choose your time carefully and make suitable preparation. Your affirmation perhaps needs to be considered even more carefully than before, since you are beginning to touch into areas of yourself that you may have chosen not to explore before. One suggestion is to make arrangements to have someone you can rely on and trust (possibly someone who also practises lucid dreaming) around during the ensuing period so that you can discuss what has been happening to you.

Emotional needs can be divided into three categories.

- Inclusion – do you belong or not?
- Control – do you like being in control or controlled?
- Affection – do you trust other people, are you receptive to people around you or do you dislike warmth and affection?

It may be that considering the following points will give you a framework in which to work.

1. Some people need to feel part of a group and dislike acting on their own; some can be part of a crowd but are perfectly happy to be by themselves if necessary. Others do not need to be part of a group and indeed can be quite uncomfortable in such a situation.

2. Many people are natural leaders, dislike taking second place and will tend to take control whether it is appropriate or not. When there is a degree of lack of clarity about control many people will take control if necessary, but pass authority to someone else if they feel that person is more able. Quite a number of people prefer to be told what action to take, and will never try to impose their own will under any circumstance.

3. Individuals who have strong needs for affection will form

open intimate relationships, and will need friends. Those with lesser needs will have some friends with whom they are intimate but others with whom they are more distant. A third group with fewer needs for affection will have much reserve in forming relationships and will be more detached.

With the help of the table below, decide what your own needs are and then seek the help of a friend to check your findings. You could use creative dreaming to clarify this. To complete the table you only need to use one word (high, low or medium) in each box. Only if your feelings are ambiguous should you use more than one category in the same box (i.e. high to medium, medium to low).

	INCLUSION	CONTROL	AFFECTION
What I express to others			
What I want from others			

In working to develop your creativity, the answers to these statements will show you under what circumstances you are likely to be most creative. For instance, you may work well by yourself but need affection from others to feel that you have succeeded in your task. Alternatively, you may need to work in a group but take private pleasure in your projects.

Self-awareness

This concept is different from that of self-image in that it is an awareness of just what the potentials are which are held within oneself, and of those things which one may be able to complete within the future. It is here that lucid dreaming begins to really come into its own, for it opens up possibilities and themes which we can experiment with to see how we can improve them or allow them to work more efficiently. The Creative Projects exercise in Section 8 gives you a basis to work from.

The preparation of yourself and of your affirmations is similar to the way shown above in Self-image. There is, however, less need to question yourself quite so stringently and more requirement to think coherently about who you are and what your talents and abilities are. By using the following brief questionnaire, you will develop a fairly clear picture of your capabilities, and when deciding to dream lucidly, you will be able to focus on some of those things you may wish to change.

Use the following phrases to start thinking about your own philosophy or rules that you may have.

If (I had power, was happy, etc.) then...

What I want is...

What I need is...

I should...

What gives me pleasure is...

What distresses me is...

I like myself, therefore...

You may also like to focus your ideas and develop a more positive attitude to your creativity. The following exercise will help you to do this.

Write a summary of the main events in your life; then record your feelings about them. Separate those feelings into those you want more of and those you don't want to experience again. Identify the behaviour you need to get the good feelings again.

Then, thinking of yourself as a business, write a statement of your company aims, your business philosophy, a motto, a logo. Work on these to extract a vision of how you want to be.

You may, for instance, wish to be more creative in your approach to your work. Let us suppose that you are aware that you are not as committed to your latest work project as you would wish to be. You might begin to use the idea of light and lucidity to 'shed light on' the subject and to develop ways of perhaps being more committed to the completion of it rather than to the project itself.

Self-expression

Since true creativity is the expression of your ability to make real something which starts off as an idea – and therefore something rather nebulous – creative dreaming at this level of awareness truly opens up all sorts of creative possibilities. One of the biggest lessons to be learned is the ability to integrate the inner self with the demands of the external world, and to be able to communicate what one is aware of on the inside with what is appropriate on the outside.

Many creative people have difficulty in translating what they perceive inwardly into something tangible, yet through creative dreaming the process of translation can be refined and honed. Almost everybody has experienced the frustration which occurs when our creation is not as beautiful or as clear as it seemed to be at first. With dreaming lucidly and with full awareness, you will be aware not just of how to put it right, but also of how to experiment with your perception of it.

The preparation for this process is similar to the previous techniques. During the day, you might like to remind yourself that you will give your creative self its own expression or find new ways to do so. Before you go to sleep, your affirmation might be something like, 'Tonight I will dream lucidly in order to release my creativity'. The result may be that your dreaming self, which usually remembers dreams, may not be aware of any change, whilst in the waking world opportunities come to light which are highly creative in their outcome. You have given yourself permission to succeed.

Objectivity

Objectivity about yourself, your circumstances and the people around you is one of the finest tools which you can develop. You are able then to make non-judgmental assessments and decide on a particular source of action which allows you to get the best out of whatever is going on around you. It is really a matter of using the energies correctly. The art of creative dreaming – for by now it is turning into an art form – helps you to create the correct environment to be at your most creative.

Preparing for this stage is very similar to the techniques you have used so far but is somewhat more focused and specific. Constantly remind yourself during the day that you can dream with lucidity. Also remind yourself that you wish to develop the art of perception which is, after all, objectivity. This will allow the energy which can sometimes get blocked to flow more freely. Your declaration of intent might take the form of 'I shall dream lucidly to enhance my perception of the world around me. I wish to see...more clearly'.

The possibility is that during your dreams you may well experience a great deal of light. It is more than likely that the information that you need will simply arrive without the help of images. It is as though you 'know' the information. You may also find that in actually trying to execute some project the energy simply flows well for you, thus giving you a great sense of satisfaction. Again, do be aware that the answers have a habit of coming in their own time and cannot be forced. One side-effect of work on this level is that the ordinary everyday world becomes brighter, more colourful and more bearable.

The Future

The highest level that most people wish to attain through creative dreaming is the level which should strictly be called that of Cosmic Responsibility. This is that part of you which is prepared to take responsibility for the world in which you live and, having successfully navigated the past and dealt with the present, is now prepared to develop a future.

Creative dreaming on this level consists not so much in having lucid dreams as in dreaming 'in the light'. The experience of light, or lightness, is much stronger on this level and really puts you in touch with energies that you may not have experienced previously. Here you are able to develop an idea, make it tangible and infuse it with the energy that will have it manifest in the waking world.

The preparation for this level is again similar to that previously experienced, but is now focused on creating a future. You dream your future into existence, so the declaration of intent must reflect this. Using an affirmation such as 'I am what I can be' or 'I use my full potential in everything I do' helps to focus the energy into true creativity. This does not necessarily mean being artistic, which is a mistake that a number of people have in their thinking, but does mean that life takes on a new meaning. Sleep at this stage is often dreamless in the conventional sense of the word, but is equally full of power. This state is discussed more fully in Section 7.

SECTION

5

HEALING THROUGH DREAMS

The potential to use lucid dreams for a variety of purposes is huge. When we begin any journey, we need to plan our route and to work out the quickest way to arrive at our destination. We can use dreams, particularly lucid ones, to help us chart a course which enables us to overcome difficulties with those parts of our personalities which prevent us from living life to the full. Dreams often alert us to the fact that there is something which needs to be adjusted or confronted. Once we have identified a problem, we can use lucid dreaming techniques to help us to understand or overcome the difficulty.

Let us suppose that you have identified the fact that your self-esteem is low, perhaps because you have received a series of setbacks at work. You might first instruct yourself to have an ordinary dream to give you a handle on the problem. For example, you may take into sleep the image of a door which is stuck and will not open. Then, using the relevant techniques, you incubate a lucid dream using this image, which allows you to overcome the difficulty. (How to do this, and the difference in the techniques, is shown below.) In your lucid dream you may dream of another obstacle which is in your way. You know that you are dreaming and refuse to believe that the obstacle needs to be present, or you are able to shrink it to manageable proportions. You now know that you have done the work necessary to remove the difficulty that is blocking you. In waking life, and in due course – because you have empowered yourself at a very deep level – your self-esteem improves tremendously, and you achieve a degree of success.

As a further example, for those who have an interest in personal development, creative dreaming can be used to enlist the help of those parts of yourself which can give you information which is not necessarily consciously available to you. It can also be used to bring an errant part of your personality under control. It is possible, in other words, to access or reprogramme a part of the personality through dreams. Being aware that one is dreaming means that appropriate action can be taken. To dream of a tenant in a flat which we own could mean, for instance, that an idea or principle has 'taken up residence' within us. To decide from a lucid perspective that the tenant should be evicted means we no longer need to subscribe to that particular way of thinking.

Dreams are said to be a clearing-house for impressions which we have accumulated during the day. It should be possible to use lucid dreams to deliberately clear away what has become known as the 'day's residue'. True mental and spiritual health means that we are prepared to take responsibility for the way we live our lives. A way of doing a 'Daily Audit' is shown in Section 8. For those things of which you are proud you can incubate more actions of the same calibre. For those thoughts, feelings and actions which you have disliked, or which have upset you, you can try lucidly dreaming about them and, during the dream, increase the will to do better. You might feel that you have treated someone badly, for instance. By going to sleep with this on your mind, you can seek forgiveness through your dreams.

You do not need to feel guilty, but to be aware of a wish to make amends.

There are many well-documented stories of creative problem solving through dreams. It is perhaps here that the napping or short-sleep technique used in studies of lucid dreams can come into its own. The answer to one's problem may come through having rested one's body either by a night's sleep or a period of complete relaxation, then having a short sleep of about 90 minutes with the intention of dreaming with lucidity. With many of these techniques, it is worth remembering that lucid dreaming can be a bit erratic, so be patient if the answer does not come immediately; it may come during a later session of sleep. The short-sleep technique does seem to enable the dreamer to focus more fully on the issues in hand.

Proof that creative dreaming can aid and enhance physical health is difficult to come by, purely because the results are so subjective. However, many people believe they have healed themselves through the use of dreams, both lucid and otherwise. As is mentioned later in this section, dream imagery about bodily problems can be quite specific. Healing imagery can therefore be substituted lucidly to help in the healing process. For instance, one might, having dreamt of burst pipes, substitute the mending of the pipes being carried out. This would enhance the body's own natural ability to heal, thereby creating an inner environment conducive to fast recovery.

For many, however, along with the ability to move through time and space without restraint, it is enough to experience the freedom which lucid dreaming brings. Creative dreaming may help an individual come to terms with disability of one sort or another. The techniques of flying or spinning, both of which are used in lucid dreaming, are particularly helpful to people with physical disabilities, enabling them to experiment with the mental adjustments necessary for coping with the frustrations of mobility problems.

Another area where lucid dreaming has a long proven history is in the handling of bad dreams and nightmares caused by trauma. This is dealt with more extensively later in this section but there are certainly enough anecdotes to prove that facing our fears through dreams can obliterate them altogether. It is as though the mind recognizes that it no longer has the power to distress the dreamer.

Healing and dreams are very closely interlinked. Through dreams we are able to put ourselves in touch with the hidden, more unconscious parts of our personalities. We are capable then of healing a problem from within, rather than only dealing with the symptoms and their effects. For instance, something may have happened during childhood which, because it is too difficult to handle, we have buried deep within us. Only when a similar trauma happens in adult life does that part of us which knows and remembers everything look through its records and present the original trauma (often in symbolic form) for our consideration.

When we have learnt to understand this process, and also the symbolism of our dreams, we can carry our what is popularly called 'dreamwork' and heal that frightened, damaged part of ourselves. It is this damaged part that may be stopping us from having successful relationships or gaining promotion at work or experiencing contentment. Dreamwork consists of being able to:

• Change your attitudes – either to yourself or your external world.

- Develop insight into what makes you the person you are.
- Solve problems and make choices in the light of such insights.
- Use your dreams constructively to change the reality of your everyday life.
- Deliberately choose to dream about something which is worrying you.

Not only can dreams be used for healing yourself, but with practice can be used to help other people. Insight into somebody else's condition – physical or mental – can often come to you through dreams, because there is a part in all of us which is alive to subtle vibrations and imbalances in the people and environment around us. Our own experiences may have given us clues and techniques to deal with such imbalance and we can thus help the other person. Many people would call these clairvoyant dreams.

Some people are more able to interpret others' dreams through the use of intuition and knowledge of symbolism. In what might be called dream therapy, based variously on Freud and other more modern psychoanalytical interpretations, the use of group therapy can help to heal. In this, meaningful dreams are shared with others for interpretation. It is then up to the dreamers themselves to choose out of the many suggestions the most relevant ones.

Perhaps one of the most important ways of using dreams for healing is the recognition that individuals will almost inevitably try to make themselves better. This type of dream occurs most often during times of illness, before or after surgery or after some life crisis, such as a family bereavement. It is as though the body is doing its best to re-establish an internal balance. An example of such a dream might be the image of leaking pipes at the onset of a heart condition.

Finally, if one is of a mind to look to the future, more able lucid dreamers may one day be able to create a world through dreams which could become a matrix for the preservation of the planet. But, first of all, we must empower ourselves.

INNER BALANCE

When you come to look at your dreams there are inevitably some questions which will need answering sooner or later. These are largely to do with those issues which arise, such as what the physical implications are for you through your particular dream, and also what the spiritual ramifications are.

We will explore later in this section how the body will do its level best to restore itself to wellbeing and will when necessary use dreams to warn of impending difficulty. Aristotle recognized that this was possible all of 2,300 years ago and Hippocrates (the father of medicine) also suggested that dreams were influenced by illness. Modern-day psychologists are also aware that dreams can be affected by modern medication. Some of the well-known beta-blockers so much used today have, as one of their given side-effects, the production of lurid (not lucid) dreams.

Creative dreams can play a very effective part in this area of holistic being. The techniques and methods used to prepare yourself for lucid dreaming are in themselves a way of making an assessment of your own health. By careful monitoring of your physical body, and continually doing a reality check as to the state of your physical being, you should be in a position to recognize when physical difficulties are becoming a problem and to take whatever avoiding action you consider necessary. The more in tune with your body you become, the quicker, for example, you will recognize the need for extra vitamins or a particular food. You can then incubate a dream which will give you the information you need as to what you should do in order to deal with the problem.

One of the interesting things about using dreams is that what may seem to be a physical problem – or the onset of one – can often be dealt with from an emotional viewpoint or even a spiritual one, using dreams as the healer. Let us suppose that you have a physical problem which has proved difficult to make better, for example an ulcerated leg which will not heal.

Trying to heal such a problem simply through dreams will not bring about any change on the physical level because action is not being taken from the right perspective. When you look at the symbolism of the ulcer, however, you are aware that something is 'eating you up'. You might at this point need to look for a cause within your emotional makeup as to what this might be. If you can identify it you have a headstart, but you may need to spend some time asking your dreaming self some questions. You could ask, for instance, for a symbol which represents the ulcer, the emotion, or the reason for the difficulty.

Because, without training, the dreaming self is somewhat unruly it will often highlight multiple answers (or possibly none at all!) but being patient will eventually bring results. With a little thought it is usually possible to identify which of the three things previously mentioned your dream image or images are – sometimes the images can represent all three. As a further example, your dream might have been of entering a dark room with a pile of dirty clothes in the corner. In ordinary dreaming you are full of distaste and wish to leave. With the help of lucid dreaming techniques, you could choose to stay and sort through the clothes. Keeping what is good and throwing out what is rotten may symbolize sorting through your emotions and dealing with negative feelings. You might decide that the room represents the ulcer, the clothes the stagnant emotions and the sorting action the willingness to deal with the emotional issues.

On the other hand, you may decide that the room is yourself, the clothes are the ulcer, and the sorting is the ability to clear away what is distressing you so that you can move forward with confidence. Your interpretation is, as always, the one which really matters; the point being that you now have a positive image with which to work. Your dreaming self has given you a very clear image of a way of working with the problem and subsequent dreams could be used to clarify the process.

Let us now move on to dealing with spiritual issues – wider topics to do with our inner ability to respond to and influence the world around us and to deal with its more subtle aspects. It becomes obvious, if we give ourselves permission, that our inner being will make available to us the information we need to handle such things. An inner sense of rightness or wrongness is the birthright of every person. Though this will be affected by our own nature and by external factors such as the culture in which we live, ultimately the spiritual self is fully aware of its purpose in life and is struggling to make this apparent. The closer we live to that ideal, the more satisfied we are and the greater our sense of inner balance.

Dreams will often clarify this sense of inner balance and warn us when we are transgressing our own code of behaviour. To take a simple example, let us suppose that you have in waking life lost your temper with an old friend. Consciously, you feel justified in your reaction, yet that night you dream of having lost something which is very precious. The dream has identified the outcome of the difficulty. You then have a choice of action. You might simply apologize to your friend and hope that the bond between you is repaired and nothing has been lost. You might, on the

°Mercury and Neptune

other hand, recognize that this is more a matter of you losing something of yourself, and wish to explore what that is. You may identify that losing your self-control is the real issue or that, where you had thought that you were extremely tolerant, in fact this is not true. You might then choose to deal with this issue by further 'dreaming it out' either lucidly or otherwise. Creative dreaming might be used, for instance, to lay down a matrix for better behaviour in the future.

We do need to understand how dreams can work for us. If you have ever taken the time to have a natal astrological chart cast for yourself, you will find that it holds a wealth of information about you, your personality and the way that you relate to others. The chart is drawn up to show the position of the planets at the moment at which you were born. Each planet is believed to indicate certain traits of character and to have an influence on particular aspects of our lives. Some of these influences are more overt and some hidden – the more we understand the hidden aspects, the more we will be in tune with ourselves. In the next section we give a list of qualities and meanings associated with the planets and their positions.

Through meditation and lucid dreaming, you may be able to recognize how you have been affected in a very unique way by those birth influences. As an example, Neptune in a position opposite to Mercury often gives an ability within the psychic field. Contemplating the images of Mercury as the messenger and Neptune as the mystic, first of all each in isolation and then as a partnership, might give an insight into a personality in a new way. Using lucid dreaming to enhance such insights enables one to make better use of those qualities within. You might give yourself the instruction one night that you wish to work with the qualities of one of the planets and really fix those qualities within your personality.

SHAMANIC HEALING

Shamanic healing also helps us to take the necessary actions on our own path towards harmony and balance. It reinforces our faith in our own inner knowledge and healing power.

We will see in Section 6 that archetypal energies are met most successfully in the dream state. It would seem that most shamanic priests are able to meet these forces through a technique akin to that of creative dreaming. The shaman travels between two worlds to meet these archetypal guides and spirit animals with a view to gaining their help and guidance. Much wiser than the ordinary mortal, these guides are capable of answering questions and imparting information which helps the individual to live his day-to-day life successfully.

Shamanic practitioners will undertake a journey on behalf of another person to help with blocked energies preventing progress, illnesses both chronic and repetitive, healing and preparation for major surgery among other things. They will also help to find the correct way to manage what are called rites of passage and to deal with difficult issues connected with old behaviour patterns. They will practise a method called 'soul retrieval' which is necessary when part of the soul energy has been lost through trauma or stress. The light that is one's birthright is diminished when part of the soul is lost.

It can be seen that all of these practices are ultimately healing. This healing occurs on a very deep level. Before shamans can help others, however, they must ask the spirits to help with learning, healing, support, strength and so on. They will often call on the spirits of plants or totem or power animals. They will have already had to face their own demons with the help of a guide and will have used techniques which have been handed down through the ages. As part of their training they will have met and come to know and trust their own totem animals.

The process of healing is remarkably akin to the passage through dream stages that psychologists have identified, and with which we deal later. The shaman will use these dreams of healing with the addition of movement through dance and the use of drumming or percussion. This last act is known as the 'Spirit Horse'. This combination of energies induces a trance state which is an altered state of consciousness akin to the mediumistic trance. Through this the shaman is able to empathize with the person seeking treatment, often acting out what the problem is. In most shamanic cultures this is done within a sacred space, or at a specially designated time, so there is an element of control in the process. While in that sacred space or time what modern psychologists call madness or psychosis is permissible and can then be dismissed, thereby healing the patient.

Dreams play an important part in this process – both those of the shaman and of the supplicant. The shaman's visions and dreams enable him or her to perceive the problem clearly and to call on their own helpers. The supplicant will be enabled, in the waking or lucid dream state, to confront whatever it is that is bothering him. The lucid dream therefore has a twofold function. It enables the shaman to call on energies which would not otherwise be available to him, to allow him to assist the supplicant in his healing. It also puts at the latter's disposal energies from which his illness or disorder has isolated him.

As in any healing process, the practitioner must learn to be free of ego and must exercise power in an ethical fashion. By and large, this will depend on which culture he or she belongs to, but certainly acknowledgement must be made to a transpersonal power and self-deception rigorously eradicated. Inevitably this means learning new behaviour and accepting new concepts of belief. In modern society this may require a return to basic beliefs and simpler world views and spiritual insights. This return can often be done with the help of a human guide, but in the long run, individuals must find their own way of living their life. This can be tested and practised through the sensible use of creative dreaming.

What is and is not reality is something that can only be decided in the light of the individual's perception and what he or she learns from a cultural perspective. Healing therefore takes place when individuals accept the reality of their own wellbeing and acknowledge that their sickness has left them. If the sickness is seen as having a reality of its own – that it has adopted a form – then it can be got rid of or banished. This is similar to the various branches of spiritual healing which require that an illness is taken away or lifted. Lucid dreaming can help in this process, since the idea of light or lightness can be substituted for the illness.

One of the most important ways in which shamanic belief can be of assistance is in helping the individual to grow from a spiritual perspective. There are various rites of passage which must be gone through and in shamanic societies they are marked by ceremony. In modern societies we do not have the benefit of such ceremonial activities and this can lead to various problems within the transition states. Shamanic practices and the understanding of dreams can allow us to make the changes of consciousness in a much more gentle way than normally happens. We deal with those changes of focus later, but for now we suggest you introduce yourself to the idea of your own totem animals.

TOTEM AND POWER ANIMALS

In shamanic and primitive belief, information is shared with us by the Great Spirit through dreams and visions. Animals are often used to show the necessary course of action. They are messengers of the Great Spirit and are on Earth to teach us simplicity and dignity. Today, many Wiccan practitioners are tending to adopt shamanic practices. The cat, of course, has always been known as the witches' familiar. Other animals such as bears, deer, eagles and fish can also perform this function. These guides provide us with links to the animal kingdom and let us tap into their inherent power.

Obviously it is not always practical, or sensible, to keep these animals as pets, and many people choose to work with their animals on the astral plane and therefore in dreams. It is the power of the animal which is more important than the actual animal itself. In shamanic societies, totems are not specific animals but representations of mystical powers. Such powers are very good at giving sensible advice.

One way of finding your own totem animal is to pay attention to your everyday waking life. Sometimes your animal makes itself felt spontaneously during the day and sometimes through dreaming. You may find that more than one animal appears. If this should be so, work with one at a time – once you are familiar and comfortable with it, move onto another one. Various animals could come and go as necessary in your life; equally you could find that other animals stay with you throughout your life. There is no 'right' or 'wrong' way – it is whatever is most appropriate for each individual. So the trick is to become aware of any animals which make themselves apparent and perhaps use these as a basis for creative dreaming.

Also think about how you react to certain situations and how you behave. Do any of the animals you have discovered behave in the same way as you do? Are you drawn to particular animals or they to you? Modern shamans believe that we all have totem or power animals – we may simply not be aware of them.

By paying attention to small details, you can pick up many clues to your totem animal. Gradually you will perceive its influence in your life. Changes in behaviour will crystallize for you which animal is of most meaning in your life at that particular time and almost inevitably you will begin to dream about it. Meditation is also a good way of finding your particular animal – such a meditation is given in Section 8. Don't forget that your totem animals can, and often do, change, so don't be put off if you receive images of several different animals.

Your communication with your totem animal is very personal. Again, there is no right or wrong way to do this. The first step is to try to 'talk' to the animal in your head. You will probably feel very silly at first and wonder if you are talking to yourself. As time goes on, however, you will recognize that the communication is two-way and that the second voice is slightly different. Learn to differentiate between the two and you will gradually learn the art of listening properly. Experienced workers with the spirit world will recognize the phenomenon of this type of duality.

We have already spoken of meeting a totem animal on the astral plane and in truly shamanic societies there is often some challenge in meeting such an animal. It may appear in a terrifying or frightening aspect initially or, alternatively, as a helper when the initiate is in some difficulty. Even today it seems as though there may be some kind of test which has to be undertaken in order to acknowledge, and honour, their power. This can often be done on a dream level. On this level, you can meet your power animal as an equal and, following old traditions, take on the power and wisdom of your animal.

Having met your animal in the meditative state, and also learnt how to talk to it, you might now like to try to develop your own ritual for approaching the animal in the ordinary everyday world. Again, this is where lucid dreaming can be of assistance because it acts as a link between the inner and the outer state. Allow yourself to feel the power of the animal (the inner) and develop your own ritual or way of calling on its power (the outer). Creative dreaming can allow you to refine the process.

As you become more proficient in all of these processes, you will find a certain synchronicity operating; that is, there will be very subtle ways in which the animal will make itself felt. Some examples might be: reading about the animal's habits, seeing instances of its presence or being threatened by it. This in turn may create dream images for you with which you can work and get to know your animal better. It is worthwhile recognizing that power animals are not only mammals. Insects and reptiles are some of the oldest images known and are very efficient power animals. Children work quite happily with animal energies without realizing they are linking into that power.

Listed below are some significances according to shamanic traditions for power and totem animals. These are slightly different from conventional dream interpretation meanings.

Ant – Industrious and hard-working.
Badger – Courageous.
Bear – Guardian of the world, watcher, inner-knowing, healing.
Buffalo – Possesses great strength.
Crow – Justice and fair dealings.
Deer – Compassionate. Physical pacing, grace.

Dog – Loyalty, guardian.

Dolphin – Wise and happy, explores deep emotion, psychic abilities, initiator.

Dragon – Rich. Qualities of Fire, knowing the answer to many universal riddles.

Dragonfly – Imagination, breaks through illusions, thus gaining power through dreams. Teaches higher aspirations.

Eagle – Expectation of power, high ideals, spiritual philosophy.

Fish – Graceful, going with the flow.

Fox – Elusiveness, agility, cleverness, sometimes deviousness.

Hawk – All-seeing, perception, observation, focus, protection.

Heron – Intuition, organisation.

Horse – Freedom, stability. Courage.

Hummingbird – Fierce warrior. Pleasure.

Jaguar – Wisdom of the shaman, focused power.

Lion – Nobility, symbol of the Sun. Protects through courage.

Lizard – Vision.

Lynx – Keeper of confidential information, perspicacity.

Mouse – Innocence, faith, trust. An eye for detail.

Owl – Symbolic wisdom, works with the Shadow, keeper of silence, riddler, beloved by Athena.

Panther – A good, protective animal, suggesting the feminine.

Puma – Shaman's companion on journeys to the other worlds, spirit of grace and silent power. Strength, elusiveness.

Rabbit – Faith, fertility, nurturing.

Raven – Inner journeys, dreams. Mystery, though sometimes the Trickster, messenger and watcher for the gods.

Snake – Transformation.

Spider – Fate, weaver of destiny.

Stag – Masculine power of regeneration, giver of spiritual gifts, beauty and mystical signs.

Swan – Guide into dreamtime, dignity.

Turtle – Shyness.

Wolf – Earth wisdom, protection. Leader of the Way. Knowledge.

For those who cannot accept these more 'way-out' explanations, we also include in Section 6 some more conventional interpretations for dream animals. For now, we would suggest that in considering stages of transition such as puberty, pregnancy and death, which in shamanic societies were marked by initiation ceremonies, totem animals can be a great deal of help.

TRANSITIONAL STAGES

Within each of our lives there are certain times when potentially we have a great deal of energy available to us to deal with our problems. These are the times of transition and while, by and large, the energy sets out to be positive, if it is not made use of to create the type of life that we want, it can go negative and cause problems for us and those around us. We need to have some technique which is going to help us assess and quantify our lives that is not going to be harmful and create difficulties for those around us. This is where lucid dreaming comes into its own and we learn how to traverse these transitional periods with comfort and ease.

PUBERTY

Perhaps the most important stage of growth that a person goes through is that of puberty. At that time literally everything changes. The body begins to do some very strange things indeed – it would seem independently of its owner. The mind throws up all sorts of new concepts for consideration, and what may previously have seemed to be a relatively safe environment no longer is. Spiritually, there is no longer the clarity of carefully nurtured belief and everything is up for grabs.

Small wonder, therefore, that the youngster either rebels or retires to the sanctuary of the bedroom. There he or she can quantify or dissect what is happening and can put into some sort of order what presents itself as absolute chaos. It is at this time that learning the art of lucid dreaming can be of inestimable benefit. Not only can it give a way of sorting chaos, but it also enables the young person to practise appropriate modes of behaviour before allowing them loose upon the world.

As the various bodily changes happen there are often dreams – sometimes lurid and over the top – which can occur. Often the dreams are to do with changing sexual awareness, the balance between the masculine and feminine energies within – or, more accurately, the dynamic between drive and intuition – and the changes which occur in family relationships. Even if looked at in terms of 'day's residue' – the material that the brain needs to process in order to make sense of the environment – there is a tremendous amount of information and new experience to be dealt with. When one also takes into account that theoretically it is at this time that the teenager should be laying down his or her potentials for a successful future life, it is hardly surprising that the mind has difficulty in functioning fully on a conscious level. Sleep will quite naturally take over, as will daydreams and fantasies.

Day dream and fantasy

In the process of the manifestation of desires there are several stages we go through. These range from day-dreaming, through to fantasizing about something, visualization, then creative dreaming coupled with creative dreaming, to a proper full-blown manifestation.

These are very close to one another: day dreaming is allowing one's mind to idle gently around an idea, whereas fantasy has much more of a focus to it. There are those who may find it easier to fantasize first and then allow the mind to idle around the idea, making refinements as necessary. It depends on the individual which one is found easier – if the technique is learnt in puberty, it becomes a very valid tool for later life.

The next stage is visualization, where you actually perceive yourself doing or being whatever the desired idea was in the first place. Now you have at your disposal all the energy which you have developed during the previous two stages and you can really concentrate on the matter in hand. Normally you will know whether you have gone over the top or whether what you are trying to create is feasible or not.

You will see how close this process is to the preparation for lucid dreaming, so the next stage is to decide to dream creatively and to have a proper lucid dream on the subject. Do not worry if a lucid dream does not happen or what you want does not come about immediately. It may be that you have not quite got all the details correct, or that a little time needs to elapse before you can have what you want. Just wait and try again later.

Now all you need to do is to wait quietly until your desire manifests, making sure that you reinforce your visualization as often as you feel it necessary. Try to keep focused on one aspect of manifestation, because if you are to diffuse in your thinking your cherished wish is less likely to manifest. A woolly instruction manifests a woolly reality.

Conflicts

We have already mentioned the fact that dreams with a sexual content often occur at this time. The young person is quite naturally widening his or her circle of acquaintances and accepting the influence of people other than parents and family. When there is conflict between family values and other authority figures this may show itself in dreams of conflict. When there is too much information to assimilate, dreams may contain images of bombardment. This, mixed with increasing desire for closer union with another person, can lead to some very confusing dreams. One such example, submitted through the Internet and slightly edited, is given below:

I dreamed that I saw an old high school friend, that I was very attracted to while in high school, although I never dated him. In real life he was also attracted to me.

In the dream I saw him again, and we were at the ages that we are now. We didn't look very different than we did in high school, though. I met him and was walking around the streets of a large city. We came upon his little sister (he doesn't really have a sister, only brothers), and she asked me what the meaning of the song 'The night they drove old Dixie down' was. I began explaining that it meant freedom for the slaves (why I don't know??)

Then as I was talking to her, I saw my ex-sister in-law in the street amongst many other people that I didn't know. The ex-sister in-law was juggling, and we were taunting her. My friend from high school began 'making out' with me in front of my ex-sister in-law. We became very sexually intense and then the dream switched to his apartment. We were sexually active there as well. Then switching back to the street, I began realizing that no one knew where I was or had been, and I thought of calling my mother. But I didn't want to tell her what I had been doing, and began thinking of a lie to tell her, although I couldn't think of one, and never did call her. The entire dream centered around having sexual encounters with my male friend from high school. I was in much enjoyment of this and did not want to wake up.

It is important to note that I frequently dream of him, but not with this much sexually active behaviour. In reality I didn't date him or have any sexual encounter!

Such a dream could, it is true, be tackled conventionally and interpreted as such, but it could also be dealt with from a creative dreaming perspective. If the young lady had already developed the art of lucid dreaming, she might have decided to ask herself for an explanation of her feelings for this young man when she knows that there is no future in the relationship. She might also have decided to become lucid at the point in her dream where it departs from reality by introducing the fact that in the dream her friend had a sister, and explored this by asking herself several questions according to the exercise 'Questioning Your Dream Characters' in Section 8. Also, where she questions her own knowledge about freedom, she might have questioned her dreaming state.

She may then have a better idea of what was happening on an inner level, rather than just taking things at face value. She might then, for instance, recognize that the sister represents her own search for awareness and freedom. There are obviously certain qualities and abilities that she admires within the young man. However, she is also mindful of the fact that she wishes to keep something secret from her mother – in this case, the authority figure within her dream. Being aware that she might wish to develop these masculine attributes within herself, she might ask for further clarity within her dreams.

Fears and doubts can be of tremendous impact within puberty. Probably one of the commonest doubts or difficulties is dislike of one's own body. This could range from something small and simple like disliking the size of one's nose to a major phobia about – for instance – sexual or social inadequacy. Obviously creative dreaming will not change any of these things, but it can help make them easier to tolerate.

Let us take our first example of dislike of some part of our body.

In this case the problem can be tackled from more than one direction. Firstly the questions might be asked 'Why do I dislike this quite so much?' 'What does this do to me?' The obvious answer that it is too big, too small or whatever may not be the real problem. It may be that there is some emotion that is associated with that particular body part which clouds the issue. The presence of the apparently grotesque, the bizarre or the out of place, at a time of life when anything may happen, may be disturbing. The body therefore becomes a focus for attention. Not being able to deal with such a problem could give rise to problems such as the eating disorders.

Just as in preparing for lucid dreaming one learns to check reality through looking at the hands and feet, so also the teenagers reinforce their own reality by finding something odd or different about themselves. This can be something of a double-edged sword in that there is a strong need to be seen as unique and therefore meaningful, but also a fear of being perceived as being too different. In slightly more spiritual terms, the very necessary bodily changes which occur very quickly at this time are perhaps less easily assimilated on a mental level, and young people need time to catch up with themselves. What may have seemed overwhelming at one time may be less troublesome once one has opened up to the potential for change. If the young people can understand that in creative dreaming other body forms can be experimented with then much comfort can be gained. Here they could suggest to themselves what it might be like to be smaller, taller, thinner or whatever. While some may believe that the body will eventually respond to the instructions given, it is probably the change of attitude which is more important. Affirmations along the lines of 'The size of my nose no longer matters to me' used before going to sleep will often be sufficient to help. An extension of this, but working on a more subtle level, might be 'I instruct my body to be as healthy, vibrant and beautiful as it can be.' Even if after such an instruction there are no lucid dreams on the subject, there will have been enough input to have effected changes at a very deep level.

One of the other sets of dreams which occur during puberty is to do with death. The young person may dream of the death of a parent, often the one of the opposite sex. This is, in fact, quite a natural adjustment to make, since the relationship with parents is often changing very rapidly, and on an inner level the child is beginning to recognize that the parent no longer has the same authority as he or she moves into adulthood. Dreams therefore reflect the perceived change of status. Also the young person's focus needs to be on someone closer to their own age, in order to fulfil the need for procreation. Learning to see themselves in relation to others takes time and patience, and often requires the 'death' of a previous relationship.

Particularly in cases where there has been personal or sexual abuse, the youth may require that the former 'safety image' gives way to something real. Guilt about their part in such abuse can lead to dreams of suicide or death as a way of escape. Incest and other such abuse can give rise to dreams of the death of the perpetrator, or if a member of the family has not been supportive, to a dream of that person's death. These are times when the techniques for handling nightmares might come in useful.

It is often during the teenage years that death is encountered in the real world. The death of close relatives such as grandparents can have a profound effect on the inner psyche – the child has to accommodate both to loss and to the absence of a support mechanism. Coming to terms with such a double-blow for the first time can often be assisted by the use of lucid dreaming. It is possible to work with both types of loss in different ways and to achieve a recognition of the future without the presence of the recently deceased.

Not all childhood dreams are bad, and indeed a secure childhood can give a basis of comforting and comfortable images which stand the individual in good stead in later life. Dreams with a recurring theme can be used to create an environment in creative dreaming which is stable and secure. Returning to a home which has held a great deal of emotional contentment is a good starting point from which to make changes which may affect the way life is lived in the future. As young people approach the first demands of adulthood and the new impressions which are assimilated, their dreams will change and become more adult in their content. They will learn to develop a firm identity, to protect themselves from physical injury, to live with painful feelings and to cope with hostility. For young people who have already practised spinning themselves into new environments in dreams, there will be much easier accommodation to the changes in environment in the real world which occur as they leave the family nest. As new responsibilities are taken up, the young people can practise new behaviour and ways of being, and can deal effectively with the fears and doubts which might prevent them from becoming successful individuals. In addition, of course, they can also use creative dreaming to enhance their creativity by following the methods shown in this book.

PREGNANCY

One area in which dreams have been found to have a great deal of relevance is in the area of pregnancy and birth. Throughout the ages women have had meaningful dreams at this time, and indeed there are reports of many mothers dreaming of fame and fortune for their offspring, or of knowing that their sons or daughters would be long remembered for their actions. Some examples are:

- Samson's mother dreamt he would be the saviour of Israel.
- Olympias, the mother of Alexander the Great, dreamt her son would be a prominent leader but that his empire would rise and fall.
- Nero's mother dreamt that he would be a monster, which he later proved to be.
- Monica, mother of St Augustine, dreamt of his great wisdom, foretelling his later actions.
- Amina, mother of Mohammed, knew of his leadership of men.
- The mother of the violinist Paganini told an angel which appeared in a dream that she wanted her son to be a great violinist.

Some women know that they have conceived before the fact has been physically confirmed, because the information has come to them through dreams. It is as though the woman recognizes the very subtle signs which her body gives her of the conception and actual pregnancy. If one believes in the more spiritual idea that the child chooses its parents, it may be that the mother senses the approach of the child's soul. It would be wrong to think of these dreams as foretelling the future, however, and easier to think of them as the sealing of a creative pact between mother and child. This is true of both women who actively wished to be pregnant and those who had no particular desire to be so.

Dreams during pregnancy seem to help the woman to accept the changing relationship between her body and her mind. Robert Van de Castle, in a study of dream diaries of more than 150 pregnant women, identified dreams of very different content during each separate period of pregnancy.

In early pregnancy the references to a woman's condition are often symbolized or hidden. She may dream of planting seeds, playing with small fish or caring for young animals. Dreams of fish are very archetypal and are clear symbols of the embryo within the womb. It seems that these dreams pick up the basic growth process of the foetus. Water metaphors are so much part of the pregnancy process, both as a reflection of the child in the womb and of the changing emotional state of both parents, that it is hardly surprising that they appear in the dreams of both men and women.

In the early stages, women often dream of strange alterations in the size of their bodies – sometimes dreaming of becoming massively fat or dreaming of symbolic images which represent motherhood. The Great Mother – as in Mother Earth – is a frequent symbol. It is as though the mind has linked into a particular stream of being and is trying to make sense of its present circumstances. Even women who are delighted to be pregnant may have dreams of such things as rats and monsters or of being engulfed. Pregnancy is such a major change that fear of the unknown has to be dealt with in some way or another.

The dreams of pregnant women's partners also seem to contain more references to the womb, enclosed spaces and other containers – all representations of the feminine. Such images may also reflect the feeling of being trapped or lonely and left out. Early in their partners' pregnancies the dreams of fathers-to-be often display their wonder and reverence about pregnancy, particularly if it is the first time. Images often consist of those that represent the subconscious, such as cellars or hidden rooms, or that suggest new beginnings.

During the second three months, women dream more immediately of the birth of their child. In their first pregnancy they will often see their new baby in dreams, sometimes as a small child and not as a newly born infant. Around the fifth month, a woman will often dream of losing or dropping the baby. It is thought that this may indicate some fear of parenthood, though in a spiritual sense it may be that the woman is dealing with a new sense of responsibility and her own ambivalent feelings. During this second term, expectant fathers tend to dream more often of babies and birthday parties and of having already had the child. They will also dream of such images as animals appearing from water or floating around in a void. Recognition of the pregnancy shows up in father's dreams once the woman's figure begins to change. Fears of exclusion also manifest throughout the pregnancy.

In the last months, a woman's fears about her attractiveness and the changes in her appearance may be echoed in dreams. At this time women often dream of former lovers and husbands. Men also tend to have more sexually orientated dreams at this time, covering such topics as potency, fear of loss of the partner and of his own masculinity. Here dreamwork and the ability to dream lucidly can act as a reassurance and support, in that any negative outcome can be changed for the better.

Dreams about being the centre of attention occur quite frequently in pregnant women, perhaps because in real life she has to accept more attention from the medical world and indeed the world at large as a matter of course. Sometimes a woman will dream of being the centre of an experiment, perhaps a specimen, or head of a team.

As the woman draws closer to giving birth, particularly in a first pregnancy, she will often have what might be called a transition dream and find herself in dark places such as caves or cupboards, having to find her way through a dark passage or past obstacles. It is here that lucid dreams might be used to deal with anxieties and fears. Since during pregnancy a woman is far more in touch with her own body than at possibly any other time of her life, this period could also be used to maximize her post-natal health.

Anxiety dreams during pregnancy often consist of the baby disappearing, or of the baby being deformed. It is thought that there may be some tie-in between an easy birth and such dreams during pregnancy. It is as though the dream serves not as a warning but as a rehearsal for the birth itself and if a woman has been allowed to face her fears and to deal with them, she is able to concentrate her efforts more fully on the task in hand.

Since post-natal depression can take some time to manifest, it may be helpful to keep a dream journal both before and after the birth. Dreams often show anxiety states before they have become conscious. Therefore taking the time to work with your dreams at this time – whether they are lucid or not – is a very effective way of discharging the excess energy which builds up. When post-natal depression presents itself and the individual has no knowledge or awareness of creative dreaming, the learning of the techniques associated with lucid dreaming can be used to gain understanding. From a medical point of view, the appearance of 'voices in the head' and other such symptoms are evidence of a mental disorder. Once the mother understands that such a condition is, in fact, probably psychic in origin – that is, arising from a deep hidden side of the personality – she will be able to recognize that she is experiencing a different reality and deal with it. Lucid dreaming and meditation can then be used to help the condition.

It is now accepted that women are often more in touch with their spiritual and psychic side around the process of pregnancy and birth and lucid dreaming is one way of grounding the self within the new role. Because sleep can be very broken at this time it is more than possible that dreams are particularly vivid and meaningful. Using dream recall and some of the methods given later in this book, it is possible to make sense of what is going on at a very deep level. It may also be that groupwork and the realization that such dreams are not peculiar to the individual may help to avert the problems of early parenthood. Dramatizing or acting out both mother's and father's dreams may lead to greater understanding between them.

Creativity has been perceived in many different ways. When a woman is being her most creative and fertile during pregnancy she is quite literally growing a new life, both within and for herself. It is worth remembering that – if she is willing – many issues which she and her partner may have as a result of their childhood or which they may have inherited can be addressed.

DEATH

Perhaps the greatest transition, and the one that holds the greatest fear and apprehension for many people, is that of death. Our attitudes to death are very much part of the culture to which each of us belongs.

The issues surrounding death are many. The modern attitude to it is very different from that of, say, in Victorian times – contemporary thought about death has changed in Western society over the last ten to twenty years in a quite phenomenal way. We are now facing our own mortality with honesty and integrity rather than pretending that it is not going to happen. As Eastern philosophies have become more well known and better understood, the attitude to death has widened to encompass ideas which previously might have seemed ridiculous. Perhaps one of the biggest changes is in the belief that the individual can exercise the right to die with dignity. Changes in the management of pain and distress, whether for the individuals or their loved ones, have resulted in profound changes in how the process of dying is managed.

Mixed up in this process are our feelings about the afterlife, our bodies, dependency on others, the finality of death, the facing of the unknown, indignity and isolation, loss, separation and rejection. Small wonder, then, that dreams come to the fore at a time when there is, has been – or is about to be – a death in the family. They are a safety valve, a reassurance and sometimes even a promise of things to come.

The Tibetan culture believes that dreaming is a preparation for death and that if one has control over dreams one also has control over the manner of one's dying. There is therefore a place for what has become known as creative dreaming in this process. One of the fears connected with the act of dying is of what is going to take place afterwards. This can range from what will happen to your body to what will happen to the Essential You – your Life Force. There will always be fear associated with dying but, by working with your dreams, a great deal can be done to put things in a better perspective.

It is often said that you are only truly alone when you die, and it is perhaps useful to have clarified your own wishes and to have made them known before you die. Many people are fearful of the legal aspects associated with death, and yet to have taken care of those things would tend to leave room in one's life for other considerations such as conserving the body's energy, and discovering one's own spiritual makeup. At this time experiencing a common phenomenon, the 'tunnel of light', or that of lightness, which is similar to an out-of-body experience, can be comforting and seems to help in the transition from one state to the next. We shall discuss the appearance of light in dreams more fully in Section 7.

Taking care of practical matters might also entail ensuring that others know what one's wishes are for disposal of your body, as well as your effects. Dreams can often help you face the issues concerning your own mortality with a degree of equanimity. Lucid dreamers particularly can practise behaviour to help them to deal with their own or another's death. When death approaches, dreams of death may lay the ground to help us prepare for the transition. Such dreams can put us in a position to make our peace with or say goodbye to loved ones and to ensure that no loose ends are left. Even those who have not consciously become aware that their time on earth is coming to an end often show some awareness of impending events.

'Death' dreams are often beautiful to the dreamer, frequently consisting of stunning landscapes (possibly of one's childhood home), streams and fountains or places of learning. It is as though the spirit or soul of the individual is giving glimpses of what is to come. It is possibly from these glimpses that the idea of the 'Summerland' has arisen.

Another type of dream that can take place is that of a machine slowing down or in the process of breaking down. Bereavement counselling often needs to take account of such dreams, since it is not just the dying person who can have these dreams, but also close family members. Shown below is a series of dreams, submitted for interpretation by a friend, which occurred around the time of her mother's death.

> My mother was dying. She was in hospital. She had fought cancer bravely for over ten years, at one point spending time in a hospice, at which time she decided she didn't intend to die and discharged herself – going on to live many more years.

> My mother was a sensitive and perceptive person. Her deathbed was not a peaceful one. There had been problems in the relationship between two of my sisters and there was not a good

atmosphere. When I arrived to be with her with another sister, my mother had talked of getting better.

Her saline drip and hydration were withdrawn and we took turns to sit up with her overnight. The bed next to hers was vacant and the dividing curtains were drawn back so that this bed was within a few feet of hers. I fell asleep on this bed.

Primary dream

I dreamt that I was looking at a scene in front of me. It was a sort of cave opening of uneven 'shapes'. I would have said rocks except that whatever the cave entrance was made of was not rock but a more malleable 'plastic-like' material, with layers and gaps. (Some early Renaissance paintings have the same sort of 'moulded-looking' cliff scenery in them.) The entrance was three-sided on a flat surface and the colours of all this were blues and greens. I knew this cave entrance went into a tunnel. In the centre of the cave shape, I saw the back of someone – this person was not going forwards into the tunnel, but moving very slowly backwards out of the tunnel, although I felt the movement should have been forward.

I woke up and looked over at my mother's bed. My sisters were whispering. I knew there was something significant about this dream. I went back to sleep and the dream reappeared. It was a 'stronger' scene, the outlines were clearer – I tried to see exactly what they were. I knew then that figure was my mother, although somehow it seemed to be me as well. I could see into the tunnel and it led towards a piercing pinprick of light. Around me were these uneven layers of rock-like formation and the figure was now moving forward.

When I woke up, I sensed that I had been dreaming my mother's dream. I wonder if I had – we were very close. I felt a sense of wonder unlike anything else I'd experienced, almost a sort of exultation. My mother died two days later.

Interpretation

While this dream was not what might be called typically lucid, it does have elements of lucidity within it. The awareness within the first part of the dream that the person should have been moving forward shows elements of awareness, as does the fairly typical image of a tunnel leading towards 'a piercing pinprick of light'. The dreamer's recognition of the material of which the cave was made as being plastic-like, but also similar to early Renaissance painting, shows that she is aware of the illusory nature of the scene that she is observing.

Waking up, recognizing the significance of the dream and going back to sleep immediately, only to have the dream reappear, is typical of lucidity. Her sense that she had been dreaming her mother's dream and the sense of wonder that she felt shows a heightened sense of awareness not typical in ordinary dreams.

As to interpretation of the dream, it would seem that the dreamer was being called upon to help her mother to move forward into another dimension. There was initially some reluctance in the first instance for the person she saw move forwards and who in fact was moving backwards. Only when she had reassured herself of her mother's condition did the dream figure move forward. This does show a particularly close connection between the dreamer and her mother. The dreamer experienced other dreams and occurrences which highlight this close connection.

1. Some days later, my partner thought he saw me sitting up on the side of our bed. He asked, 'What are you sitting up for?' but, looking again, saw that I was actually in bed sleeping.

2. I dreamt of my mother. She said to me, 'It's all right (or it could have been I'm all right) R. (My name)'.

3. In another dream, which came at a time when my grieving for her was so overwhelming, she was stern in the dream and said, quite sharply, 'Get on with your life'. The stress on 'life' was in the tone that she used about something that was being 'consumed', like food, work or a task.

4. About a month after my mother died, I dreamt I was in the living room of a little house we lived in in the Yorkshire Dales. Two of my sisters were with me. I was half-asleep on the floor. They said 'We'll go shopping now', and I said I would prefer to stay with my mother. I had looked to her earlier for an answer – some sort of advice or confirmation or something – and she had shaken her head as if to say 'no'. I went to see her in the next room, where she was sitting behind the door in a foetal position. Her head and her feet were criss-crossed with tape. I thought at first that she was wearing red latticework boots, but saw that it was tape. The tape was red. When I woke up I wondered about the significance of the colour of the tape. It was an electrical red.

5. Almost nine months after mother died I had another dream about her. She was in a doorway – a higher-than-usual doorway, but with no door. She had a lovely, light summery dress on – I think it was her favourite colours of blue and green and she looked younger and lovely as she was. She was holding a baby she said was hers. It was a baby but could walk. She said she hadn't been treated well. I said that in this new (epoch, age or something), it was wrong that the period of her pregnancy should have been so awful and I was going to do something about it. I put the child to sleep in a bed. I was told its name but I couldn't remember the name when I woke up. It was one syllable, hard-sounding and not familiar to me – in fact, almost not a Western name. The baby was fair-haired. When I woke up, I told my husband about this dream and went back to sleep again when I dreamt of a long narrow freshly dug grave, filled with growing shoots of brilliant green.

Interpretation

These dreams are wonderful examples of the type of healing dreams which can occur when there has been a death of a loved relative or friend. They also show how the dividing wall between one dimension and the other can be penetrated.

1. Here the dreamer's partner seems to have witnessed and experienced her dream body as well as her sleeping body. We do not know whether the lady had on this particular occasion been dreaming or not.

2. This dream is a 'reassurance' dream, which often occurs shortly after a death. Opinions vary according to belief as to whether the dreamer's psychological makeup dictates such a dream or whether the deceased person is communicating with the dreamer. Suffice to say that at times of extreme emotion the veil between the two worlds of earth and spirit is very thin, and the dream would have brought a good deal of comfort.

3. This particular dream moves into much more of an encouragement framework for our dreamer. She is aware that she herself should be moving on, and that although her grief is tremendous, the message she receives from her mother is that she must tackle life in an 'all-consuming' way.

4. The emphasis in this dream has moved from the dreamer to her mother. Here it becomes obvious that our dreamer should no longer be considering her mother as a source of wisdom and clarity. This is an interrelationship between her and her mother that does not include her sisters at all. Conveniently, her dreaming self sends them shopping. The Yorkshire Dales is a known environment for the dreamer which makes her feel safe. The next room, where she goes to speak with her mother, shows that although the latter is ready to move into a new phase of life (the foetal position), she is bound by physical or possibly legal constraints, by the red tape. In the dream, the dreamer realizes that she is half-asleep – that is, in an altered state of consciousness – even within the dream. This is an example of Dream-Induced Lucid Dreaming.

5. This last dream indicates that her mother has indeed moved on to a new state of being (the higher doorway) and is now spiritually much more settled. Her mother has created a new life (the baby) of which the dreamer is aware, but not part of (the non-Western name). This new life has progressed several stages – the walking baby. It is now time to acknowledge the difficulty of the preparation time – the pregnancy probably represents her mother's life and the problems that had surrounded her illness. It must now be let go. The final dream suggests that there is now both new life (the green shoots) for the dreamer and her mother.

Children will often have dreams around the time of a death in the family where they perceive the sick person as flying. This ties in very closely with their childish perceptions of what adults call out-of-the-body experiences or astral travel.

Life Appraisal

Many dreams prior to death are comforting dreams of meeting old friends or relatives. In Spiritualist belief this is because the veil has thinned between the spirit world and this, making the transition easier. In psychological terms, it would seem that the dying person is reviewing their life in some way, and in spiritual terms it is giving them the opportunity to make amends for anything they may feel they have done wrong. This appraisal can be done very simply by using an adaptation of a technique developed by Rudolph Steiner so that one does not take issues from this life onto the next stage of existence. The technique is as follows:

1. When time and energy permit, starting from the present day, begin to review your life in stages which are comfortable for you – for example, three to five years. Thus you would go back over the last three to five years, then six to ten, then nine to fifteen and so on.

2. Divide these periods into yearly segments, taking the year immediately past first, then the previous year and so on.

3. Look at each yearly period for high points and low points, things you did that you enjoyed and things that you did not. Look also at how you dealt with people and situations and, if necessary, ask for forgiveness or understanding both from the person concerned and from yourself if you feel you have behaved badly.

4. Do not let yourself dwell on such matters but be as honest as you can. Often you do not actually need to speak to the person concerned to ask for forgiveness or understanding, but can do it through the power of thought. The intent is as important as the act itself.

5. When you have completed this action, let it go. It is important to do this to clear yourself from the baggage you have been carrying, perhaps for years. You will have made your peace.

6. You do not have to – or need to – deal with the whole of your life in one go. Nor need you fret over issues you have not handled or cannot handle at this time. You will be able to deal with them as and when you are ready.

This exercise is also an extension of the technique called 'Daily

Audit', which is shown in Section 8. Creative dreaming can help in the process, giving both clarity and the opportunity to call upon memories to clear the situations.

Dreams of death

We have already mentioned the presence of dreams of death in the period of puberty. Any great change can be signified by dreams of death. Because death marks such a transitional stage in life, it is often perceived in dreams as an image of change. The end of such things as a relationship, divorce, change of residence or indeed a job, may bring about some frightening images. The feelings of failure, loss of self-esteem and other negative feelings are characterized in dreams by the death of the loved one or one's own death.

Such dreams alert us to the fact that we may have allowed parts of ourselves to be killed off – perhaps as a compromise – for the sake of the relationship or for apparent peace of mind. Thus a dream of this sort can be the start of a healing process which takes the dreamer away from depression and uncertainty into clarity. At this stage, practising the art of creative dreaming can hasten the healing process. There is thus no necessity to be fearful of such dreams when they are seen in this positive light. It was fully recognized by the ancients that dreams had a healing function, and modern investigation has revealed that there are several stages which go on in the individual in the process of 'unwellness' and the journey towards health.

ILLNESS

Serious illness or trauma usually results in more intense dreams when the body tries to re-establish a state of good health. This may or may not be for the reason that modern medications tend to suppress dreams because they have an effect on REM sleep. There is then a kind of rebound effect, where REM sleep tries to re-establish itself. This has given rise to the knowledge that the body seems to restore itself through REM sleep.

Each kind of illness and becoming well again can be followed in the dream imagery which occurs. The imagery in dreams changes and shifts with each stage of recovery. Researchers have noted seven distinct degrees which provide images. The images are different in each stage.

Dream stage 1

These are usually forewarning dreams. At one time or another, we all become susceptible to accidents or illness, and dreams are useful in forewarning us of when these periods are likely to happen. They provide us with the opportunity, if we are sufficiently sensitive to our own dreams, to escape from harm – to take avoiding action. Anxiety and stress, be that through working too hard or neglecting physical health (or indeed both), is clearly shown in dreams. These types of dreams are probably responses of the brain that are activated during dreaming in response to minute bodily sensations not discernible in the conscious state. The Greeks had a name for such dreams that predict illness, calling them 'prodormal dreams'. Some examples of such dreams are: images of being in a car that is out of control; falling off a cliff; being in the middle of a thunderstorm; being aware of an imminent explosion. If one has developed the ability to control one's dreams, it is possible to work with such images in order to prevent the problem from getting any worse.

Dream stage 2

These are diagnostic dreams. In many ways, they are extensions of the first stage, in that they can alert the dreamer to the fact that there is something wrong. It is quite sensible to monitor dreams for clues to bodily disturbances, and analyzing dreams for danger signals in illness can allow the dreamer to stop the process sooner. These dreams often depict images showing that some kind of damage is taking place. Examples of such dreams might be a falling building, injury to one of the dream objects or something not working properly, extremes of temperature or arid barren landscapes.

Dream stage 3

This stage contains crisis dreams. When in real life the wellbeing of the body is compromised in any way, the unconscious mind portrays the circumstances as a crisis. Any injury to the body is perceived as a physical attack, and the mind immediately sends out an alert. Dreams take on an image of seriousness, particularly when the individual is about to undergo surgery. Often images showing cutting implements are very strong in such dreams – perhaps meat being carved, the loss of a limb, inadequate restoration of a building and sawing old wood.

Another dream that can occur is sometimes scary. Surgery usually requires hospitalization, and terminal illness can need institutional care. This often puts the patient in a position of vulnerability, which can be reflected in their dreams. Feelings of being trapped or lost translate themselves into dreams as wandering through a maze, a forest or some other dark, unknown environment. They may also surface as dreams of being in prison, caught in an animal trap or suspended over water, especially a whirlpool. Serious illness gives rise to dreams of disaster.

Dream stage 4

This stage consists of post-crisis dreams. The body appears to have a defence mechanism which controls the dreaming process in the first two weeks after surgery or trauma. This is perhaps why dreams seem to be absent after surgery and do not surface immediately after traumatic events but are experienced later. Disrupted dream patterns are quite common at this time and are often affected by the various types of medication, such as morphine, needed to control pain. Many painkillers, however, suppress the body's production of its own natural pain controllers and make the body dependent on the drug. Their continued use can disrupt the natural linkage between healing and dreaming.

Another side-effect of pain is that it can affect sleep patterns. Major sleep deprivation affects REM sleep and can cause violent nightmares. It is as though the body and brain try to catch up on lost REM sleep. A few hours of deep sleep are then followed by wild dreams. These dreams often contain fear and anxiety images highlighting the individual's fear of death and radical change. As the patient's condition improves dreams will return to normal.

Dream stage 5

This is experienced as a time of healing dreams. During a period of recovery from injury or of convalescence after surgery, the part of the body that has been affected will often be brought to notice in dreams. They often indicate that the individual is capable, at least in dreams, of returning that part to normal use. Such indications can be enhanced by the use of lucid dreaming. Other images in dreams often reinforce this idea of a return to health, such as a new, fresh environment, spring-cleaning, finding lost belongings or finishing off a project.

Dream stage 6

These are convalescence dreams. They occur when the body and mind become aware that they have begun to return to health. This process is gradual and is shown by a change of focus in dreams. The content of the dream usually demonstrates something new happening, such as a new job, a new home or one's appetite returning to normal. These dreams are more often than not ones that can be worked with lucidly in order to enhance their effect. Also at this time affirmations of intent, including such phrases as 'I have the right to be well', or 'I sense a complete return to health', work well to improve the body's ability to heal.

Dream stage 7

This stage is that of dreams of wellbeing. It is the final and most important stage, since it would seem that the individual has here given himself permission to return to health. Often dreams will go back to the types of dreams that one was having before the illness, sometimes with a more positive twist. At this time, having undergone the experience of serious illness, it is possible to utilise what one has learnt to create a positive dreaming framework. Creative dreaming, with all its techniques, moves us gently towards taking charge of our lives in a completely different and perhaps more spiritual setting.

These seven stages give a framework in which to consider one of the other highly important difficulties of life – that of mental illness. It is not a good idea to feel that such problems can be cured through the use of dreaming, lucid or otherwise. It is true, however, that dreaming can give us clues about what is happening on an inner level and also an indication of the way forward towards the healing of the illness.

MENTAL DISORDERS

While mental instability is not a rite of passage in the same way that puberty, pregnancy and death are, it is certainly a transitional phase of existence that many people go through. The definition of being clinically sick is very different to 'not quite feeling oneself' or being off-balance. What is one person's stress is another's challenge. It would be very wrong to suggest that lucid dreaming can be used as a cure-all for such periods in our lives and certainly we have no intention of suggesting that sufferers substitute it for proper medical attention. What we are suggesting is that, since we have already seen that the body has an innate ability to heal itself through dreams, this ability can be harnessed and enhanced through lucid or creative dreaming.

There are certain illnesses where the dreaming faculty is seriously disturbed and it is those which should perhaps be dealt with first. In the section on death, we spoke of bereavement, and while this in itself is not an illness, the effects of it can be. Often in bereavement of any sort – whether it is the loss of a job, the ending of a relationship, an actual death or a radical change in lifestyle – there can be an absolutely devastating sense of loss and perhaps alienation. This is why so many women, when their children leave home, are completely confused, because not only have they 'lost' their children but they have also had to make a huge adjustment in their primary role in life – that of mother.

Often dreams will try to compensate for such losses and the individual will dream of the missing person or aspect with great clarity. If the loss has been sudden or dramatic, dreams will reflect the element of shock. This is often depicted as ropes breaking, shipwrecks and not being able to save someone from disaster. If the dreamer can be encouraged to use dreamwork or creative dreaming to let go or to expect a better outcome, healing can then begin and the person should recover. The technique for facing nightmares outlined in Section 8 can be used to good effect.

Below are some of the more common conditions which might be helped by lucid dreaming.

Acute stress reaction
This is a reaction to any sudden shock in response to an exceptional physical, mental or emotional event. The risk to the

individual is increased when there is physical exhaustion or other imbalance present. Such a reaction usually resolves quite quickly with little ill-effect but can leave behind a legacy of dreams as a way of clearing the psyche. It is often wisest to use dreamwork and the understanding it gives to help in the process of healing. It is probably best not to attempt creative dreaming until such times as the individual is ready to tackle residual fears in this way, but the RISC technique (see Section 2) could be used to good effect. Simplicity is the watchword.

Delusional disorders

These are either single or a set of related delusions. They are usually continuous and sometimes lifelong. Their structure is often very varied, and there is often the sense that the individual's body is misshapen, that he or she smells or is somehow sexually deviant. Such delusions commonly happen in middle age, but sometimes begin in early adult life. They can often be related to the individual's life situation at the time the delusions first occur.

There is also a rare delusional disorder which can be shared by two or occasionally more people with close emotional ties. Generally only one person actually suffers from a genuine psychotic disorder, commonly schizophrenia, and the delusions are induced in other people. They disappear when the people are separated. This may explain the mass suicides and deaths which occur in certain religious cults.

The techniques associated with creative dreaming might be used to help deal with some of the most distressing symptoms.

Delirium

In delirium there is an impairment of consciousness and attention ranging from 'clouding' to coma. There is a reduced ability to focus, to sustain, direct and shift attention. There is disorientation so far as time is concerned and sometimes place as well. There may be illusions and hallucinations. There are also perceptual distortions and changes in thinking. Marked changes in activity can occur – there being unpredictable shifts from low to high activity. Reaction time to stimuli may be increased or decreased. Perhaps the one condition of interest to most dreamworkers is the disturbance of the sleep pattern, involving insomnia, total sleep loss or reversal of the sleep/wake cycle. There are disturbing dreams and nightmares which then may become hallucinations in the waking state. Since this condition usually occurs in the elderly it may be a little difficult for them to learn the necessary techniques to break the cycle. However, with help, it may be possible to give the sufferers some relief by suggesting to them that they learn to constantly remind themselves that they are dreaming. Medical practitioners will not necessarily approve of such action, yet it will enable the elderly to retain a better hold on reality.

There are other conditions regarded by the medical profession as disorders which can be helped or improved by either lucid dreaming itself or some of the techniques associated with dreamwork.

Personality disorders
Most of us have at some time or another met with people who seem not to fit into any particular life category and may seem to act somewhat strangely. Specialists in mental disorder have attempted to fit people into such categories. They have broadly defined people with personality disorders as needing to fulfil at least some of the following criteria when there is no brain damage or disease and no psychiatric disorder which would account for odd behaviour. In personality disorders there are recognizable indicators, which are:

- Markedly incongruous attitudes and behaviour, such as in the way sufferers are affected by circumstances, how their impulses are controlled and how their thought processes operate. Their ways of perceiving their surroundings and the way they relate to others may differ from usually seen patterns of behaviour.
- This type of behaviour pattern is not restricted only to periods of mental illness and has gone on for a considerable time.
- Abnormal behaviour is extensive and does not allow the individual to act correctly in either social or personal circumstances.
- The occurrence of odd behaviour always appears during childhood or adolescence and continues into later life.
- The disorder leads to a great deal of personal suffering, but this may only become obvious later in the course of the illness.
- Work and social performance is almost always affected badly.

It is perhaps somewhat disturbing to think that some of these criteria also define acceptable eccentric behaviour! Some sub-divisions of personality disorders are shown below.

Emotionally unstable or borderline personality disorder

In this type of disorder there is emotional instability and lack of impulse control. In the impulsive type there are outbursts of explosive and aggressive behaviour, while in the borderline type there is often additionally poor self-image and lack of direction.

Teaching the individuals how to control their aggressive behaviour through practice of creative-dreaming techniques can often help this condition. In the borderline type much can be accomplished by working with the individual and their dreams to improve self-image and personal relationships.

Anti-social personality disorder

This is a disorder which shows huge differences between the

individual's behaviour and the prevailing social customs. The individual will show at least three of the following characteristics:

• Complete unconcern for others' feelings.
• Irresponsibility and disregard for the rules of society.
• Inability to maintain relationships, though there is no difficulty in establishing them.
• Low tolerance to frustration and rapid aggression reaction times.
• Inability to experience guilt and to profit from experience, particularly punishment.
• A marked inclination to blame others and offer plausible excuses for their behaviour.

As an adjunct to other therapies, the individual can tackle for himself the changes of behaviour through lucid dreaming and can practise different possible ways of controlling his deviant behaviour.

Depression

In the light of creative dreaming, the next condition which warrants exploration is what is popularly called depression. This is a mood of sustained sadness or unhappiness which is believed to be far more common in women than men. From a medical point of view, it is preferred to divide this category into depressive episodes and recurrent depressive disorder. Dream therapy and management can be of help in ameliorating both conditions.

Depressive episode

It is the custom nowadays to classify a time of depression which requires medical treatment as a depressive episode. During this time, there is likely to be at least three of the following symptoms present:

- Reduced concentration and attention.
- Reduced self-esteem and self-confidence.
- Ideas of guilt and unworthiness (even in a mild episode).
- Bleak and pessimistic views of the future.
- Ideas or acts of self-harm or suicide.
- Disturbed sleep.
- Diminished appetite.

The low mood varies very little from day to day. Sometimes anxiety, distress and motor agitation (the shakes) may be more prominent than the depression. Other features such as irritability, immoderate alcohol consumption, histrionic behaviour or hypochondria can hide mood changes.

Short periods of being depressed are different from depressive episodes which last at least two weeks. Doctors will differentiate between mild, moderate and severe depressive episodes. Usually social and employment activities are affected. In mild episodes, the sufferer is usually distressed by the symptoms but will continue to function. In moderate depression, he will have considerable difficulty in functioning effectively, and in a severe depressive episode, it is highly unlikely that he will be able to continue with social, work or domestic activities, except to a limited extent. In a severe depressive episode with psychotic symptoms, there may delusions, hallucinations or a depressive stupor present. The delusions are usually of wrongdoing, poverty or disaster for which the patient assumes responsibility. Hearing, taste and smell are usually involved – the patient hears accusing voices, or smells and tastes what seems to be decomposing bodies and rotting flesh.

It can be seen that when the condition is acute it is unwise for the lay person to interfere. Yet it is also true that a great deal of help can be given if the sufferer is able to respond to the idea of being able to adjust their dreams. When actually in the middle of a depressive episode, the help offered should be discussed with the doctor first but can also be suggested later to enable the patient to make use of the techniques if they should so wish.

Techniques using affirmations of intent such as 'I am capable of coming through this dark period' or more simply 'I will learn to feel better' may help initially, since they have an effect on the inner being and instigate healing. They might be followed by incubating a dream with the intention of understanding the condition. There should obviously be no pressure to achieve results.

Recurrent depressive disorder

This is characterized by repeated episodes of depression as specified in depressive episode (mild, moderate or severe) without any history of independent episodes of mood improvement and mental overactivity. However, the diagnosis should still be used if there is evidence of brief episodes of mild mood elevation and overactivity immediately after a depressive episode (sometimes apparently precipitated by treatment of a depression). The age at commencement and the severity, length and time of the episodes of depression are all highly disparate. In general, the first episode occurs in the forties. Individual episodes last between 3 and 12 months; the average length of episodes being 6 months, but they then recur less frequently. Recovery is usually total between episodes, but some sufferers may develop a persistent depression, mainly in old age. Individual severe episodes are often precipitated by stressful life events. In many cultures, both individual episodes and persistent depression are twice as common in women, though this may simply be because women tend to seek help more frequently.

During times when the individual is free from depression, much can be done to give a sense of positivity by the use of reinforcement, reassurance and the sensible use of dream management. Again, if the sufferer can perceive that the depressed state is a different state of awareness and akin to a dream – and therefore will pass – the simpler techniques of lucid dreaming can be attempted.

Psychotic disorders

'Psychotic disorder' is used as a term of convenience when the psychotic symptoms have become obvious and disruptive of daily life and work. There are certain key features of this disorder:

- An acute onset – a sudden change of state within two weeks of possible triggers.
- The presence of typical syndromes (i.e. a rapidly changing mental state and the presence of typical schizophrenic symptoms).
- The presence of acute stress. This is the occurrence of a stressful event such as bereavement, loss, marriage, divorce or psychological trauma.

Complete recovery from such difficulties usually occurs within 2 to 3 months – often sooner. It may be that the more abrupt the beginning, the better the outcome. One of the problems with this condition is that there can be no indication of how long the state will last. Dream management is likely to be of help after recovery, so that the individual gains confidence in their own ability to cope. Creative dreaming should be used with caution and more as a way of affirming a healthy reality than as a therapeutic device.

There are, of course, other conditions which may be helped by dream management and/or lucid dreaming but are really beyond the scope of this book. There is, however, one syndrome which can be helped through dream management, since one of the symptoms is dream disturbance. This is post-traumatic stress syndrome.

Post-traumatic stress syndrome

There are typical symptoms including the reliving of the trauma through flashbacks or dreams. There is often a fair degree of emotional blunting and numbness and a withdrawal from others. The sufferer can be unresponsive to his surroundings and avoid activities and situations which are likely to remind him of the original trauma. Probably one of the first recognised examples of this was the shell-shock experienced by soldiers in the First World War.

The constant state of arousal and the expectation of disaster experienced by sufferers can be very wearing, leading to insomnia, anxiety and depression. These effects can be severe enough to lead to thoughts of suicide. Alcohol and drugs may be sought as a relief from these feelings. The onset of this condition can occur from a few weeks to about six months after the trauma, though these periods are not set in stone. One of the most distressing symptoms can be the continual living with the 3F response – Fright, Fight and Flight. This can be dealt with through the use of dreamwork and creative dreaming, since the fear can be faced by using the techniques for dealing with nightmares. The expectation of disaster can be helped by the use of affirmations, and the development of a new focus in life by using lucid dreaming techniques.

In many cases of mental disorder, nightmares are a particular symptom of distress. They warrant study of their causes and their management as a separate subject.

NIGHTMARES

Nightmares offer a rich source of material for study. It seems that 30 to 50 per cent of all adults experience occasional nightmares. A study of college students found that in a group of 300 subjects, almost 75 per cent had had nightmares at least once a month.

There are various factors which lay the groundwork for suffering nightmares. These are:

- Difficulties in adolescence.
- Illness of any sort, but particularly high fevers.
- Life changes such as death in the family.
- Stressful times during work or study.
- Relationships which have gone sour.
- Traumatic events, such as a car crash or personal attack.

Such events can trigger a series of recurrent nightmares, which is the mind's way of trying to come to terms with the trauma. If there is little respite from such night terrors, then there is often a strong need for therapy or counselling, although the situation can be much helped by the learning of lucid-dreaming techniques in order to face the perceived danger.

Unpleasant dreams and nightmares can also be triggered by some drugs, recreational or otherwise, and various other medications can also cause nightmares. Many drugs seem to suppress REM sleep, though there are some which seem to increase nightmares because they increase the activity of some part of the REM system. Beta-blockers, used by some people with heart conditions and those suffering from anxiety, can give rise to nightmares, as can L-DOPA, used in the treatment of Parkinson's Disease. Alcohol in particular also seems to give rise to frightening and intense emotional dreams.

This intensity may demonstrate the difference between exciting and frightening dreams. Research has shown that lucid dreams seem to occur during periods of intense REM activity, and it does seem to depend on the attitude of the dreamer whether the dreams will be fear-filled or challenging. There is also some reason to believe that certain drugs may facilitate lucid dreaming, thus allowing us to work through our fears and difficulties.

Nightmares arise out of our own fears. Fears are illogical and are often illusions, so what better place to deal with them than in the land of dreams? At one and the same time, we are able to recognize that they are not real and yet they have a reality of their own. They are negative expectations which can be allowed to take on a gruesome aspect if we let them spiral out of control. Often in waking life, we have no opportunity to face our gremlins, and so they will surface in dreams and will not be gainsaid. Even when fears are apparently useless they have a function to perform, in that we are using them to protect ourselves from harm. However, sooner or later they must be dealt with and eradicated, and lucid dreaming creates such a way.

Facing fear is probably one of the most satisfying acts of confrontation permitted to us, and the method is quite simple. You must learn to face the nasties little by little. Bearing in mind that the object manifested in your dream is a personification of your fear you can take action to make it smaller, to bring it under control and to get rid of it, in that order.

By using creative dreaming, you can acknowledge that this 'thing' is a figment of your imagination and therefore is an illusion. This may be enough to make it disappear, perhaps for good, but sometimes it may return in a different guise – perhaps smaller, perhaps larger – to be dealt with in a different way.

If it returns, you may need to continue with the second phase of bringing your nightmare under control. You might address it using an affirmation such as 'I am in control of you' or 'I choose not to be afraid.' You may choose to visualize it shut up in a box and helpless, or you might wish to hold it and befriend it. Always do or say something which you know you are capable of doing, since if you are not, you will only frighten yourself all over again. Always bear in mind that the idea is to control the fear and not necessarily at this stage to get rid of it. If it does disappear, that is an added bonus. Incidentally, there is a belief that you should not turn your back on a nightmare figure lest it approach you unawares, though this is probably simply a manifestation of fear.

An alternative method using the principles recommended by anthropologist Kilton Stewart is shown below. In his work with the Senoi of Malaysia – who were a relatively primitive tribe – Stewart contended that they worked extensively with their dreams. Although much has been written about the Senoi's reliance on dreams as a guiding force in their lives, some anthropologists do question the validity of Stewart's study. However, his method does have merit in confronting nightmares.

1. Do not attempt to escape from a threatening dream figure. It is better to try to confront it bravely. Look at it without fear, asking the question 'Who, or what, are you?' As you become more proficient, you will begin to recognize your own fears and doubts.

2. Never ever surrender to an attack by a dream figure. Firstly, show that you are prepared to defend yourself by looking at him or her straight in the eyes and demonstrating that you are prepared to defend yourself. If you cannot avoid a fight, try to get the better of your dream antagonist, although many believe that under no circumstances should you try to kill it. This is because, in effect, you would be attacking the frightening part of yourself.

3. Try offering understanding to your adversary. If you feel it is possible to communicate with your dream figure through words, thoughts or gestures, attempt to reach some kind of compromise. Do not internalize any insults or threats but recognize any well-founded complaints. If you cannot agree, try to structure the conflict as an open dispute. Try to reach harmony with the hostile figure.

4. If reconciliation is impossible, try to separate yourself from the figure in some way, by, for instance, stepping back. It is probably wise not to turn your back on this figure in your dream, since that will tend to make you vulnerable.

5. If you do achieve reconciliation, ask the dream figure to help you, rather than fight you. It may be worth mentioning specific problems in your dream or waking life with which you need help.

This method of confronting negativity is very close to the principle of Neuro-Linguistic Programming. In this system, introduced in the early 1970s, you learn to re-frame aspects of your own personality and to recognize that you have no need to fear them. Using creative dreaming gives you an additional measure of control in your attitude to yourself.

Anxiety is one of the biggest causes of nightmares. Frank anxiety affects both the mind and the body, causing unease, quivering and sickness. Often such symptoms are part and parcel of other illnesses and unfortunately these can increase fear, meaning that a sufferer becomes locked in a never-ending spiral of anxiety which affects both sleep and dreaming.

Anxiety is a problem when it affects everyday life. Ideas which keep reoccurring, for instance, that you might have a grave illness or be in real jeopardy, tend to increase the feelings of anxiety and affect your dreams. However, anxiety of itself does not cause heart attacks or strokes, nor does it cause nervous breakdowns. It does make you feel tired by using energy needlessly. Anxiety may also be one of the symptoms of disorders of depression, difficulty with the thyroid gland and also menopausal changes.

In the absence of real fear, or when fear is still present long after a danger is past, it is possible to suffer from various negative thoughts and phobias. In waking life these can lead to various types of conduct which have an inhibitory effect on day-to-day activity. It may be that in trying to avoid places or situations which bring on an anxiety attack, the individual actually gives himself even more of a problem because the place or situation becomes harder to face the next time around. Avoidance becomes a habit rather than a defence mechanism.

Sometimes by choosing to face the difficulty with the help of lucid dreaming, you are able to lay to rest whatever is giving you difficulty. You might, for instance, with help, be able to give yourself the suggestion that you can face whatever the problem is with courage and dignity; because you know that you are dreaming, you can practise different ways of acting until you are comfortable. You might also have the realisation that your anxiety is over what might happen rather than what is happening.

It takes some time to rework any change in behaviour; you also need to remember not to become anxious over the new behaviour. To regenerate confidence it is imperative that you take things very gently indeed. By firstly practising easy things in which you become competent in dreams and then doing them in waking life, you are able to move on and tackle slightly more difficult tasks. After you have acquired proficiency in those small things, you can later attempt even more difficult tasks until such times as they no longer make you anxious.

Try first of all moving your attention away from tense, worrying thoughts to concentrate on something else. Use a representation of a time when you were particularly happy since this can also form the basis of a situation for creative dreaming. Any picture which makes you feel calm and relaxed is good. You might use any of the alternative therapies such as aromatherapy, massage, cranial osteopathy, healing or homeopathy to help to control anxiety.

Having dealt with day-to-day anxieties, you may find that a periodic dream theme is that of some form of anxiety. Anxiety dreams are often the precursors of nightmares and have a different feel from nightmares. More often than not they allow us to act out, and thus control, those aspects of our lives which cause us distress. If acknowledged and worked on early enough, nightmares need not even occur. A number of our dreams seem to be about things we fear, but this is most likely because they have more impact than others and we therefore tend to remember them. Dreaming can allow us deliberately to access and explore our anxieties. The images may often seem to form the significant part of such a dream, but it is actually the emotion experienced which needs to be faced and recognized. This can often be done by adapting the RISC technique already outlined to help us towards successful lucid dreaming.

When you become proficient in perceiving what effect your imagination has on your emotions and body, you can start the process of handling anxiety. If you are not capable of allowing yourself to handle your feelings of fear or pain at some level, they will begin to control you. This is when the monsters and gremlins begin to appear and, if allowed free rein, will take over the dream scenario until you are prepared to deal with them. Often by deliberately facing your hidden anxieties, dreams will give you information about what action needs to be taken to enable you to avoid making mistakes. Knowledge of your future may be revealed through hidden anxieties. Using a technique such as that shown above for handling frightening figures in dreams can be very helpful. The anxiety experienced in nightmares proper can be appreciated as an indication of a failure to react properly to the dream situation.

We experience anxiety when we are unable or unwilling to take responsibility for some aspect of our life. We have no way of coping with feelings which arise when we feel helpless and hopeless. Anxiety dreams can bring the real problem to the fore, allowing us to re-evaluate it in the light of knowledge gained through the dream. Lucid dreaming can then help us to create new attitudes and new patterns of behaviour in order to cope with the situation around us. Working in this fashion is a more efficient way of dealing with this type of problem – if one is brave enough.

Anxiety dreams often occur when there is some degree of phobia; that is, an irrational fear of something. Overcoming such a fear can be accomplished with some success by tackling the dreams first of all by confrontation. This means accepting that your fears are surfacing in your dreams and therefore they have to be managed. Then you could possibly use creative dreaming to take each frightening element and deal with it using the technique already given for confronting nightmares.

It is up to you whether you choose to decipher the images that arise in your anxiety dreams through straightforward interpretation or not. It is best that you use your own judgement in something like this. You might find that identifying the fear is not enough to stop the anxiety and that you need further information to help you to deal with it. You also might give the anxiety itself an image, and ask yourself the following questions:

- What does it look like?
- What does it sound like?
- What does it feel like?
- What do I want to do to it?
- What do I want to say to it?

This should give you a much better sense of control both over yourself and over the anxiety.

Speaking of control, it is worth while looking at how we handle negative thoughts and what we can do to alleviate them. This is really tackling a problem at source, since it enables us to handle those thoughts which give rise to anxiety problems in the first place. There are certain characteristics which belong to negative thought patterns and some of these can be dealt with through creative dreaming. The characteristics of negative thoughts are as follows:

- They occur very quickly and are automatic.
- They are hard to stop.
- They commonly contain significant bending of truths, false conjectures and usually come about through inherited philosophies.
- The individual who has the thought processes welcomes them as acceptable, making no effort to question the judgement behind the reasoning.
- They are nearly always linked to the current situation.
- There is no particular direction to these thoughts; they are

merely present, often blocking problem resolution.
- They may appear excessive to others but the individual concerned often sees them as perfectly reasonable.
- The person is usually oblivious of or neglects the effect his judgements can have on his life, until they cause crises.
- Negative thoughts are often prevalent among close family and friends.

Contemplation, reasoning or examination on their own do not necessarily produce negative thoughts, but are often used as an instinctive, unintentional way of producing anxiety. A degree of anxiety in life is necessary, as it has the effect of keeping us on our toes and focused on the situation in hand. Physiologically it keeps the body in a state of alertness and the mind – in theory at least – clear. Only when anxiety takes over in other areas of our lives do we have to take action to confront it. This can best be done through creative dreaming, though sometimes this has to be done as straightforwardly as possible – as though through the eyes of a child. A monster is therefore faced as a monster and not just as a figment of the imagination; a bizarre situation is therefore treated at face value. Then the situation can be changed to one's advantage.

Lucid dreaming gives us the courage to get rid of the terror of nightmares forever by recognizing that the disturbing images are created by our own mind. It is the dreamer's choice as to whether he wakes from the nightmare, having dreamed himself free from his fears.

Particularly in nightmares, the dream atmosphere or scenario gives us important clues as to our psychological state or those things which worry us at a very deep level. It is a good idea to use lucid dreaming to help us to deal with those aspects of our lives presented to us in this way. Understanding the various scenarios can mean that we take steps to change them. After reading the following explanations, you may choose to change the scenarios to something more in keeping with the more positive you.

DREAM ATMOSPHERE	INTERPRETATION	PSYCHOLOGICAL ANALYSIS	POSSIBLE RESOLUTION
Adventure Discovery, pursuit, voyaging across lands. Strange people, exciting situations, dangerous conditions and you triumph over all.	Your mind is looking for more exciting stimuli in either your work or social life.	The first indications of the need for change. The start of a more extrovert period in your life.	Actively seek to make changes, even in small ways, to your waking life.
Attack An unexpected or violent attack by a known or unknown assailant.	You are vulnerable to other people's aggression or emotion.	Your personality is causing your vulnerability. By refusing to run away, you develop understanding.	Develop a readiness to defend yourself and/or to deal with the aggression shown.
Bombardment By objects or real bombs. Object flying towards you too fast to stop.	You are under pressure from external circumstances or other people's needs.	Stress is not allowing you to take control of your life.	Avoid disaster by strategic planning and relaxation. This may warn of possible breakdown.

DREAM ATMOSPHERE	INTERPRETATION	PSYCHOLOGICAL ANALYSIS	POSSIBLE RESOLUTION
Children Depends on the action of the dream child or children. If happy, there is the need to be child-like. If lost, old fears may resurface.	You need to be in contact with the information that the inner child or being a child has.	Issues from childhood need to be dealt with to enable you to enhance your life.	Spend some time looking at yourself in childhood, whether it was good, bad or indifferent. Accept the ability to move
Death Your own or of a loved one. Looking down into an open grave. Fear of death in the atmosphere. Reading of a sudden death.	A dream of radical change or fear of such change. The end of a relationship or situation. Carrying on with a course of action is unnecessary.	Literally something within you has died and there is a need to make adjustments in behaviour and thought.	Review the whole life and how it is lived to become aware of the potential for change, but be prepared to grieve for the old life before moving on.
Explosions Similar to bombardment, but there are actual explosions occurring. Being aware of the potential for explosion.	There is anticipation of being continually opposed. Pent-up emotions within mean you are reaching danger point.	There is emotional overload which must be released appropriately.	Develop and use stress management techniques as a matter of urgency though you may have to go through some kind a of crisis first.

DREAM ATMOSPHERE	INTERPRETATION	PSYCHOLOGICAL ANALYSIS	POSSIBLE RESOLUTION
Falling Through space, down a long flight of stairs. Being surrounded by falling objects. A feeling of weightlessness.	Often thought to be sexually based, this may also suggest the lowering of standards. Also the transition from the spiritual to the mundane.	There is a need for freedom from old, possibly learnt, patterns of behaviour and the development of new ways of thinking.	Decide whether you are letting yourself down and practise flying rather than falling. Relax and let yourself go. Practise landing gently.
Grotesque Images are distorted and out of true. You feel you are part of a fantasy or bad dream.	You are not being true to yourself or using your talents properly. This is causing a distortion in perception.	There is a highly imaginative side to your nature trying to make itself felt. Initial feelings about your own creativity are inadequate.	There are probably hidden creative talents which need to be expressed. Try to translate the dream through your own creation.
Nakedness Finding yourself completely naked or becoming naked in the middle of a dream.	There is a fear of exposure or of being found wanting in some way. Being inadequate.	Something in life is not being done well enough or properly, giving rise to fears and doubts.	Decide what is the problem represented and resolve to overcome the fears in whatever way is appropriate. Practise better ways of acting.
Paralysis There is a sense of being unable	You are in a situation from which you	You are limited by your own perceptions or	Decide how you are preventing yourself from

DREAM ATMOSPHERE	INTERPRETATION	PSYCHOLOGICAL ANALYSIS	POSSIBLE RESOLUTION
to move or of being trapped.	cannot escape. You are not yet fully oriented within your waking body.	restrictions. Your physical body may be out of balance.	functioning properly and explore ways of improving performance.
Pursuit Being chased by something or someone. Often unable to escape.	You are threatened either by external circumstances or a part of your own personality.	When part of the personality becomes neglected, it presents as a threat to your integration.	Work with the images to re-integrate the aspect of personality or to understand the circumstances.
Unprepared for an event Often for an exam or public appearance. Not having done enough work.	There is a sense of insecurity in you and a sense of not being good enough. There is a need for high achievement.	You may have a poor self-image or a tendency to belittle your abilities.	Look carefully at situations in waking life to decide which are appropriate. Take steps to change the situation or the handling of it.

It can be seen that in each of the examples shown above work on your dreams is necessary to resolve the problem, not just to change the scenario. Such work can then be followed by creative dreaming. Through this, you can either learn new behaviour or reinforce the decisions you must make in waking life. Such changes can be very helpful in making your life easier and more fulfilling. We would dare to suggest that it may well be possible to effect significant healing of many imbalances through lucid dreaming as an adjunct to the use of images and the imagination. There are those who would call these the tools of the psyche.

THE INNER HEALER

Having looked at what could be called the negative aspects, we now need to consider the use of dream images in healing. Research work carried out on symbolism of images in connection with healing and dreams has found four components to be essential in the efficient use of such healing energy:

1. The image should be intense and work for the dreamer. It must have personal relevance.
2. The patient must be able to make a commitment to carry out the procedure.
3. The image should appear unprompted and be accepted by the dreamer so that they become competent in its use. A personal image will work better than one given by someone else.
4. The image dreamer should feel that they are in charge of the process. This is obviously of greater importance in creative dreaming.

Carl Simonton was probably the first exponent of the use of symbolism in healing therapies. He found out quite by chance that the attitude of patients who believed that they had power over the course of their disease did better than those who did not. The patients who felt they were in control also appeared to have a stronger will to live. In other words, they were committed to their recovery.

This contrasted with those who claimed to be committed, but in fact continued to smoke, drink and abuse their bodies in other ways. Other patients suffered from depression after becoming disenchanted with the world, even though they acknowledged they had a part to play in it. They also missed therapy sessions and doubted the help they received.

Ultimately, Simonton and his wife, Stephanie, a psychotherapist, decided to try and help patients who lacked positive thought patterns. The Simontons evolved their own therapy for fostering such patterns after much study into various psychological approaches, including biofeedback, meditation, and group therapy. They also used a combination of visual imagery and relaxation techniques. In their book *Getting Well Again*, written with James L. Creighton, they explain the process: 'Essentially, the visual-imagery process involved a period of relaxation, during which the patient would mentally picture a desired goal or result. With the cancer patient, this would mean his attempting to visualize the cancer, the treatment destroying it, and most importantly, his body's natural defences helping him recover.'

Such techniques have since been developed and tried and tested with mixed results. The parameters of many studies were somewhat flawed; it has certainly been proven that those patients who have a positive attitude to whatever disease they are dealing with do get better faster, and in cases of terminal illness there is a greater chance of their condition going into unexplained remission. It is this faculty that is utilized in lucid dreaming. It would seem that the individual is able to link into his or her own healing process and facilitate the innate ability we all have to return to health.

It is also true that not everyone manages to succeed at beating major illnesses using such techniques; perhaps for them there is a need to heal the spiritual rather than the physical self. In these cases, lucid dreaming may help in the management of the disease.

Some people subscribe to the idea that the body mirrors certain difficulties and tensions. To say that something is a 'pain in the neck' may be very accurate and lead to problems in that area. Deafness might be an inability or unwillingness to hear what is going on. Here creative dreaming can enhance the healing process by first using creative visualization as a preliminary focus. To help you do this, in the next section we suggest ways of putting yourself more in touch with the tools of the psyche. It can be seen that the branch of healing that we have been dealing with can be widened to include many other aspects of healing and self improvement. It is worth remembering that you need to think carefully about taking responsibility for your own healing and to decide for yourself whether you wish to substitute other methods for medical attention or whether you should use these methods as an adjunct to conventional medical attention. We suggest that each may be effectively used as support for the other.

SECTION

6

THE TOOLS OF
THE PSYCHE

Almost inevitably when working with images and dreams – and also in the field of self-development – the individual has to find and cultivate the tools that work best for them. In this section, I am putting forward some of my own particular favourites which have helped in my search for self-fulfilment and knowledge. Because the truths they articulate are so universal, these tools are widely used, albeit probably tailored to fit individual requirements. Any errors or biases you may suspect in this section are totally mine, so I suggest you check your own facts and make your own judgements accordingly.

At difficult periods in one's life, such tried and tested ways forward are both comforting and challenging. Having a positive frame of mind when trying to make progress inevitably helps. So, having left behind the difficult transition periods of life and come to an understanding of some of the traumas and vicissitudes that most of us face at one time or another, you may like to widen your own search to encompass some aspect of universal knowledge.

There are many schools of thought to do with lucid dreaming.

Some hold that it is useless to start with an image, while others feel that it is easier to affect the dream if one has an image to start with. Simply let it be said that, as always, it is a matter of personal preference, and whichever way works for you is right. If both are equally good, then you are particularly fortunate.

Please bear in mind that the techniques are good not just for creative dreaming but also for developing the art of dreaming creatively. All of the suggested tools in this section – Archetypes, the balance between the masculine and feminine sides of ourselves, the Tarot, myths and astrology – are closely inter-connected. Over the years, they have been used by numerous individuals in many different ways to help in the understanding of the art of being human. They are offered here in the spirit of discovery in order to help the reader onwards on his or her own journey.

ARCHETYPES

As blueprints of various parts of the personality, which can be brought into play at different times of your life, you may like to make use of the archetypes. These appear as disparate aspects of a person's makeup, giving a particular expression to the personality under certain circumstances. Three aspects of a human being's character show themselves independently in dreams. Sometimes they surface as people the dreamer knows, occasionally as imaginary or fabulous characters or spirits. Working with the archetypes through lucid dreaming is a rich source of help and information.

The most forbidding aspect of the individual has been called the Shadow and is the characteristic of the most basic of our defects and shortcomings. It is that aspect of us that holds the same sexual properties as ourselves, but is being subdued because of its shocking and unruly qualities. Then there is the Anima in man and the Animus in woman – that component of the opposite sex inherent in the dreamer. In a man, it is all that is intuitive, feminine and perceptive. In a woman, it is her masculine properties of reason and impartiality. Lastly, the True Self, the part which most often makes its appearance in dreams, is the most truly creative of all once it has been allowed the right to express itself.

The most meaningful characteristic of the Inner Self is pure energy, and each of the above dream icons personifies a different form of those dynamic energies that the personality has at its disposal. Particularly through lucid dreaming, each image is capable of sparking this 'total' energy into action.

The Self initially arises as most probably pertaining to focusing on the future; then, as the other aspects become more efficiently amalgamated, the individual is capable of developing into a whole, much more rounded personality. If the dreamer is willing to make use of the archetypal figures and work with them, the dream characters can then begin to assist in producing a combined potential that exists beyond any of them individually. Such archetypes will then have accomplished their purpose and so will be unlikely to surface again in dreams, other than at times of tension.

Inner development happens as we grasp and harmonize each of these aspects of our identity. Each part of the character has to develop on its own without confusing the purpose of the others. As each aspect expands, we are able to make use of more and more energy, but it is important to manage any initial disharmony which may arise. When this disharmony does make itself felt, there is no way that the individual should be harmed by the process, for while the effect may be distressing, it highlights an inner difficulty which, when handled, is ultimately beneficial. The communication and flow of energy between the various parts should increase and sharpen the constitution to the point where those aspects of the character first seen as separate entities can be blended into a harmonious and powerful whole.

The Ego

When in the dream state, you become aware of what is happening, the part that notices is the Ego. The Ego, being the most conscious aspect of us, tends to be more observant in dreams of the hostility it shows up with other aspects.

When the Ego has become divided from other aspects of the psyche, we do not appreciate the world in which we live in the best way possible. There is the danger of one becoming self-seeking and discouraging, having problems in connecting to others and often unable to tolerate anything other than one's own personal point of view. When this type of response goes too far, other attitudes come into effect and dreams make an attempt to redress the balance. If we are wise we will at that point use the skill of being able to dream with lucidity to hasten the process.

The Ego is the aspect inside all of us that monitors our waking life and how we fit into the world, but often this can become grossly distorted and inaccurate. Being prepared to work with impartial self-criticism, taking note of the way in which we create fantasies and develop inner peace of mind can help us to control the wayward parts of the personality.

The correct self-control needed to balance the internal self and the one which deals with the external world is the delicate equilibrium between rationalism and emotion. This means that the Ego must be controlled, but can never be totally given up.

The Shadow (a figure of the same sex as the dreamer)
In the first instance this figure appears to be the opposite sex to the dreamer and consequently becomes misconstrued as the Animus or Anima, depending on the gender of the dreamer. Only later is it acknowledged as the same sex. It becomes visible in a dream as the character who the dreamer cannot identify and sometimes appears behind the dreamer. It is the disregarded part of his being that the dreamer has failed to cultivate. Within it is hidden much that has been subdued and prevented from reaching maturity – as well as those aspects which have never been understood.

Everybody has their personal Shadow and it is generally the most negative side of them that has deliberately not been recognized. Confronting the Shadow is distressing: it is the torment of viewing ourselves as we actually are at our lowest ebb. When we are capable of facing this gruesome entity with control, we are able to believe in ourselves, because from that recognition we acquire the ability to see the rest of existence genuinely. This leads to better consideration of others, and of new perceptions of the unconscious. When the nerve to confront the Shadow is acquired, admitting its reality and recognizing it for what it is, we are then adequately equipped to produce a genuine state of being rather than some tortuous fantasy. Those creative instincts that we have can then be resurrected – artistic aptitudes and potentials that have up till now consciously been repressed and buried along with the spiteful and damaging aspects of the self. This essential energy, when controlled and learned, becomes an impetus for forward progress rather than a hazardous foe. We are able to face our demons and prevail.

One way to consciously meet the Shadow is for you to ponder all the things you despise most about other people. Then add to that all that is found difficult to come to terms with in the human race's management of itself – this person is the representation of the Shadow. This will be a reasonably correct image of your own personal Shadow. Your first response is to be grateful that you are most definitely unlike that, but if you ask those close to you if those attributes are inherent in you, the reply is likely to be yes. When we can genuinely highlight examples of the same type of behaviour within ourselves the movement to totality is gathering pace! Often there will be an unforgettable disgust of a certain set of distinctive peculiarities which, if we are honest with ourselves, alarm us because they are simmering beneath the surface within ourselves. Homophobic conduct is an example in many men, because many are troubled by their own sensitivity and artistic ability. The Shadow frequently shows itself in dreams as someone we unreservedly dislike, are scared of, or are jealous of and as someone we can't ignore. A true growth process is begun when one embraces a significant transformation in life that will give a chance to bring the Shadow to the fore rather than hoping that it will disappear. When negative dream images are actively encouraged and dealt with, these harmful energies need not be projected onto others and thus can be utilized to diffuse defensive behaviour. Within the environment of lucid dreaming, experimentation and 'playing' with different sets of behaviour can take place, learning to cope with the grotesqueness of the Shadow before finally gaining its help.

Without the creativity that comes with using the Shadow, we place ourselves in jeopardy of living in a world of delusion. Our lives lose substantial weight when we only centre on one type of perception – either internal or external. Different people look at things in opposite ways and often gain from a change in viewpoint. The introspective character benefits from encountering life changes from the 'outside' and vice versa for the extroverted. Experiencing creative dreaming allows us to practise new behaviour without harming anyone.

The Self

The Self is the archetype of the capabilities we possess. Always present, but hidden behind the prerequisite progress of the personality, the Self holds the secret of the integrated personality. The Shadow and Animus/Anima have almost always been neglected on purpose, whereas the Self is only gradually revealed. Because the latent possibilities beckon from the future, the first experience in dream form may be a figure encouraging us to move forward. Later it can develop into an icon of completeness with which we are capable of working in the present day to create a sustainable future.

There is within everyone an unknown, unknowable higher spiritual quality which becomes available to each person as he makes the effort to reach out further and further beyond himself to try to understand the world he lives in. His own experience and the use he makes of his awareness is unique but it is based on universal knowledge. It is an inner guidance which cries out to be understood, and gives access to unfathomable information which must, with practice, be applied to everyday life.

Often this aspect presents itself in dreams as a holy figure according to the individual's perceived belief. Thus it may be recognized as Christ, Buddha, Krishna or some similar figure. As you become more efficient at dealing with – and understanding – the information you receive, your perception of the energy of the manifestation changes and you are more likely to perceive it as light. You no longer have need of a personalized image on which to focus. This is akin to the perceptions present in the state of witnessing, and is an awareness of the fact that we are all part of a multi-faceted totality. Each of us is at one and the same time an individual but also part of a greater interactive whole.

When images of this archetype, such as a guru, god, an animal with virtuous qualities, a cross, a *mandala* or other geometric shape begin to appear in dreams, you are ready to face the process of becoming whole. By becoming more aware of a greater spiritual reality, you are capable of moving beyond a self-centred approach to life. There is at this time the potential for a great deal of confusion, but if you have taught yourself lucid dreaming you are able to separate reality from illusion and thus recognize the call of the material world contrasted with the requirements of the spiritual. By recognizing that you are dreaming, you are able to prioritize your responsibilities in such a way that you can achieve a conscious balance between the two. You can then use lucid dreaming to work out the correct course of action to maintain that balance.

When negative or destructive images occur connected with this element of the personality, you need to be aware that you are neglecting the power of the Self. It is often at this point that you will make a decision to advance and to change for the better. Unfortunately if you do not, change will usually be forced upon you.

The Great Mother/Mother Earth

This archetype is the essence of all the attitudes of the feminine, positive and negative. It presents the symbol of totality in a woman, and is the aptitude for using all aspects of her character. In aiming for this excellence, woman must use and promote all the separate functions of her being. She must attempt to use perception, opinion, intelligence and intuition as ways of being rather than as offensive implements. This archetype is not the wholly matriarchal aspect of woman, but is a more enhanced ethereal inner sense of her Self. Her domain is all of life's pattern, including an innate perception of the way it works. This can be accomplished in as many diverse ways as there are women.

A Woman's Self

Each and every woman is the essence of feminine dynamism. Her prime concern is the intangible quality in life and her intuitive and feeling-oriented abilities. Her abilities manifest themselves through her capacity for perception, empathy, intelligence and intuition. Her icons tend to be of fertility and caring but also of the erotic and earthly. She senses the fulfilment of life, death and of regeneration. While perceiving her prime function as being that of procreation, she also understands herself to be ruthlessly destructive of anything she beholds as imperfect.

Each individual woman attempts to express each function as fully as she can, compensating for her supposed failings by pursuing balance in her relationships with men. These relationships will only work if she has succeeded in developing that deficient side of her personality. Her partner must grow and change with her, lest his lack of understanding prevents her from developing her true potential.

Creative dreaming is a wonderful tool for helping the individual to work with these aspects of the personality in seclusion and safety.

The Wise Old Man

Like the Great Mother, the Wise Old Man is the synthesized figure of all the masculine characteristics when they are both recognized for their power and integrated into the personality. When a person understands that the best guidance arises from deep within oneself, the Wise Old Man puts in an appearance in dreams, sometimes as an authority figure, sometimes as magical.

Only when he has learnt to access the deeper recesses of his unconscious does the dreamer become able to consult his own personalization of a mentor and friend. Sometimes this personalization appears in times of deep trouble, offering help and solace when all other forms of help have disappeared. All of the functions of sensation, feeling, thinking and intuition appear in the Wise Old Man, who thus gives a suitable focus for lucid dreaming.

A Man's Self

Many men have found themselves pushed into situations where they must deny the more sensitive and intuitive aspects of themselves. When this happens, this latter side will tend to surface in dreams and unless a conscious effort is made to make use of what, in business, are called the 'softer skills', he is likely to lose access to a very important and viable tool. Creative dreaming can help him to balance himself out and to combine the twin tools of logic and intuition.

Man to be whole must accommodate himself to understanding that the first separation in his earthly life was his detachment from his mother. This echoes his disconnection from his spiritual source, however he perceives that. To return to an integrated state of being he must regain a sense of autonomy rather than struggle for control.

The unconscious mind is constantly searching for some kind of internal balance and often makes sense of information by comparing and contrasting. Some kind of necessary inherent balance exists which classifies this material. Such classification enables us to return to a harmonious whole and means that we may dream in pairs (e.g. masculine/feminine, old/young, clever/stupid). Lucid dreaming means that we can follow a line of enquiry in order to achieve and maintain that balance.

Anima/Animus (a figure of the opposite sex to the dreamer)

There is a representation of wholeness belonging to yoga which expresses almost all that needs to be said about internal balance. This is known as the *pak wa*, below:

Each part, positive and negative, contains within it an element of the other. In Chinese philosophy the feminine is negative and passive, and the masculine is positive and active. It is now generally accepted that from a psychological point of view each person holds within themselves an idealized version of their opposite – the Animus or Anima represents that part of the Self which is the opposite sex. This is part of the inner self which must be revealed and understood if the personality is to achieve a proper comprehension of itself.

Through dreams you are able to grasp the idiosyncrasies and quirks of character which differentiate you from everybody else. There may often be disharmony between the inner and outer being; there is always a danger that you will project onto others that part of yourself which is not easily found or the disharmony that is not easily managed. In personal relationships this can cause misapprehension and difficulty in seeing your partner clearly. Once, however, some kind of balance is established, the whole character can become more integrated and, indeed, more of an entity.

No one person can quite approximate to the feminine side of any masculine personality or vice versa. If you can allow yourself to come to terms with the hidden masculine or feminine and accept them for what they are, they become the basis of your understanding of the opposite sex. They also help you to open up to your inner realms. These inner figures are known as the Anima and the Animus.

It is unfortunate that when the potential for balance between the masculine and feminine aspects of a personality is overlooked or mistreated, in due course the individual will probably not be able to appreciate significant aspects of the opposite sex. This is likely to affect their attitude and conduct within intimate relationships.

Anima

Dreams try to heal conscious attitudes which are not properly aligned. The Anima - that is, the emotional and intuitive side of man's nature — tends to appear in dreams as a completely unknown woman, aspects of women the dreamer has known or as feminine deities when he is not paying sufficient attention to the feminine side of himself. When he ignores the attributes of tenderness, obedience and sensitivity which are available to him, he puts himself in jeopardy and runs the risk of moodiness and temper tantrums.

As he becomes more aware of the feminine principle, he will realize that principally his mother, but additionally all the women he has known, have helped to form his perception of the feminine, thus giving focus to all the feminine forces within himself. With understanding and the ability to work with them, particularly with lucidity, his dreams will show him how to be more able to develop warmth and genuine feeling and to accept the feminine qualities of openness, sympathy and other such sensitive and adaptable characteristics. Should he not be able to harmonize these feminine qualities, he may well be viewed as inflexible, obstinate or indecisive.

Often, instead of recognizing the Anima as an aspect of his own self which should be an accomplice, a man will project it onto an unobtainable 'object', avoiding proper contact with the opposite sex. Alternatively, he will cast his own distorted image of the feminine onto any woman he encounters, not understanding when all women seem to have the same faults, that it is his projection. When that inner feminine is frustrated the Anima turns into a completely negative, destructive illusion. The Anima becomes a guide to inner wisdom only when the man learns how to handle the energy he has available, and stops his projection.

Animus

The Animus usually appears in dreams when there is the necessity for a woman to recognise and develop the masculine side of herself. This does not mean becoming loud and aggressive but does mean understanding the rational, considered parts of her personality and being able to make use of them. Her masculine side is influenced primarily by early contact with masculine energy. If, for instance, the men in her immediate family have made no effort to develop an understanding of themselves, a woman's Animus will later show evidence of that lack of understanding, perhaps in her behaviour towards others, including men. While the Animus manifests completely differently for each woman, she will be capable of using it as an inner guide only when she has taken pains to appreciate that side of her personality.

There is a danger of a woman not having the courage of her own convictions sufficiently to question conventional belief, such as her perceived lack of success. She has accepted other people's viewpoints but does not develop her own judgement. This can be destructive for herself and others. When able to develop her own determination she can then use the masculine within to manage her life better.

Relationships will fail over and over again for the same reasons until a woman can accept that she continually projects her own misperceptions onto her partners. Continuously she will suffer disappointment and disillusionment from her man until she realises that she is only trying to reflect her own masculine side – her Animus, in fact. When she is prepared to mature and grow, the relationships she has will do likewise.

When in dreams the Animus continues to make itself known, it is time for a woman to make use of creative dreaming so that she gives herself the opportunity to develop clarity of thought and a workable strategy for life, by deliberately making use of her intuition. If, however, the negative side of the Animus dictates her way of thinking and planning, she may become stubborn and self-opinionated, feeling that men and life owe her fulfilment.

Masculine/Feminine Archetypes

There are various aspects of being which correspond to the four functions of sensing, feeling, thinking and intuition. As an easy way of coming to an understanding of how you handle relationships, it is possible to build up a kind of map of the interaction which goes on between these functions and how you use them in everyday life. Following C. G. Jung's work to identify these functions, it has been accepted that we hold within us at a very deep level a series of basic pictures which symbolize each function. Depending on the culture of the dreamer, these functions will present themselves in dreams in recognizable ways to enable the individual to work with the distortions which may have been forced upon them through experience, perception and socialization.

Each of the masculine and feminine sides of the personality has these four functions. In addition each function has a 'greater' and 'lesser' quality which have been designated as 'positive' and 'negative'. This is not strictly correct but does pick up on the idea that some types of personality are less appropriate and meaningful than others. Each of us would do well to explore our reactions to all of these aspects of our personality in an effort to achieve an inner balance, since there are 64 (8 x 8) interactions possible.

Some of these interactions you are less comfortable with than others, and these will give you most difficulty in everyday life. For instance, you may find that you are continually in situations in the work place where you make your boss angry. With understanding, you will be able to discover whether your view is the distorted one, and you have been relying too heavily on the competitive side of your personality, or whether his or her perception of you is at fault and their Ogre or Destructive Mother is coming to the fore (see below). In other words this clash of personalities is in fact a projection of an inner conflict in both of you. By learning to use lucid dreaming properly to resolve the conflict, you will both learn to cope with your own distortion and not accept the other's projection of their difficulty.

Perfect balance would be achieved by using all aspects of the personality as shown below, but in order to do this it is first necessary to have a concept of the archetypes or basic pictures.

MALE	FEMALE	POSITIVE/ NEGATIVE	FUNCTION
KINDLY FATHER	KINDLY MOTHER	+	SENSATION
OGRE	DESTRUCTIVE MOTHER	-	
YOUTH	PRINCESS	+	FEELING
TRAMP	SIREN	-	
HERO	AMAZON	+	THINKING
VILLAIN	COMPETITOR	-	
PRIEST	PRIESTESS	+	INTUITION
SORCERER	WITCH	-	

Feminine Archetypes

The feminine archetypes, in more detail, are:

Kindly Mother: This is the conventional picture of the caring mother figure, forgiving transgression and always understanding. Because much has been made of this side of femininity, until recently it was very easy to overdevelop this aspect at the expense of other sides of the personality.

Destructive Mother: This woman may be the 'smother-mother' type or the frankly destructive, prohibitive mother – the mother who prevents the adequate growth of her children. Often, it is this aspect that either actively prevents or – because of its effect on the dreamer – causes difficulty in other one-to-one relationships.

Princess: The fun-loving, innocent, child-like aspect of femininity. She is totally spontaneous, but at the same time has a subjective approach to other people. When thwarted, she will often become petulant and difficult.

Siren: This type is the seductress, the sexually and sensually aware woman who still has a sense of her own importance and power. In dreams she often appears in historic, flowing garments as though to highlight the erotic image.

Amazon: The self-sufficient woman feels she does not need support or the male; she often becomes the career woman. She enjoys the cut and thrust of intellectual sparring, and is often known as the strategist.

Competitor: She is the woman who competes with all and sundry – both men and women – in an effort to prove that she is able to control her own life, and probably those of others around her.

Priestess: This is the highly intuitive woman who has learnt to control the flow of information and use it for the common good. She is totally at home within the inner intuitive world.

Witch: This intuitive woman uses her energy to attain her own perceived ends. She is somewhat subjective in her judgement and therefore tends to lose her discernment. Often seen as negative, she can nevertheless be a tremendous force for change.

Masculine Archetypes

The masculine archetypes, in detail, are:

Kindly Father: This side of the masculine is the conventional kindly father figure who is capable of looking after the child in us, but equally capable of being firm and fair.

The Ogre: This represents the angry, overbearing, aggressive and frightening masculine figure. Often this image has arisen because of the original relationship the dreamer had with their father or father figure. The ogre particularly represents masculine anger used negatively.

Youth: The fun-loving, curious aspect of the masculine is both sensitive and creative. This is often the 'Peter Pan' figure who has never grown up. There is a sense of adventure about him.

Tramp: This is the real freedom-lover, the wanderer, the gypsy.

He owes no allegiance to anyone and is interested only in what lies around the next corner. He owes loyalty to no one but himself and is often seen as the pleasure-seeker.

Hero: The hero is the man who has chosen to undertake his own journey of exploration. He is able to consider alternatives and to determine his next move with relative ease. Often he appears as the Messianic figure in dreams. He will rescue the damsel in distress, but only as part of his own growth process.

Villain: The villain is completely arrogant and self-involved, not caring who he tramples on in his own search for autonomy. He is often the aspect of masculinity a woman first meets in everyday relationships, so can remain in dream images as a threatening figure if she has not come to terms with his selfishness.

Priest: The intuitive man is the one who recognizes and understands the power of his own intuition, but who usually uses it in the service of his god or gods. He may appear in dreams as the shaman or pagan priest.

Sorcerer: This is the man who uses discernment in a totally dispassionate way for neither good nor evil, but simply because he enjoys the use of his inherent power. In his more negative aspect, he is the Trickster or Master of unexpected change.

Discover your attitude to relationships

Your way of relating will depend on many factors: your perceptions as a child, the way your family handle such matters, how you have expressed your own gender and even the way your astrological chart dictates your life.

The question you ask yourself each time is 'Do I think that (Archetype) has a good/bad/indifferent relationship with (Archetype)?' Depending on whether you are masculine or feminine, you will score the chart slightly differently. You might find it easier to use two pens of different colour to score your results.

If you are a man, you will place the masculine archetype first and decide on the relationship with the feminine, thus 'Does Kindly Father have a good/bad or indifferent relationship with Kindly Mother, Destructive Mother?' etc. Then, 'Does Ogre have a good/bad or indifferent relationship with Kindly Mother, Destructive Mother etc.?' Do this for each masculine archetype.

The next step for a man is to score the chart from his feminine viewpoint. The question then becomes 'Does Kindly Mother have a good/bad/indifferent relationship with Kindly Father, Ogre, Youth etc.?' We suggest that you use a tick for a good relationship, a cross for a bad relationship and a dot for an indifferent one.

if you are a woman, scoring will be slightly different, in that you will place the feminine archetype first. 'Does Kindly Mother have a good/bad/indifferent relationship with Kindly Father, Ogre, Youth etc.?' Then, 'Does Destructive Mother have a good/bad/indifferent relationship with Kindly Father, Ogre, Youth etc.?' Then score the chart from a masculine viewpoint: 'Does Kindly Father have a good/bad/indifferent relationship with Kindly Mother, Destructive Mother?' etc.

There are 8 x 8 (64) relationships which occur within each of us led by our gender (sex), and 8 x 8 (64) which occur led by our Animus or Anima depending on our gender. There will be 128 marks of one sort or another on the matrix. There are no right or wrong answers, and you are now ready to score your matrix.

To experiment with your own interrelationships, try filling in the matrix on the next page.

YOUR ARCHETYPE MATRIX			
	KINDLY FATHER	OGRE	YOUTH
KINDLY MOTHER			
DESTRUCTIVE MOTHER			
PRINCESS			
SIREN			
AMAZON			
COMPETITOR			
PRIESTESS			
WITCH			
Score			

TRAMP	HERO	VILLAIN	PRIEST	SORCERER	*Score*

- Add up the number of ticks in each column and row and enter the total in the appropriate box.
- Add up both crosses and dots and enter into the appropriate box. For the purposes of this part of the exercise, bad and indifferent relationships are considered together. When you have time, you may wish to consider the indifferent relationship score to discover whether you wish to work on such relationships and how they manifest in your life. The totals will always reach 16. Broadly, any score on the right hand which is eight or over needs consideration. Your score box for the bottom line will look something like this.

	KF	O	Y	T	H	V	P	S	Score
A									9/7
C									4/12
P									8/8
W									11/5
Score	10/6	5/11	12/4	10/6	8/8	7/9	14/2	3/13	

- Thus, if the scorer is male he is likely to have problems with his own anger, recognizes his potential to be a Hero but can be totally ruthless if necessary (Villain) and is not likely to like using his own inner powers or may use them badly (Sorcerer). In his relationships with women, he will have difficulty with those who try to compete with him, but will be able to handle women who are more altruistic than maternal (Priestess).
- If the scorer is female, she might have difficulty in handling masculine anger and be attracted to, but at the same time repelled by, the manipulative male (Villain/Sorcerer). Her response is likely to be to try to compete with someone showing these qualities. This would make for a very lively relationship.

Anyone looking at this exercise from a scientific viewpoint would recognise that our methods could be seen to be flawed. However, as a rough and ready guide to enable you to make changes in your life, it is an effective tool. Using the technique of lucid dreaming, you might structure your dream to confront an archetype with which you have considerable difficulty. For instance, in the examples above, the male might wish to confront or get to know his Sorcerer in order to enhance his life. If he were very brave, he might incubate a lucid dream by using the phrase 'I wish to understand competitive women'. Being aware that he is dreaming would allow him to have some control over the process and in the dream perhaps turn negative responses into positive ones.

THE TAROT

The Tarot (which means 'truth') is possibly one of the most fascinating triggers which can be used for creative dreaming. Recognised as a kind of universal record which has resonated for many centuries across numerous cultures, the representation of the meanings of the cards is usually very beautiful. Though at one time there was a conventional sequence in which the cards were designed for use, this no longer applies. It is often a matter of personal preference for the designer.

For the purposes of creative dreaming, we suggest using only the Major Arcana, which consists of 22 cards which traces Man's journey through life. Later you may progress to using the Minor Arcana – a further 56 cards – but only when you feel ready to explore your own psyche further.

There are many different packs you can choose from. To choose your own pack you should give yourself the opportunity of looking at and handling as many packs as possible. There are now so many available that it would be impossible to suggest which one might be suitable, but we would suggest that you choose a simple one to begin with. You will usually find yourself drawn to the right ones. Any New Age store or bookshop will usually have examples for consideration and will order the less easily obtainable for you. If you are going to use your cards solely as a tool for lucid dreaming, then it is suggested that when you first buy them you spend a little time with them just appreciating them for what they are. Keep them with your dream journal, so that working with them becomes part of your nightly routine.

The Fool
This card shows a traveller on a journey without an agenda in the world. Like the joker in ordinary playing cards the Fool travels light. Often shown with a bundle in his hand and with a dog at his feet, he is seen at the beginning of life's journey. As he sets out with great naïveté not realizing the pleasures and the difficulties which lie ahead, he has no concept that at the end of that journey he will have no qualms about flying when he steps forward into a new beginning.

I. The Magician
Man is distinct from the beast because he has both mind and spirit which, with training, he can use. The magician shows his duality by being part of heaven and earth; and is capable of untold potential. He is often pictured indicating both heaven and earth (as above, so below), sometimes wearing a hat that represents infinity. He is often perceived as Mercury, the messenger of the gods. By the time the traveller reaches this stage, the magician is able to offer the gifts of intuition; those inner resources must be used as a guide to the best way forward.

II. The High Priestess
The High Priestess, as she stands in front of the doorway to the

unconscious, represents hidden or secret knowledge and the occult sciences. She is pictured as a young woman, often holding a pomegranate (suggesting the fullness of life). Seen by many as Persephone in her role as Queen of the Underworld, sometimes veiled, she depicts all the potential of our dreaming selves. As the first representative of the feminine in the Tarot, her image leads us deeper in to the unconscious and all the wisdom that it reveals.

III. The Empress

Here we have woman and mother and also domestic happiness – the female life-giving force. She is the feminine ruler, counsellor, open to all, practical and decisive. Shown often as a pregnant woman, richly dressed, she epitomizes fertility. In her negative aspect, she may be destructive and vengeful but nevertheless holds out a promise of things to come. As the archetypal mother, she offers an understanding of the mothering function for male and female alike. (See illustration on page 241.)

IV. The Emperor

Crowned and seated, he represents man in his positive aspects: willpower, authority, strength and courage. Usually depicted facing towards the reader, he suggests the benevolent father figure, though sometimes in danger of abusing power and becoming tyrannical. He offers a concept of authority in worldly matters, coupled with intelligence and sensibility. Sometimes it is important to come to terms with our father or father figure before we can become adults in our own right.

V. The Hierophant

The hierophant characterises knowledge, enlightenment, asceticism and inspiration. In the quest for spiritual understanding, we need to build bridges and form bonds we would not necessarily otherwise make. Often depicted as a priest with power over temporal life, he gives the impression of understanding and knowing his own mind. While not connected with religion as such, it is often in meeting the hierophant that the traveller along the way clarifies his attitude to spiritual belief.

VI. The Lovers

Here the masculine and feminine unite together in harmony, each having learnt about themselves and each other. Usually portrayed as two young people hand in hand, there is often a third figure in between. This represents the dilemma caused when someone else must be considered. Also standing for youthful indecisiveness, uncertainty and instability, it can mark a new stage of existence.

VII. The Chariot

Suggesting the successful balancing of alternatives and forward progression, this card represents the harnessing and control of forces. It is also conquest and advancement over physical nature through using the finer forces controlled by one's spiritual nature. Usually shown as a man controlling two horses – sometimes pulling in different directions – the chariot is often canopied, suggesting protection of the highest order. This card can also indicate the choices that one must make in moving forward to a better future. Seen as Apollo riding daily across the sky, he promises better things to come.

VIII. Justice

Depicted as a wise figure holding scales with which to weigh one's choices and a sword, this card is encountered when we need to establish equilibrium in our lives. Impartiality, balanced judgement, integrity and arbitration are all qualities associated with the card of Justice. Also suggesting fairness and discipline, it represents the ability to discriminate and to make wise choices. Such choices do, however, require a dispassionate approach, and if this is absent there can be poor judgement or legal trouble.

The Empress

IX. The Hermit

Derived from loneliness, fear, poverty and despondency, this is an isolated character with few possessions. Often shown as a cloaked figure carrying a lamp, he represents the passage of time and especially times of solitude. There is a duality about this card, in that the hermit can rely totally upon himself or can choose to accept alms from other people. We must all spend time alone in order to appreciate the richness of relationship.

X. The Wheel of Fortune

This is the card of chance, fate and luck. It also represents the wheel of life with its ever-changing fortunes. Usually shown with one figure climbing the wheel and another falling off, it stands for the cyclical nature of life. It is sometimes shown with a figure strapped to it when it stands more for the Karmic wheel – those things in our lives which bind us to a physical existence. Sometimes it represents the unlucky influences that we draw towards ourselves.

XI. Strength

The card of strength depicts the natural energy of willpower and courage. Often shown as a man overcoming a beast, usually a lion, it stands for those inner qualities of passion and dignity that must be tamed before the individual can continue on his journey. Those lower animal impulses need to be channelled, not with aggression but with compassion and understanding. Only in this way can the seeker of truth recognize 'higher qualities' which will enable him to develop into the person he knows he can be.

XII. The Hanged Man

This card suggests sacrifice but also an element of dedication. The image is usually one of a man hanging upside down with his hands tied behind his back. However, he never appears to be in distress, having accepted his fate and the need to cast off material values. In the journey towards truth, it is a turning point where limitations are recognized in favour of a simple act of faith. Understanding this brings inspiration and regeneration, but he is no way a martyr, for he recognizes the value of a new life.

XIII. Death

Death in the physical sense is nothing but a new beginning; so the real meaning of this card is actually radical change. Seen as a transition from one stage of life to another, it also stands for liberation and transformation. Usually shown as the figure of the Grim Reaper or as Time, death marks the end of life as we have accepted it until now. Also signifying loss, this card suggests the loss of the ego in favour of something finer and greater.

XIV. Temperance

This card represents the first stage of a new existence, picturing life, fecundity and balance. Always somewhere within the image is shown water flowing in two directions – often between two chalices, vessels or cups. This signifies the flow of life between the two dimensions of the physical and the spiritual. Energy in its purest form is an integral part of the way that the traveller empowers himself to move forward, and this card gives the first intimation of future pleasures.

XV. The Devil

Following the first glimpse of bliss, the traveller then must meet the Devil. This is his own internal gremlin, his base instincts, especially those of a sexual nature. The Devil personifies all his fears rolled into one. The picture, often seen as the conventional devil figure, usually suggests that there is some ambiguity over whether we are ruled by our basic instincts or have power over them. This is again a point of choice where the traveller can either return to the pleasures of the flesh or move towards a more spiritual existence.

XVI. The Tower

The lightning-struck tower demonstrates the breakdown of structure which may have been seen as suitable until now. The image is a powerful one, showing how previously held ideals and concepts can be swept aside by some kind of revelation. Things will never be the same again, and the traveller must accommodate himself to new sensations, feelings and emotional problems. Often seen as a negative card, the outcome of such a breakdown is in fact usually ultimately positive.

XVII. The Star

After the cataclysm of the Tower, the traveller must now recognize hope and a new aim or objective. The image is regenerative, showing a gentle light cast upon those things which until now have remained hidden. Possibly at a very low ebb, all the energies must now be concentrated into faith in the future and new beginnings. There are, or rather will be, new opportunities to prove our worth. Previous transgressions can be forgiven or left in the past.

XVIII. The Moon

The journey of the soul now begins to return to a consideration of aspects of the feminine as part of a greater duality. The moon is often pictured as a mysterious feminine figure with three faces representing the maid, the mother and the crone. In actuality, the moon signifies the unconscious and all of the deeper understanding of life that that entails. She is intuition, limitless knowledge and a sense of inevitability. Since it represents dreams, daydreams and fantasies, it is an ideal card with which to practise creative dreaming. The moon suggests obscurity, but is also the door between the unconscious, inspiration and prophecy.

XIX. The Sun

The Sun stands for the energy and power of the consciousness to overcome the darkness. In contrast to the darkness of the moon, the sun stands out in all its bright glory. It is masculine and powerful in its intent. It enables the weary traveller on life's journey to grow in stature and to appreciate the sheer joy of life. Even when adversely affected, it still bodes well. It foretells a time of clarity, trust and optimism – a coming to terms with all that we are.

XX. Judgement

Before the traveller can take his place within the world, he must stand in judgement on himself – only he can judge his actions, joys and sorrows. The representation is usually of a figure of judgement revealing the skeletons from the past. With new knowledge, we can forgive others and ourselves for our lack of perception and understanding. Past deeds must be looked at and justified in the light of present knowledge before we move on.

XXI. The World

This is the final card in the Tarot journey before the Fool begins again on another cycle of existence; it signifies completion. Usually shown as or named The Universe, the image is one of totality. The problems and difficulties of the journey have been conquered, enabling the individual to take up the position he has won in the cosmic dance. He has attained a state of unity and is within the world, but not of it. He now has the right to a well-regulated life and ultimate success.

Dreaming with the Tarot

Combining the images with the basic meanings gives a starting point for the imagination, and what comes up can then be taken into lucid dreaming for further consideration. The best way to do this is probably as follows:

This exercise can be done with each card, as many times as feels right. As time goes on, you will find that you are appreciating more and more detail within the card, and will therefore take that detail into your creative dreaming.

- Sit quietly where you will not be interrupted.
- If you are attempting to follow the Tarot journey – man's journey through life – take each card in the order set out above. What comes to mind as you do so? Working in this way is a progression in understanding.
- If you prefer to work with random images, simply shuffle the Major Arcana and, asking for an image which is appropriate for you at this point in your life, select a card for consideration.
- Think about your own life at this moment and how the particular card applies to you. How can you apply your knowledge of the meanings of the card to the situations in which you find yourself?
- Contemplate the card for a short time and allow yourself to internalize the energy and power of the image. Try to take in as much of the detail and information as possible.
- Now close your eyes and try to visualize yourself as part of the action of the card. How does it feel to be part of that scenario? What emotions and sensations are you conscious of at this time?
- Now tell yourself that you will have a lucid dream about what is most relevant to you or your situation at this time.
- Go to bed, allowing your last thought to be of the card's meaning.
- Remember when you wake up to make a record of your dream whether it is lucid or not. You may find that an ordinary dream on one night leads to a creative project or to other lucid dreams on a subsequent occasion.

Affirmations

You may like also to use occasionally an affirmation or statement of intent which epitomizes the qualities of each card. Such affirmations can be made the focus of your creative dreaming. We suggest you might like to try some of the following:

The Fool
'My freedom is to be an individual; my task is to use that freedom wisely.'

The Magician
'I have at my command all the tools I need to create the existence that I want.'

The High Priestess
'I hold the secret of all knowledge within and guard it with integrity.'

The Empress
'I am the nurturer of all, the giver of life and of love.'

The Emperor
'I have the power of life and therefore responsibility for all things of the earth.'

The Hierophant
'I am inspired and guided by my highest wisdom for the greatest good, finding it within myself and the world.'

The Lovers
'I love both the feminine and the masculine parts of myself, and wish to share my integration with others by demonstrating how accepting I can be.'

The Chariot
'I conquer my instincts and emotions with the intentions of my higher self and achieve physical goals.'

Strength
'My greatest fears and weaknesses provide the energy which enables me to express my higher self and my dreams.'

The Hermit

'I look within for the guidance of my higher self to elevate my moods and direct me to the light.'

The Wheel of Fortune

'As I experience the fluctuations of my physical, emotional and mental life and accept the process completely, I am enabled to manifest my full spiritual potential.'

Justice

'I am balanced and able to understand the outer manifestations of my inner issues, and subsequently to take the correct action.'

The Hanged Man

'I relinquish my attachments and fears, in the faith that this sacrifice of invalid patterns will open me to a new life.'

Death

'I leave my needs and relationships behind and seek the higher light within myself. The more I let go, the freer and more luminous I become.'

Temperance

'I integrate and blend the diverse polarities of my life to create balance, unity and harmony in creating who I am and manifesting what I do.'

The Devil

'I will transcend the chaos of my darkest fears and transform my weaknesses and vulnerabilities into a clear channel of light penetrating through the gloom.'

The Tower

'Sudden realizations about inadequate past ideas and patterns free me instantly from self-created limitations and physically-binding circumstances.'

The Star

'I am a living, breathing being radiating pure energies and giving sustenance to myself and others through the inspiration of my light.'

The Moon

'I value both my positive and negative feelings as expressions of the world around me, and accept their enrichment and fertilization.'

The Sun

'I understand my physical limitations but look to heaven to find the inspiration to trust and live with my inner child. Personal growth comes through relinquishing my rigid personal boundaries.'

Judgement

'Beyond illusion, reality allows me to doubt and the dream does not allow me to doubt. Illusion does not exist, only reality exists.'

The World

'I am a co-creator of the world, and know that I will be nurtured and supported by it as I acknowledge my identity with all its actions.'

MYTHOLOGICAL FIGURES

Once you have learned to meet and understand those mythological figures associated with your own astrological chart and with the Tarot, you have a further rich source of study in the mythology and legends of your own and other cultures.

These can allow you to learn a little of the complexities of both human and divine nature. Using creative dreaming to explore the very deep layers of human nature makes us realize that the mythological stories are as relevant today as they have always been. Somewhere within each of us we are able to find our own version of a beautiful woman such as Aphrodite, a fearless hero such as Jason (of the Argonauts), or a dreadful monster like the gorgon.

When we are learning to put ourselves in touch with the forces of nature we shall no doubt come across the nymphs and satyrs. The former are perceived as semi-divine maiden spirits analogous to aspects of nature, particularly trees and rivers, and the latter as libidinous woodland spirits associated with Dionysus. Again, when we are searching for the more creative side within us we may need to consider the qualities of the Muses. Traditionally these were the nine goddesses who presided over the arts and sciences. They were said to be the daughters of Zeus and Mnemosyne (Calliope, Clio, Euterpe, Terpsichore, Erato, Melpomene, Thalia, Polyhymnia and Urania) and their images form a rich source of material for dreaming with awareness.

This is partly a light-hearted exercise, but also partly serious. As you read the brief entries below, perhaps your imagination will take flight and then you can use your newfound skill of lucid dreaming to play out the stories. You may gain a new understanding of how life could have been in those times

You can also apply the essence of the story to your own life today. When thinking of these stories, put yourself in the position first of all of the main character and explore what it feels like to be that character. Use as a basis the IFE technique shown in Section 8 but, instead of becoming a dream object, become the mythological character of your choice. You might also try playing out one of the minor characters of the story. With this sort of preparation, you should soon be able to experience a lucid dream incorporating your favourite, or most relevant, characters. You may even learn a great deal about yourself in the process!

It does need to be said that the list below is by no means comprehensive and is geared towards Classical mythology. You may wish to build up your own library of favourites or stories which have a particular relevance for you.

Achilles (Greek mythology): During his infancy, in order to make him invincible, his mother plunged him into the Styx, holding him by the heel. Achilles as a soldier withdrew from fighting in the Trojan War after a fierce quarrel with Agamemnon. His friend Patroclus, clad in Achilles' armour, was killed by Hector, whereupon Achilles re-entered the battle, and was later wounded in the heel – the only vulnerable place in his body – by an arrow shot by Paris. He died of this wound.

Adonis (Greek mythology): A beautiful youth loved by the goddess Aphrodite and by Persephone. Killed by a boar, he had, by the decree of Zeus, to spend winters with Persephone in the underworld and summers with Aphrodite. He is often identified with the Babylonian god Tammuz, and his cult involved the celebration of the seasonal death and rebirth of crops.

Amun or Ammon (Egyptian mythology): A god who became identified with both Zeus in Greece and Jupiter Ammon in Rome. As a national god of Egypt, he was associated in a triad with Mut, his wife – a mother goddess – and Khonsu, their son. This triad echoes the interrelationships necessary within a family.

Andromeda (Greek mythology): Her mother Cassiopeia bragged that she herself (or her daughter) was more beautiful than the nereids. Poseidon, god of the sea, thereupon sent a sea monster in retribution to ravage the country. To soften his anger, Andromeda was tied to a rock and offered in sacrifice. She was rescued by Perseus. This story highlights several archetypal actions – the pride of the mother, the sacrifice of the maiden, the anger of the masculine and the heroic rescue.

Antaeus (Greek mythology): A giant, son of Poseidon and Earth, living in Libya. He forced any who crossed his path to wrestle with him. He overcame and killed them all until he was conquered by Hercules.

Anubis (Egyptian mythology): Often represented as having a dog's head, he is the protector of tombs and the god of mummification. He is known to weigh the soul of the departed against a feather. If found wanting, the soul is consigned to the underworld.

Aphrodite (Greek mythology): Identified by the Romans with Venus, she is the goddess of beauty, fertility and sexual love. She is also identified with Astarte, the Phoenician goddess, and the Egyptian Ishtar. Her name probably means 'from the foam' although she is also held to be the daughter of Zeus and Dione.

Apollo (Greek mythology): The son of Zeus and Leto and also brother of Artemis; he is seen as the epitome of masculine beauty. His main responsibilities were with the arts, prophecy and medicine.

Arachne (Greek mythology): A talented weaver who challenged the goddess Athene to a contest. Athene in anger destroyed Arachne's work, whereupon she tried to hang herself. Athene compassionately turned her into a spider instead.

Argus (Greek mythology): There are two beliefs pertaining to this figure; both equally relevant within the sphere of creative dreaming. The first is that he was a watchman with numerous eyes who was slaughtered by Hermes. After his death, Hera took his eyes away to be preserved on the tail of the peacock. The second is that he was Odysseus' dog, who recognized his master on his return from Troy after an absence of twenty years. Both stories focus on the importance of the power of vision in mythology.

Ariadne (Greek mythology): She helped Theseus to overcome the Minotaur (a fabulous beast and also her half-brother) by giving the former a ball of golden thread to help him navigate and escape from the labyrinth. Theseus and she were forced to flee together, but she was abandoned on the island of Naxos. Found by Dionysus, she then married him.

Artemis (Greek mythology): She was the goddess of hunting and is associated with abundance and childbirth. She was identified with the Roman goddess Diana and also with Selene, goddess of the moon. She is often depicted with a bow and arrows.

Arthurian legend: Based on the life and times of Arthur, King of Britain, the legends are a rich basis for lucid dreaming. The quest for the Holy Grail, the Round Table and the interrelationships between the various knights and their ladies have all entered folklore as romanticized perfection. Camelot as an idealised environment, Merlin as the archetypal magician and Lancelot as the most courtly of Arthur's knights who ultimately betrayed him with Guinevere, are also well worth considering.

Asclepius (Greek mythology): The son of Apollo, he is a hero and god of healing. Often pictured wearing a staff with a serpent coiled round it – the *caduceus* – he sometimes also carries a scroll or stone tablet, thought to represent medical knowledge.

Atalanta (Greek mythology): A huntress, fleet of foot and averse to marriage, who would marry only someone who could beat her in a race. One of her suitors won their race by throwing down three golden apples given to him by Aphrodite. These were so beautiful that Atalanta stopped to pick them up and was thereby beaten. This story, and the one which follows, give many triggers for creative dreaming.

Athene (Greek mythology): She is the goddess of wisdom and strategy. She is usually depicted as female, but armed, often carrying an owl – the figure of wisdom. She is said to have sprung, fully armed, from the head of her father, Zeus. She represents that part of woman that is the thinker rather than the intuitive.

Atlas (Greek mythology): As a punishment for wrongdoing was condemned to supporting the heavens for eternity. Later stories suggest that he was turned into a mountain – the Atlas mountains. This image of him bearing the world on his shoulders is one that will often surface in dreams when someone is under extreme pressure.

Bacchus: A Roman alternative name for Dionysus.

Balder (Scandinavian mythology): A son of Odin and god of the summer sun. Like many other gods, he was vulnerable to one thing only – in his case, mistletoe. Loki, the trickster god, had the blind god Hodur kill him.

Bastet: An Egyptian goddess, usually shown as a woman with the head of a cat, wearing one gold earring. While initially destructive, if you are prepared to challenge her, she is said to work with you and not against you. She therefore forms a useful focus for understanding the negative side of femininity.

Centaur (Greek mythology): A kind of composite creature, a Centaur has the head, arms and torso of a man with the body and legs of a horse. Often representing Sagittarius in dreams, Centaurs are often seen as being uncontrollable and drunken, although this seems to be a confusion with satyrs.

Charon: In Greek mythology there was a belief that the dead soul must be ferried across the River Styx to Hades. This task fell to Charon, an aged ferryman who was paid for his services by a coin being left in the mouth of the deceased. In lucid dreaming this image can help us to effect necessary change in our lives.

Chimera (Greek mythology): A Chimera is a composite being composed of several parts of other animals. Such a being is often seen when one first experiments with lucid dreaming. This demon or bogey often needs to be confronted before one can progress properly.

Chiron (Greek mythology): Given the task of teaching the gods healing, Chiron was injured by one of his pupils and has become the archetype for The Wounded Healer who is often too proud to allow himself to be healed by others.

Cronus or Kronos (Greek mythology): The leader of the Titans, he was the youngest son of Uranus (Heaven) and Gaia (Earth). He overcame and castrated his father, married his sister, Rhea, and fathered many future gods, including Zeus, by her. Cronus swallowed his male children immediately after their birth because it had been foretold that he would be conquered by one of them. When Zeus was born, Rhea deceived Cronus by giving him a stone wrapped in cloth and took the baby to Crete. Zeus eventually deposed him as ruler of the universe. This story gives many images suitable for working out the dynamics of family relationships.

Cupid: A Roman god who is identified by the Greeks with Eros, the god of love. In both cases he is represented as a naked beautiful boy with wings, carrying a bow and arrows. He wounds his victims by the use of these weapons and is seen most often today in images connected with St Valentine's Day. He represents true, if capricious, love and has been known to appear unexpectedly in dreams.

Cyclops (Greek mythology): In *The Odyssey*, Odysseus escapes from the giant Cyclops Polyphemus by stabbing him in his single eye while he was asleep. It is thought that this single eye may be a cross-cultural reference to the Third Eye now recognized in psychic development. In other tales the Cyclops are depicted as one-eyed giants who made thunderbolts.

Daedalus (Greek mythology): Considered to be the instigator of carpentry, he is credited with many works of pure craftsmanship. He is said to have built the labyrinth for Minos, King of Crete, in which to imprison the Minotaur. Daedalus and his son Icarus were imprisoned by Minos, but escaped on wings fashioned by Daedalus. Icarus flew too near the sun and was killed, although Daedalus reached Sicily safely. This story gives some good triggers for experimental flight in creative dreaming.

Demeter (Greek mythology): The corn goddess, whose symbol is often an ear of corn, was the mother of Persephone. She is identified with Ceres and also Cybele; she is said to have mourned the defection of her daughter to such an extent that the world suffered from famine. She thus epitomizes the archetypal Destructive Mother.

Diana (Roman mythology): Goddess of the moon, she was also identified with Artemis and is connected with the principles of hunting and virginity.

Dionysus (Greek mythology): A Greek god who was known originally by the Romans as Bacchus. He was initially a fertility god given to excess and became linked with wild and uninhibited religious ceremonies. He therefore became known as the god of wine and inspiration.

Echo (Greek mythology): Deprived of speech in order to stop her incessant talking, she was left able only to repeat what others had said. Falling in love with Narcissus and being rejected by him, she faded away until only her voice was left. In another version of her story, she rejected the love of the Nature god Pan, who had her torn to pieces, each of which could copy other sounds. This is a good image to consider when working with blockages in communication.

Electra (Greek mythology): In order to gain revenge for the murder of her father Agamemnon, Electra persuaded her brother Orestes to kill her mother Clytemnestra and Aegisthus (their mother's lover). This myth gives rise to the psychological Electra Complex, which is extreme love for the father figure.

Eros (Greek mythology): See Cupid.

Frey (Scandinavian mythology): The god of fertility and giver of rain and sunshine.

Freya (Scandinavian mythology): The goddess of love and of the night, sister of Frey.

Frigga (Scandinavian mythology): The wife of Odin and goddess of married love and the home, she is often identified with Freya. She gives her name to Friday.

Furies (Greek mythology): The spirits of chastisement, often depicted as three goddesses with hair created from snakes. They carried out the punishments meted out upon criminals, tortured the guilty with pangs of conscience and caused famines and plagues.

Gorgon (Greek mythology): Any of the three sisters with snakes for hair, of whom Medusa was the only mortal one. They had the ability to turn anyone who looked at them into stone. Medusa was killed by Perseus, who looked at her reflection in his shield in order to find where best to wound her.

Graces (Greek mythology): Goddesses, usually three daughters of Zeus, representing charm, grace and beauty, qualities which they gave as physical, intellectual, artistic and moral attributes.

Hades (Greek mythology): He was a son of Cronus and master of the underworld, the home of the spirits of the dead. He is represented as stern and uncompromising rather than evil – he later gave his name to the place in which he resided. As an image for creative dreaming, such a place or personality gives numerous opportunities for consideration.

Hecate (Greek mythology): A goddess of dark places and destructive femininity, her name means 'the distant one'. She is often associated with spirits and magic and acknowledged by gifts at crossroads. She is sometimes identified with Artemis and Selene.

Helen (Greek mythology): Believed to have been born from an egg, the daughter of Zeus and Leda, the swan. Her beauty was legendary and is said to have caused the Trojan War. Her name connects her with the Hellenic goddess of vegetation and fertility. As a subject for creative dreaming she forms an image of feminine gracefulness.

Helios (Greek mythology): The sun personified as a god.

Generally represented as driving a chariot from east to west across the sky on a daily basis, this image is a common one in ancient belief systems, though the names may be different in each system.

Hercules (Greek and Roman mythology): He was a hero of extreme strength and bravery. Known as Heracles by the Greeks, he undertook 12 labours which are said to give us the basis of the zodiac. He therefore offers a potent image for the Hero's journey in creative dreaming.

Hermaphroditus (Greek mythology): He became joined in a single body which retained characteristics of both sexes when the nymph Salmacis fell in love with him and beseeched the gods to be forever united with him. As an image of wholeness, he can appear often in dreams.

Hermes (Greek mythology): Called Mercury by the Romans, he was the messenger of the gods. He is recognizable in mythology through his winged rod and sandals, and by his hat which is often depicted as the sign of infinity. He is sometimes also perceived as a fertility god as well as the god of merchants, thieves and the right to communicate.

Horus (Egyptian mythology): His symbol was the hawk or the eye. As the son of Isis and Osiris, he avenged his father's murder, overcoming evil and in the process himself becoming a god. The Eye of Horus, being a magical symbol, is an effective image in lucid dreaming.

Hypnos (Greek mythology): The god of sleep, son of Nyx (Night), gives his name to hypnotism, hypnopompic and hypnagogic states. These last two states have particular importance in creative dreaming.

Icarus (Greek mythology): See Daedalus.

Isis (Egyptian mythology): Wife of Osiris and mother of Horus, she was initially a nature goddess. After Osiris was killed by his brother, she was required to rescue the disparate parts of her husband's body in order that he could father Horus. Her worship therefore became one of the major mystery religions, re-enacting the rites of death and new life.

Jason and the Argonauts (Greek mythology): The Argonauts were a band of especially chosen companions whom Jason took with him on board his ship Argo in his hunt for the Golden Fleece. Their story is one of the oldest Greek sagas and may reflect early exploration in the Black Sea. Jason had himself tied to the mast of the ship in order to gain passage past the Sirens, so that he could see the way forward but could not be overcome by the Sirens' feminine wiles. As a heroic journey this story can give rise to much material for creative dreaming.

Juno (Roman mythology): Identified also with Hera by the Greeks, she was originally an ancient Italian goddess. Wife of Jupiter, she was seen as a marriage goddess and the queen of heaven. As an image of the woman of power she is a wonderful icon to work with in lucid dreaming.

Jupiter (Roman mythology): Also called Jove, he was originally a sky god. Identified by the Greeks as Zeus, he is associated with lightning, the thunderbolt and excessive actions. The giver of victory, as an image in creative dreaming he opens the way to the completion of successful ventures.

Kali (Hinduism): Best known in her destructive aspect, she is the goddess of the graveyard. The wife of Siva, she presents another aspect of herself as Durga, an equally fierce goddess, and as Parvati who is more benevolent. Presenting three aspects of femininity, her story gives plentiful substance for lucid dreaming.

Lilith: In Jewish lore she is the first wife of Adam. Capricious and mysterious, she is frequently shown as the murderer of newborn children. In psychological terms, it is this aspect of womanhood that both men and women fear and with which they must come to terms. She can be comfortably confronted through lucid dreaming.

Mars (Roman mythology): Initially an agricultural god, he is the god of war and the most significant god after Jupiter. The month of March is named after him and his greatest importance nowadays is in the field of astrology.

Mercury (Roman mythology): See Hermes.

Midas (Greek mythology): Best known for the story of how everything he touched was turned to gold, as an image for use in creative dreaming he epitomizes the folly of ill thought-out wishes and desires. Since he could neither eat nor drink, he then had to subject himself to indignity in order to escape from his own greed.

Minos (Greek mythology): A legendary king of Crete who, having irritated Poseidon, became the father of the Minotaur (half-man, half-bull). Until Theseus was brave enough to challenge this monster, many innocent young men and women were sacrificed.

Minotaur (Greek mythology): See Ariadne, Minos and Theseus. As an image for lucid dreaming this creature epitomizes uncontrolled desires and sometimes the Shadow.

The Minotaur

Morpheus (Roman mythology): The god of dreams and later also the god of sleep. He gives his name to morphine and its derivatives.

Narcissus (Greek mythology): Traditionally a beautiful young man who fell in love with his own reflection, he illustrates the futility of false self-love. Both the flower that bears his name and his image of beauty can be considered through lucid dreaming.

Nemesis (Greek mythology): A goddess usually seen as the bringer of divine justice for misdeeds or arrogance. Following this idea, creative dreaming can be used to confront the principle of retribution through her.

Neptune (Roman mythology): See Poseidon.

Odin or Woden or Wotan (Scandinavian mythology): Usually represented as a wise one-eyed old man. He is the ultimate god and creator, and is also god of victory and the dead. He gave his name to Wednesday.

Odysseus (Greek mythology): Called Ulysses by the Romans, he is the central figure of the Odyssey, which are tales of his and his followers' exploits. Barred from returning to his home for ten years by Poseidon following the Trojan War, he was forced to travel through the ancient kingdoms, learning much along the way. His is a typical Hero's journey.

Oedipus (Greek mythology): Left to die on a mountain by his father, who had been informed through a prophecy that he would be killed by his own son, Oedipus was cared for by a shepherd. Famed for solving the riddle of the Sphinx, he eventually returned to Thebes, killed his father and married his mother, both by mistake. On discovering what he had done, he punished himself by gouging out his own eyes and banished himself as an outcast. In psychological terms, his name gives rise to the Oedipus Complex (inappropriate love of the mother). The story gives an objective focus for lucid dreaming.

Orion (Greek mythology): A giant and hunter. He was changed into a constellation of stars when he died. His myth survives today in the belief that sacred sites all over the world are linked to the position in the sky which is known as Orion's Belt.

Orpheus (Greek mythology): The story of Orpheus and Eurydice echoes many ancient tales of the female being rescued from the dead or the underworld by the male. In Orpheus' case, he rescued his wife and, against instructions, looked back into the underworld and therefore lost her for a second time. Used in lucid dreaming, this story can clarify the mixture of good and evil in human nature.

Osiris (Egyptian mythology): Father of Horus and husband of Isis, he was initially known as a fertility god. His death and resurrection through the persistence of Isis clarifies the concept of continuing life and is a potent creative dreaming image.

Pan (Greek mythology): A shepherd god, he is pictured as half-man, half-goat. Considered by many to be untamed and unregulated, he represents all those forces of nature with which man must come to terms. His music is usually haunting and ethereal.

Pandora (Greek mythology): The first mortal woman. She was given responsibility by the gods for a box. Some say it was filled with blessings, others say with difficulties. Against instructions she opened the box and released into the world many problems. However, Hope was left behind in the box in order help to heal the world. Using this image for lucid dreaming helps to give an understanding of wanton behaviour and deliberate misdeeds, but also hidden talents.

Pegasus (Greek mythology): A magical winged horse which sprang from the spilt blood of Medusa when Perseus killed her. Pegasus is said to carry the soul to uncharted realms. As a 'safe' image for flying, Pegasus is an excellent representation for use in lucid dreaming.

Penelope (Greek mythology): The wife of Odysseus, Penelope cleverly avoided her many suitors while he was banished from her side by Poseidon. She did so by promising to marry once she had finished her weaving, but in fact she unravelled her work every night. As a symbol of industriousness and strategy, she offers material for creative dreaming.

Persephone (Greek mythology): Called Prosperina by the Romans. She was kidnapped by Hades and made queen of the underworld. Unwilling to return permanently to Earth, she lied to her mother, Demeter, saying that she had been forced to eat some pomegranate seeds, a symbol of fertility, in the underworld. She had, however, done so voluntarily. In order to appease both her mother and Hades she agreed to spend half the year on Earth and half as queen of the underworld. Her story highlights relationships between mother and daughter and the need for autonomy.

Perseus (Greek mythology): A hero fêted for many daring deeds. On instruction from Athene he cut off the head of the gorgon Medusa and gave it to her. Having Pegasus, the winged horse, as his constant and faithful companion, he rescued and married Andromeda.

Pluto (Greek mythology): The god of the underworld. Also known as Hades, he was a force for transformation and sometimes retribution. Equal in power to Zeus, he often could not be ignored.

Poseidon (Greek mythology): Identified by the Romans with Neptune, he was the god of the sea, water, earthquakes and horses. Often depicted with a trident in his hand, Poseidon is seen as vengeful when thwarted.

Psyche (Greek mythology): A beautiful maiden beloved of Eros, who had been sent to kill her. She disobeyed his instructions to remain in ignorance of his nightly form and thereby he was forced to leave her. This meant she had to perform what seemed to be an impossible task in order to redeem herself. Released from mortal form, she has become the personification of the soul as female. As an image for lucid dreaming she puts the individual in touch with those inner qualities which give freedom to self-expression.

Ra (Egyptian mythology): The sun god, worshipped as the giver of life and a supreme deity. Travelling across the sky during the day and voyaging through the underworld at night, he is often shown in his ship with other gods.

Romulus and Remus (Roman mythology): Twin sons of Mars, they were abandoned at birth near to the River Tiber. They were found and nurtured firstly by a she-wolf and then by a shepherd family. Remus was killed before the founding of the city of Rome, which was named after his brother.

Saturn (Roman mythology): Somewhat stern and unyielding, he is an ancient god often identified with Cronus. His festival in December, Saturnalia, marked a turning point (around the time of the shortest day) towards spring in the cycle of the year. This celebration ultimately became one of the components of Christmas.

Sisyphus (Greek mythology): Punished in Hades for his transgressions in life by being doomed throughout eternity to rolling a large stone to the top of a hill, from which it always rolled down again. In terms of lucid dreaming this demonstrates the futile task from which there is no escape.

Sphinx (Greek mythology): Originating in Egypt, the myth of the sphinx became known throughout the Mediterranean basin. It had a human head and the body of a lion and was thought by the Greeks to be female. It is said that it killed anyone who could not answer its riddle to do with the three ages of man. When this riddle was solved by Oedipus, the sphinx had no reason for living and killed itself.

Theseus (Greek mythology): Also see Ariadne and Minos. In some accounts, the son of Poseidon, he is most famed for his conflict with, and conquest of, the Minotaur. This depicts a typical Hero's journey. He was helped by Ariadne but later abandoned her in order to complete another heroic task. In some stories, he is also reputed to have married an Amazonian woman who was killed in his stead. Looked at from the perspective of lucid dreaming, the stories associated with him can give a view of masculine energy used perhaps unwisely.

Thor (Scandinavian mythology): The god of thunder, he is shown as armed with a hammer. Also the god of agriculture and the home. Thursday is named after him. Used in lucid dreaming, he is an image of masculine power and energy.

Tir-nan-Og (Irish mythology): The Irish equivalent of the Greek

Fields of Elysium, the Valhalla of Norse legend or the Summerland beloved by Spiritualists. This is a land or place of total happiness – a state of bliss. It is a good starting point for those interested in Celtic mythology.

Titan (Greek mythology): Any of the older gods who preceded the Olympians and were the children of Uranus (Heaven) and Gaia (Earth). See Cronus.

Trojan Horse and War (Greek mythology): A hollow wooden horse was used by the Greeks to enter Troy towards the end of the Trojan War – the ten-year siege of Troy. The Greeks were striving to recapture Helen, who had been abducted by the Trojan Paris. The horse was apparently abandoned outside the walls of Troy. The Trojans themselves opened the gates of their city. The group of men hidden in the horse overcame the city's defences, thus defeating the Trojans. As a trigger for lucid dreaming it is possible to learn much about one's own strategy and to expect the unexpected.

Troll (Scandinavian folklore): A grotesque entity, usually living either in a cave or under a bridge. An image often used to frighten children, in creative dreaming it can be utilized to make sense of negative behaviour.

Tyr (Scandinavian mythology): The god of battle, identified with Mars, after whom Tuesday is named.

Unicorn: A mythical animal, usually pictured as having the body of a beautiful white horse with a single straight horn in the middle of its forehead – thought to represent the Third Eye. The Unicorn had, by common belief, medicinal or magical properties. It is said that only virgins can control Unicorns.

Uranus (Greek mythology): The first ruler of the universe and of uncertain temperament, he was a personification of Heaven. He was overthrown and castrated by his son Cronus. In creative dreaming, he enables us to confront our own uncertain temperament.

Valkyrie (Scandinavian mythology): Odin's twelve handmaidens. They transported those who were slain in battle after performing courageous deeds – and who were deemed worthy by the gods – to Valhalla, the place of eternal glory. As an image for lucid dreaming they correspond to the Amazon in the archetypes.

Venus (Roman mythology): The goddess of beauty and sexual love, she is identified with Aphrodite, the Greek goddess of love. Initially the spirit of kitchen gardens, she later came to represent all that was womanly and fine. While herself sexually profligate, she later became the goddess of chastity and was revered in many forms. As an image in creative dreaming she is the idealization of woman with all her charms.

Wayland the Smith (Scandinavian and Anglo Saxon mythology): A smith with supernatural powers, he is a version of the Green Man – the depiction of nature. He is reputed to have his forge in a Neolithic barrow called Waylands Smithy, from where, on clear nights, he can be heard working.

Yggdrasil (Scandinavian mythology): A representation of the Tree of Life, this an enormous ash tree at the centre of the earth. It has three roots, one extending to Niflheim (the underworld), one to Jotunheim (land of the giants) and one to Asgard (land of the gods), thus representing body, mind and spirit. Although it is constantly under threat from an evil serpent gnawing at its roots, as well as deer feasting upon its leaves, the tree is able to survive because it is watered from the well of fate. As a focus for meditation and lucid dreaming there are many fruitful images available.

Zeus (Greek mythology): Identified by the Romans with Jupiter. He is the supreme god, the protector and ruler of mankind. Destined to kill his father Cronus, he eventually deposed him as ruler of the universe. All-powerful, he is the distributor of good and evil and the god of weather and atmospheric conditions. He is depicted as mating with both goddesses and humans alike, thereby having many offspring along the way.

ANIMALS

Particularly when you begin to search for deeper meanings that can help you to understand yourself, when the bizarre sometimes becomes the norm and also as one passes from one stage of lucidity to another, the animal will often appear. It symbolizes various qualities which you as an individual may need to develop. Often such qualities can only be easily understood on an instinctive level. We have already spoken of the shamanistic societies who totally accept the relevance of animal and bird guides and guardians, so, as a brief guide to help you in the process of understanding, we have included some possible meanings for the appearance of animals in dreams. We look at some basic interpretations first and then consider the symbolism of specific animals.

Animal with a cub: such an image is usually to do with the nurturing qualities which are inherent in each of us, and may mean that we must look at the actual concept of mothering, as much as at our own mother.

Baby animals: when baby animals appear in a dream they are usually a representation of the more vulnerable, child-like aspect of the individual, which is perhaps frightened and needs support and encouragement. Often in creative dreaming such an image can represent the child we once were. What traumatizes us as children is often hidden until such times as we are prepared or able to work with the results of that trauma. Often the first inkling that we have of our ability to heal ourselves is the appearance in dreams of the hurt young animal. It may be time for us to become more mature and to face life with all its joys and difficulties. Conversely, by taking such an image into sleep we can trigger off a healing process. (This is discussed more fully in Section 5.)

Cold-blooded animals: this particular representation, shown in dreams by any species of reptile, signifies the hostile, heartless aspect of the instinctual side of our nature. Sometimes such an animal, particularly the crocodile, can make one aware of the presence of death or evil. This relates to the Egyptian myth when the genitalia of Osiris were consumed by a crocodile.

Composite animals: we have mentioned elsewhere 'the bizarre' within the framework of lucid dreaming. Composite animals, that is a combination of different types of animals in one being, appear quite frequently in lucid dreams. Such animals are not necessarily figments of an overactive imagination, but may suggest a certain difficulty in deciding the qualities that are needed in any given situation. The dreamer may need to integrate some of the qualities of two, or more, possibilities for growth. When an image which is half-animal, half-man – such as the Centaur – appears, it suggests that the dreamer is beginning to come to terms with his baser instincts and to progress spiritually. The dreamer's animal instincts are beginning to be recognized and made more human. In dreams the transformation of dream characters into animals and vice versa shows the ability to change any given situation at one's own insistence.

Deformed animals: this image may show exactly how an individual has been injured or hurt in some way. Deformity in limbs can sometimes represent sexual difficulty; by such a dream the dreamer can come to terms with impulses which he may have found offensive.

Domesticated animals: when these appear in dreams they suggest a recognition of those parts of ourselves which we have brought under control and put to good use. God-like, talking, awe-inspiring or wise animals, or those with human characteristics, appear in many fairytales and myths which highlight the wisdom and perception of the animal. As mentioned elsewhere, shamanic cultures rely heavily on this perceived wisdom, and it is certainly true that the more one attempts to understand oneself, the more likely one is to dream of such animals. There is an instinctive wisdom and grasp of circumstances that is present in each of us. This becomes covered by a layer of sophistication in the Western world, and we are thus prevented from making use of a very simple approach to life. Such animals allow us to access this simplicity. Helpful animals are an easy way for the dreamer to accept assistance from the unconscious side of himself.

Invertebrate/vertebrate animals: the emphasis on invertebrate animals in creative dreams allows us to express our instinctive reactions more vividly. In contrast, when the backbone of an animal is highlighted in our dreams we need to appreciate the presence of structure and stability in our lives.

Parts of animals: these correspond to the various meanings associated with parts of the human body. In dreams the number of animals or their limbs can offer numerological representation.

Prehistoric animals: often the appearance of a dinosaur or monster-like animal can represent a past trauma, possibly from one's childhood, or even some negative event which has occurred in family history and is now causing difficulty.

Sinister animals: the fears and doubts that a dreamer has are often translated into dreams as sinister or threatening animals. Fuller explanations of how to handle such appearances are given in Sections 5 and 8.

Taming or harnessing the animal: creative dreaming gives the individual a unique opportunity to come to terms with his doubts and fears. Aspects of himself, which may have been shelved or ignored, can be dealt with by the 'observer' in him through lucidity. Being able to tame our instincts and to harness our inherent abilities means that they can become productive and useful.

Wild animals: these are often associated with nightmares and therefore represent danger, whether that is internal or external. At this stage, if the animal is threatening, there is a destructive force arising from the unconscious. This may be a way of understanding anxiety.

Wounded or badly hurt animals: emotional or spiritual hurt can be translated into the image of wounded animals.

Archetypal animal images

Often in creative dreaming there are fleeting inexplicable flashes of information which come and go without necessarily being part of an actual dream. These archetypal images often have significance, sometimes in the same way that totem animals do, or at other times – as already mentioned – to highlight a particular quality in the dreamer. Often these appear as animals. The more common images of animals are:

Bull: killing the bull in dreams is a very powerful image. Linking as it does with festivals in ancient civilizations, it suggests initiation into the world of the mature adult. This is someone who succeeds in mastering his basic instincts such as sexual passion, creative power and assertiveness. The bull can also denote the negative side of behaviour, such as destructiveness, fear or anger. This image also links with the Minotaur.

Cat: the cat often denotes the capricious side of the feminine in human beings. Goddesses such as Bast, the Egyptian cat goddess, are usually represented as having two sides to their natures, one devious and one helpful. The refined, sensuous side of woman may also be suggested, as is the powerful, self-reliant aspect.

Cow: the cherishing mother or mother figure is often depicted by the cow. Many civilizations have revered the cow; hence as a dream image it will represent the Great Mother and fertility.

Dog: the dreamer may recognize in the dog either a devoted and loyal companion, a protector, or somebody from whom the dreamer cannot gain freedom. In the negative sense this could be something which will not go away. A dream of a huntress with dogs suggests that the dreamer is making a connection with one of the feminine archetypes, that of the Amazon. A dog guarding gates, or being near a cemetery, indicates the spiritual guardian of the threshold, or possibly death. Traditionally this creature must be put to sleep or tamed before there can be an initiation into the underworld.

Fish: when fish appear in dreams they can often manifest as one of the more bizarre elements in creative dreaming. Being water creatures, they represent the more emotional side of the personality and the ability to link with the flow of our own emotions. The fish can also be a symbol of pregnancy. Being able to connect with the collective unconscious, it is possible to take advantage of the temporal and spiritual power available.

Goat: dreaming of a goat is the recognition of creative energy and the power of the masculine. In its more negative terrifying guise the goat suggests the darker side of human nature, immoral behaviour and frank sexuality. Thus in old interpretations it would represent the Devil or Satan.

Hare: it is the luminous (light-surrounded) hare – often seen holding its baby in a cave – which tends to appear in dreams, and as such is the Mother of God. Linked with the moon, the hare can signify the all-knowing wise aspect of femininity or, in the masculine, the intuitive faculty, spiritual insight and instinctive reactions. In the context of lucid dreaming, it is worth noting that when one does not use one's power effectively, 'madness' which is founded in illusion can arise, demonstrated as an image by the mad March Hare.

Horse: the horse occurs as a very strong image in creative dreaming. Traditionally a white horse describes a state of spiritual awareness in the dreamer, a brown one the more rational and sensible side, while a black horse is the excitable side of the dreamer's nature. A pale horse usually suggests death, whilst a winged horse depicts the soul's ability to transcend the earthly plane. All of these images can manifest spontaneously in a creative dream. If the horse is under some kind of strain or is dying there may be an issue with maintaining personal direction and possibly also difficult problems which cannot be easily overcome. When the horse is being harnessed, the dreamer may be bringing part of his life under control or is perhaps focusing too hard on sensible objectives, leading to restrictions. In a man's dream, a mare will denote the Anima (feminine side), a woman or the realm of the feminine. In a woman's dream, if she is being kicked by a horse, this may either indicate her own Animus (masculine side) or her relationship with a man. A horse that can get through any door and batter down all obstacles is a representation of the collective Shadow – those demons which must be conquered by each of us. The horse as a carrier of burdens often signifies the mother, or mother archetype. Often in lucid dreaming you can, knowing what the symbolism stands for, instruct yourself to meet such a symbol in your dream.

Lion: the lion is a symbol for nobility, strength and honour, whilst also representing our egocentric feelings. If one is fighting a lion in a dream a difficult issue will soon be resolved successfully. In such a fight it is important for the dreamer to overcome the lion to show inner strength.

Pig or wild boar: the pig is an indication of stupidity, thoughtlessness, greediness and of feeling dirty in one's environment. The dreamer's conscious self may acknowledge that these aspects are coming to the fore in his everyday life. The identification of these problems is the first step in confronting them and changing oneself for the better. The wild boar is an archetypal male symbol and is therefore a negative crux in a woman's dream. A degree of escapism is evident and the dreamer may be running away from a difficult situation to be 'free' rather than confronting it.

Serpent and snake: There is a slight difference between snake and serpent dreams. The serpent in dreams is a comprehensive symbol, either male or female, that manifests from deep within the inner self. Serpents are an indication of inherent abilities and untapped energy. The harnessing of these energies allows the dreamer to acknowledge and 'accept' their sexuality and indeed use these powers to improve everyday life. In our dreams they can also express decay and destruction, thus by extension suggesting the cycle of life and rebirth. The serpent is almost always taken to signify evil, as in the Garden of Eden, yet it actually represents uncontrolled passion. By tradition man perceives himself as being frightened of these basic feelings, so the serpent suggests temptation yet also signifies the search for the spiritual. A doubt in his own instinctive or feminine qualities will often lead to a man dreaming of a serpent and he may also distrust his 'manliness'. In a woman's dream the serpent is a manifestation of a fear of penetrative sex or a doubt in her ability to seduce.

Snakes are probably one of the most universal of images in dreams. There is an image occurring symbolically in primitive societies of two snakes entwined round a central staff. This double helix has now been proved, through scientific experiment, to be the form of DNA – the building blocks of life, giving us an ancient symbolic representation of a scientific fact. This image thus becomes the symbol of the urge for life and is known as the Caduceus. Since this urge for life is frequently suppressed and thwarted, it is often understood only in its most primitive expression, sexuality. The image of the snake or serpent as sustained power, not necessarily sexual, is one of the most easily recognizable. On a more basic level it also signifies the penis.

A snake entwined around the body or limb indicates some form of entrapment, possibly being enslaved by one's baser passions. A snake, or worm, leaving a corpse by its mouth can represent the sexual act, but can also signify the dreamer's control of his or her libido. The image of a snake with its tail in its mouth is one of the oldest available to man. It signifies completion and the union of the spiritual and physical. Being swallowed by a snake shows the need and ability to return to the Ultimate and to lose our sense of space and time.

Because snakes are seen as a low form of life, while also being in some cases poisonous, they have become associated with death and all that man fears. A snake in the grass denotes disloyalty, trickery and evil. Images such as these signify the unconscious forces that are released once the dreamer reconciles the opposing sides of himself in order to create healing, rebirth and renewal. Once such images are understood and accepted, lucid dreaming allows you to deal more objectively with them.

Sheep: the sheep is known to be part of a flock, and so in dreams the importance of being part of a group is highlighted. The god-fearing 'good sheep' and also the passive and 'sheepish' may have relevance within the context of the dream. To dream of sheep and wolves, or of sheep and goats, is to register the conflict between good and evil.

Tiger: the tiger signifies royalty, dignity and power and is both a creator and a destroyer.

Wolf: dreaming of wolves, whether singly or in a pack, may indicate that we are – or feel we are – being threatened by others. The wolf may represent the dreamer's cruel sadistic fantasies without the need to take responsibility for them. The She-wolf is traditionally seen as the hussy, but also the carer for orphans and rejected young.

BIRDS AND FLIGHT

The symbolic significance of birds is slightly different from that of animals. Throughout time birds have come to represent the soul in all its various aspects. Many cultures have seen them to be carriers of the soul, perhaps because they are seen to be the freest of all creatures. Of all living animals they have the fewest ties with the Earth and therefore represent such abilities as creativity and imagination and indeed any other processes needed for freedom of thought. Therefore birds often symbolize magical and 'other-worldly' powers.

Flight has always fascinated man, perhaps because it is the only physical activity that until recently (in historical terms) he was not able to achieve through his own volition. We have already mentioned the importance of flight and flying in lucid dreams – the image of birds in helping us do this is obviously extremely important.

Certain birds appear quite frequently in dreams and the more important are shown below. A bird's conduct is entirely natural – in other words, a bird does not have to think about whether it can fly: it just does. This means that it can be used in dreams to understand man's psychological behaviour. Thus:

- A captive bird can indicate pent-up emotions or creative ability.
- A bird flying freely symbolizes expectations and needs and the soul being set free to pursue its inner desires.
- To see a full display of feathers or plumage indicates the dreamer's outer self or façade and the way he thinks other people perceive him in the outside world.
- A bird with gold wings is linked to the element of fire and therefore to the more spiritual side of the dreamer.
- If a flock of birds containing both beautiful birds and ones without feathers is seen in a dream, the dreamer is probably in some confusion over what is best for them materially or mentally. A decision needs to made quickly.
- In a man's dream a bird can represent the Anima – his hidden feminine side. In a woman's dream, however, a bird usually suggests the Spiritual Self.
- The two aspects of the Anima are often indicated by two opposites such as black and white. A black bird signifies the

neglected – or secret – aspects; the white indicates the open and friendly parts of our psyche.

- A pet bird (be it the dreamer's own or an imagined one) can show up representing both a closely held belief that the individual sees as part of his makeup and also a part of himself that constantly needs looking after.

- The Anima is again represented in dreams by the dove. The bringing of 'calm after the storm' after a particularly stressful time, or the restful part of humankind, is shown by its appearance. The dove also represents reconciliation.

- Birds of prey bring out the qualities of control and supremacy in dreams. Heightened perception and an eye for detail are highlighted by these far-sighted creatures. The eagle, being the most well known and noblest of all birds of prey, brings out these qualities in the dreamer and he perhaps needs to look at becoming more dominating and noble in everyday life. The bald-headed eagle is a symbolic and cultural representation of the USA and therefore what it means to the dreamer.

- The popular meaning of the word 'chicken' – that of being a coward – perhaps best describes the presence of this bird in a dream. In not being able to be 'free as a bird' (i.e. by being cooped up in tiny cages or by having its wings clipped and not being able to fly any distance), the chicken shows a lack of free spirit in the dreamer. There is a need to be less grounded and immovable in dealings with others. As a domesticated bird, it shares the same symbolism as domesticated animals, that of instincts curbed or subverted in the cause of duty.

ASTROLOGY

We have mentioned in Section 5 the potential for learning through the use of your natal chart. For those who wish to take this study further, there follows some information which may be incorporated into your creative dreaming.

Astrology and astronomy are linked and are both part of history. The position of the planets helped the ancient peoples, such as the Babylonians, to regulate their lives in ways which sometimes even today we would do well to copy. In the beginning, particularly in an agricultural society, it helped them to know when to plant and when to harvest, and some of the ideas developed then survive today in gardening lore and practices. As more complicated societies developed, astrology showed leaders when to go to war, when to create festivals and celebrations for their people and when to concentrate on strengthening their ties with other nations. It is more than probable that the soothsayers of old were astrologers and, as they were most likely shamans as well, practised the art of lucid dreaming.

The twin sciences formed the bedrock of knowledge of the study of history, science, art and religion, and ordinary people relied on the information they accumulated. In the 17th century, man began to move away from a sense of awe and wonder at his place in the universe. Astrology was the tool of intuition – and intuition was no longer seen as a viable learning tool. Astronomy became a pure science and astrology lost its place of importance. In the new secularization of society, it also became lost to the priests and teachers of religion. However, it survived, and now, as we move forward into hopefully a more spiritual age, it begins to assume a new importance in our drive to understand ourselves. As with so many of the older practices, it is shown to have a basic common-sense approach to all of those mysteries with which we all struggle. It is interesting that what have become known as the 'outer planets', that is Uranus, Neptune and Pluto, whose influences are seen to be generational (i.e. affecting a generation as a whole), have all been discovered since the Age of Enlightenment began in the late 17th century.

The suggestion is that you use astrology as part of your self-development tool kit along with the art of creative dreaming. By knowing the qualities of each planet, you can use lucid dreaming to 'fix' the information so that it becomes second nature to use your awareness in everyday life. Initially, having instructed yourself to have a lucid dream, concentrate in turn on each of the planets and their qualities. Allow at least three nights for each planet, and within a month, even though you may not have dreamed lucidly for each of them, you will have assimilated a great deal of information. Alternatively, you might concentrate only on those planets which intrigue you.

The planets

The two most important planets of all to astrologers are the Sun and the Moon. From Earth, the Sun by day and the Moon by night are the most visible of our helpers. Knowledge of their qualities shows us the way forward as well as where we have come from.

Below are brief descriptions of each of the planets:

The Sun: The Sun gives light, which draws us forward into what we can be. It gives us our identity, or 'self' within the world. The Sun relates to our will, consciousness, creativity, father and authority figures.

The Moon: The Moon represents emotions, feelings, instincts and day-to-day habits. The Moon in a chart shows the link with the mother and describes how a person is nurtured and how they themselves nurture others. Its house (explained in more detail below) shows the circumstances under which emotions are most likely to express themselves. The Nodes of the Moon (a calculated position used by many astrologers) show our purpose and difficulties in how we make links with the world we live in. The South Node of the Moon shows old patterns of behaviour and response. The North Node points in the direction of further fulfilment and integration.

Mercury: Mercury has always represented thoughts, ideas and the mental processes in general. It governs not only ideas, but also the communication of those ideas. All types of communication are in fact ruled by Mercury, who was recognized by the Romans as the messenger of the gods.

Venus: Venus rules our values and perception of acknowledgement of ourselves. When we make an assessment or appreciate something, whether that is another person or a material possession, Venus is behind it. It is of prime importance in relationships, enjoyment, art and attractiveness.

Mars: Mars is associated with activity, assertion, power or enlightenment. It tells us how we get things started, the way we like to work and how we express rage. Often known as the warrior planet, it gives an indication of how we face conflict.

Jupiter: This planet, often known as the benevolent one, indicates the way we can solve the questions that disturb us. It is to do with how we can make use of fortuitous happenings. The largest planet in the Solar System, it represents development, progress and expansion.

Saturn: Saturn announces the spheres in life where we are bound to learn the hard lessons of the path we have chosen. Saturn, the ringed planet, shows us our boundaries and perimeters but also where and how we need to search for stability in life. Once the lesson is absorbed we have all the help we need in being able to work with quiet persistence.

Uranus: Uranus highlights our ability to go beyond our

boundaries; it is the planet of sudden happenings, of abrupt changes. Uranus offers us opportunities for change – both personal and global. Inventiveness, freshness and freedom are all characteristics associated with this planet.

Neptune: Neptune dissolves boundaries, either self-imposed or otherwise, providing us with the means to blend with the cosmos. It is inspiration, fantasies, perfection, consideration and fellowship. In its more negative aspect it is to do with mystery, delusion and scattered thinking. In many ways, it is the planet most closely linked with the practice of creative dreaming.

Pluto: Pluto is the planet of profound alteration from the very core of our being. Touching as it often does those parts which we do not understand within ourselves and which we would not necessarily wish to change, it encourages us to rethink our values and desires entirely. Pluto is about death, rebirth and transformation.

The ancients gave each sign an element: Fire, Earth, Air and Water. Fire is active, Earth practical, Air intellectual and Water sensitive. In addition, they also divided the 12 signs of the Zodiac into Modes – Cardinal, Fixed and Mutable. Cardinal initiates, Fixed maintains and Mutable changes. For the purposes of this book, it is only necessary to remember the basic meanings of each of these ways of looking at the signs. You only need to remember that Aries, the cardinal fire sign, initiates the cycle of life. Taurus, the fixed earth sign, grounds the life spark. Gemini, the mutable air sign, heeds the surrounding environment. Cancer, cardinal water, chooses to nurture within the home. Leo, fixed fire, expresses creativity. Virgo, mutable earth, then adjusts the physical conditions. Libra, cardinal air, pulls the energy together. Scorpio, fixed water, deals passionately with the relationships so formed. Sagittarius, mutable fire, uses experience to seek meaning. Capricorn is cardinal earth and therefore builds structures. Aquarius, fixed air, sets focuses on more spiritual ideals. Finally Pisces, mutable water, connects to divine inspiration to allow the cycle to begin again.

The placing of your planets, especially your Sun, gives a particular slant to your personality. Astrologers use certain keywords which express the signs of the zodiac in ways which are easy to remember. To enhance your understanding of yourself these keywords give fertile material for dreams – either lucid or otherwise. You may like to assimilate them in the same way as you have with the planets, or to use the image given for each sign, before you choose to study your astrological chart. Do remember that study of this nature should be fun, and not something that creates a problem for you.

SIGN	REPRESENTATION	QUALITIES
Aries	The Ram	The starting point – the trailblazer and adventurer. Courage, chivalry and boldness. Independence, impelling force and energy.
Taurus	The Bull	The steady, prudent, resolute response to life. Containing and all-encompassing. Developed impetus.
Gemini	The Twins	Connective, analytical, establishing and drawing together of ideas. Endless search for information. Examination, inquiry, curiosity. Tenseness and anxiety.
Cancer	The Crab	Home and kinship. Demonstrative and sensing. Supervision. Direction. Compassion. Practice and habitual behaviour. Absorption. Intuition prior to identification.

SIGN	REPRESENTATION	QUALITIES
Leo	The Lion	Self-respect. Pride, decision, artistic energy. Declaration and acting. Drama. Bravery. Children. Sports. Humour, regality. Generosity of heart.
Virgo	The Virgin	Anxiety. Virtue, chastity and commitment. Business-like, judicious and faultfinding. Attention to detail. Crafts.
Libra	The Balance/Scales	Partnership, fellowship, unity. Tactful. Socially skilful. Appraising. On the ball.
Scorpio	The Scorpion	Transformation and regeneration. Atonement and action. Purging. Reduction to the fundamental. Dismissive. Strong protection.
Sagittarius	The Centaur/Archer	Seeker of understanding. An educator, traveller, risk-taker. Genuineness, forthrightness, philosophy and truth.
Capricorn	The Mountain Goat	Pragmatic vision. Sober and methodical. Control and power. Perseverance and hard work.
Aquarius	The Water Bearer	Objective; works with anyone. Ambitious, essential, humane. Knowledge not action.
Pisces	The Fishes	Anticipation, sympathetic and acceptance. Sacrifice and going with flow. Changeable. Absorbing Daydreamer. Inclination.

If you wish to go even deeper into self-interpretation, you might like to know the meaning of the houses within an astrological chart. The chart represents the space around us and each house suggests a particular area of life. By understanding the effect of each planet in the different houses, you can find out where your pleasures and pains are most likely to occur. Again, dreams – and lucid dreams in particular – can help us to a very deep understanding. For example, if a person has Mars in Cancer in the Fourth House you could say that their ambition and drive is expressed in a sensitive and protective manner in matters of the home and family. The houses and the areas covered in life are:

NUMBER OF HOUSE	AREA OF LIFE COVERED
First	Self-awareness. Physical characteristics. Health.
Second	Material possessions. Personal security.
Third	Mental qualities. Relation to environment.
Fourth	Home and family.
Fifth	Creativity. Happiness. Power.
Sixth	Service to others. Work.
Seventh	Partnerships. Personal relationships.
Eighth	Sharing. Legacies. Dealing with death.
Ninth	Travel. Organizations. Philosophy.
Tenth	Social status. Career.
Eleventh	Hopes and wishes. Group objectives. Acquaintances.
Twelfth	Emotions. Sorrows. Inspiration. Deception.

Finally, as a sort of *aide memoire*, here is the way that each of the signs thinks about itself:

Aries   I Am

Taurus   I Have

Gemini   I Think

Cancer	I Feel
Leo	I Will
Virgo	I Analyze
Libra	I Judge
Scorpio	I Desire
Sagittarius	I See
Capricorn	I Use
Aquarius	I Know
Pisces	I Believe

NUMBERS

For those who wish to use creative dreaming to explore symbolism on a much more esoteric level, a great deal of information can be accessed through the use of numbers. A number will often surface in dreams which has intimate significance for the dreamer, such as a certain date, or the number of a house that the dreamer once lived in. Our minds will often register the importance of the number, both esoteric and otherwise, even though this is not consciously remembered.

Numbers have significance in many belief systems as well as in most religions. Probably the most commonly recognized meanings are those which were considered to be pragmatic and down to earth. Considered by many to be pure fortune telling, the first set of interpretations nevertheless gives rich grounds for investigation when having fun with creative dreaming.

One: You will achieve notable expertise in your work.

Two: Professional or personal relationships need treating cautiously.

Three: Your thoughts for solidity and prosperity will develop.

Four: A stable and protected home is available to you.

Five: A significant disclosure, which will bring transformation, is about to be made.

Six: A meaningful relationship is about to be made possible.

Seven: Internal efforts will help explain inherent difficulties.

Eight: An extraordinary opportunity is about to enter your life.

Nine: Caution needs to be taken not to overextend yourself.

Zero: The cipher suggests that anything is possible.

All numbers can have both negative and positive connotations, and below is a table setting out some key words which can act as a focus for further thought or as subjects for meditation before using them as themes for lucid dreaming.

Working with the negative qualities of numbers – or considering that a number is negative for you – is not in itself a bad thing. When a number highlights negative qualities within you and allows you to achieve a balance by recognising them, you then have at your disposal a means of making your conduct more appropriate to each situation.

	POSITIVE	NEGATIVE
One	Independence, self-respect, purpose, unity of purpose.	Dogmatism, arrogance, narrow-mindedness, humiliation, unwillingness.
Two	Tranquillity and balance, integrity, altruism, sociability, compatibility.	Indecision, apathy, lack of dependability, bloody-mindedness.

	POSITIVE	NEGATIVE
Three	Freedom, boldness, fun, eagerness, inventiveness.	Listlessness, overconfidence, restlessness, half-hearted conduct.
Four	Loyalty, imperturbability, orderliness, honesty.	Awkwardness, monotony, conventionality, inflexibility.
Five	Assurance, energy, bravery, health, susceptibility, compassion.	Hastiness, instability, inconstancy, unreliability.
Six	Idealism, honesty, philanthropy, supremacy, faithfulness, trustworthiness.	Softness, abstraction, surrender.
Seven	Wisdom, perception, philosophy, perseverance, observation.	Sullenness, fault-finding, lack of action, antisocial feelings.
Eight	Orderliness, power, business ability, judgement, control, perseverance.	Lack of inspiration, rudeness, aloofness, domination.
Nine	Intelligence, selection, artistry, acceptance, brilliance, lofty moral sense, intellect.	Illusion, laziness, lack of concentration, aimlessness.

Spiritually, as we progress, the particular energy which is contained in numbers becomes more available to us. Most numerical systems only have significance up to nine and any other numbers are then reduced to their basics. That is, 13 becomes 4 (1 + 3) and 25 becomes 7 (2 + 5). However, other systems offer choices of a higher degree of spiritual awareness or a return to the more basic meaning. Thus, eleven is a master number for those who are prepared to take responsibility for guiding others but can be reduced to two and thus is an appreciation of duality if that responsibility is not willingly undertaken. We have taken this system of numbers only as far as twelve, since beyond that explanations become more complicated and difficult.

The more esoteric interpretations are:

One The self, the beginning; the first; singularity.

Two Duality; hesitancy; balance; masculine v feminine; two sides to an argument; contrasting elements.

Three The triangle, freedom, independence.

Four The square, vigour, stability, efficiency; the earth; reality; the four sides of human character – perception, feeling, thought, anticipation; earth, air, fire and water.

Five The human body; human emotion in the body; the five senses.

Six Agreement or symmetry.

Seven Cycles of life, mystical, ethereal meaning, human totality.

Eight Death and resurrection, the universe.

Nine Pregnancy; the end of the circle and the commencement of something new; spiritual awareness.

Ten A new beginning; the male and female together.

Eleven Eleventh hour; the master number.

Twelve Time; a full cycle or wholeness.

Zero The feminine; the Great Mother; the unconscious; the absolute or hidden completeness.

In using creative dreaming to understand numbers you might use a statement of intent before going to sleep, such as 'I wish to understand the significance of the number...and its qualities of...'. You should find that your unconscious will then give you the information you need, either lucidly or through ordinary dreams. An extension of working with numbers is to recognize the place of sacred geometry in the overall scheme of things. Dreaming gives us access to ancient knowledge without us actually knowing what we have got hold of. Shape and form are extremely important in this world of ours, and proportion is probably even more so. If something is out of proportion, it enters the realms of the bizarre and even· the ugly.

Each shape, and its resultant object – triangle/pyramid, square/cube – has its own significance. In creative dreaming, we link into something quite profound in our exploration of geometric shapes. Whereas so many people have had difficulty in learning geometry by conventional methods, experimenting through lucid dreaming with shape is a real pleasure. (In Section 8 we suggest an exercise to help you experiment in more than one way with shape.)

* * *

By the time you have practised the various visualizations and affirmations in this section, and learnt to understand how ancient teachings can help you to understand yourself, you will probably be finding that your attitude to yourself and life in general will be changing quite considerably. Work done with your dreams can help you to decide what you need to do to change those attitudes which you have already identified. These are likely to be those which have inherited from your families, both maternal and paternal, and which may be handed down through more than one generation. Examples of these are poor self-image, Victorian attitudes to sex and sexuality and the inability to communicate.

Such concepts may also have arisen from perceptions you have had as a child of the world around you and which until now you have had no reason to change. Such patterns might be: waiting for attention in a large family; recognizing that one is not going to be listened to; lack of respect; difficulties with authority figures; and displays of anger. You will find that almost imperceptibly these issues have less need of attention in your daily life. They seem not to matter quite so much.

With the help of creative dreaming, you will now be able to accept new possibilities for fresh attitudes which your dreamwork has brought up. Particularly taking into account the wider viewpoints you are developing by having studied life-affirming aspects in yourself, something quite meaningful is happening. You are now able to use intentions, affirmations or actions to change negative – or even less than positive – attitudes. Gradually this will have an effect on the way you understand your dreams and perceptions and you may find that your life begins to feel less burdensome and in many ways much 'lighter'. This is because you are moving into different stages of awareness which will be explained more fully in the next section.

SECTION

7

CREATING THE WORLD YOU WANT

Having begun to understand the more spiritual and esoteric implications of creative dreaming through practising with Tarot, Archetypes, Myths and Numbers, we can really begin to appreciate the true meaning of lucidity – 'of the light'.

In this section of the book, you are moving much more into a state of being understood so well in Eastern philosophies. This is not a totally passive state, but is one which allows you to recognize that you have total control over your spiritual being and can create the world you want. It is as though, having reached the Ultimate, when you come back into everyday existence after experiencing this state, you will be able to appreciate everything around you in a new way.

Part of the joy of this state is recognizing that far from such knowledge leading to your isolation from the 'real' world, leaving you alone and without support, you now have access to what amounts to a universal family. This family consists of other people who, like yourself, have chosen to question their parameters and have moved 'beyond the ordinary'. Creative dreaming has been the tool you have used to reach this state and, along with the refinement of other altered states of consciousness is what you will use to help you to move further towards the blissful states so beloved in Eastern religions.

Such states enable you to be in the world, but not of it. In other words, you are able to see the world in which you live for what it is – a state of illusion created by you and others like you. It is your responsibility to make it as 'real' as you possibly can. While talking about a state of lucidity, the condition of blissfulness may seem totally unattainable and unreal. We can only suggest, at risk of being thought to be 'hippy-dippy', that you experiment for yourself.

WITNESSING

For many, lucid dreaming is the epitome of how far they wish to go in understanding dreams and dreaming. However, there is a stage beyond creative dreaming which entails yet another change of consciousness. Known as 'witnessing', it is an aspect of consciousness which goes beyond the personal. Dream lucidity may only be a forerunner of this state. It is one of the stages of self-contemplation which can occur in sleep. Just as we must learn to understand the pre-lucid state and the manipulation of our dreams before we can rightly say that we have lucid dreams, so also we must achieve lucidity before we are able to reach a dispassionate observation of our dreaming selves. This state is close to that recognized in Eastern philosophies as *samadhi* or *satori*. We move along a continuum from taking part in the dream (acting within it) to observing the dream in a totally dispassionate and non-involved way.

Witnessing most often emerges spontaneously and seems to need you to go through five stages for it to be achieved successfully. The five stages of moving from 'the actor' to 'the observer' are outlined briefly below.

1. In the first stage, the focus is much more on active participation. At this stage, there is simply a recognition that the individual is in the middle of a dream. The feeling is that the dream is external – beyond oneself – and that there is also an internal 'self'. You as an individual take part in the dream. There is a greater degree of wakefulness inside, but you are still tied into the figures and situations of your dream. Becoming more familiar with lucidity means that you can make an attempt to manipulate the dream.

2. At some point, it may occur to you that what is apparently external to you is, in fact, 'inside' – it is occurring within the dream framework. This is the second stage. Two paths open up to the dreamer. You may either become fully involved in the dream episode, understanding that both the self and the dream ego are involved, or move your focus completely to the inside, allowing the dream environment to fade. While you are dreaming lucidly, you will still be aware of the dream even though caught up in its activity. It becomes easy during these initial phases to move backwards and forwards between watching the dream in an uninvolved way and being actively lucid. You can choose to manipulate the dream in some way, when the dream will continue, or you can move your attention away from the dream and become passive when it will fade or disappear.

3. Lucid dreams in the third stage are usually brief. They consist of short periods of a spontaneous state of awareness that is similar to that in meditation where there is no need to interact with what is going on. Here one is learning simply to observe and to let go, without becoming involved. A meditation exercise is given in Section 8 which can help you to refine this process. The action of the dream is not particularly gripping or important, but recognizing that you are actually in this state

of awareness of observing the various phenomena is. There is strictly no need to anticipate any outcome, to try to fulfil any desires, or to get caught up in any particular action.

4. In this fourth stage, an 'inner wakefulness' dominates, and there is no remembrance of having any dreams at all. All that is left is dreamless sleep. You should recognize that this is not the same as the dreamless sleep that occurs in non-REM states, however, but is a state of being where all imagery is completely eliminated and there is complete desirelessness. The Inner Self is still capable of perception, but is also aware that there is nothing separate from it to perceive. In other words, it is 'at one' with everything, but is also aware of nothing. It is a difficult thing to explain, but is a state wherein one is witnessing nothing but Self. It is the ability to remain in a state of total passivity, of beingness. There is a sense of having transcended the physical state and of suspension within a void or boundlessness.

5. Once the dreamer has moved into this boundless state, where there is only pure consciousness, any images perceived take on the form of abstract shapes and conceptual symbols. They are almost entirely abstract and apparently without particular meaning, except that they are part of a whole. It is only their relationship with one another which gives them meaning, since there is no emotion or sensory input associated with them. Witnessing these requires a non-judgmental appraisal of what is seen with no particular need to adjust the image. It is here that one has a real sense of what lucidity is truly like, since the sense of expansiveness and light is truly all-pervading. You sense and appreciate the way that all things are interwoven. You are part of everything and everything is part of you. There is a sense of dynamic stillness – of motion and yet tranquillity. Many people would not call this a dream

state at all, but more a state of being, though such a feeling can only be appreciated from a state of total relaxation, coupled with a suspension of disbelief. This is truly the light of awareness.

There are really no words to describe these latter experiences. Just as the 'new' sciences of psychology and sociology had to find new words, meanings and shades of meaning to explain their findings, so these higher states of consciousness move away from mere words. They become aspects much more of feeling, sensing and 'being' in that order. Feeling can be taken as an internal state. Sensing is a slightly deeper awareness – akin to the subtle energy which, for instance, alerts an animal to danger or the human to pleasure. Being is a combination of both – an awareness of internal 'rightness' coupled with a subtle knowing that all is as it should be both inside and outside oneself.

There is only one word which describes such a state, and that is 'light'. In English, the word has two meanings – 'of little weight' and 'an appearance of brightness'; both of which are manifested in witnessing. Almost inevitably there is a sense of both weightlessness and clarity which comes with this experience. It is not something which is experienced visually, but with all the senses, and is indeed 'the light which passeth all understanding'. It is unique to each individual and yet belongs to all.

The Sufi believes that the inner light inherent in all of us is of differing strengths and only shows itself to those who wish to see it. It develops according to the understanding of the individual. Those who actively look for knowledge will have an inner light that shines more vividly. It can often be found more easily in the unconscious state, and colours the dreams of those who actively dedicate themselves to the search for knowledge. Our type of intelligence evolves from this light, not vice versa.

When the individual has the courage to use the inner light to clarify the issues which intrigue him, he is better equipped to use the natural talents that he has.

Man is both spiritual and material, not one thing or the other. When his concerns are with more worldly matters he is more materially disposed and turned towards the more prosaic. He is more spiritual when he wants to escape the more mundane aspects of this mortal coil, and focuses on the wider issues. The difference is not a difference of type but of direction.

The dreams belonging to the two attitudes are different; materially-minded dreams are darker. If the dreamer becomes more spiritual, however, he will gradually see dreams containing more light in them and may eventually experience a vision of blinding light. This phenomenon is akin to the description of witnessing as given above.

The goal of the Sufi is to know his true self – the inner mind. To the Sufi the dream in itself is less important than becoming aware and conscious that we are dreaming. To experience the rich inner life that we have, we must dream, and those dreams come through different channels. The Sufis have named these as follows:

Kayhali is the Arabic word for dreams where the 'day's residue' is reproduced. This reproduction may happen very clearly or come across as totally confused and chaotic.

Kalbi means 'dreams of the heart'. They link fear and desire which, being closely related, tend to cloud reality. They are in fact the opposite of reality, being illusions created through the distorted mirror of fear and doubt. The distortion comes through emotion which confuses the picture of what is wanted and what is needed.

Nakshi denotes 'symbolic dreams only to be interpreted by the wise'. They show inner truths of which even the dreamer may not be aware on a conscious level. Interpretation will often lead to the True Self but can be painful and disturbing, particularly if the interpretation is coloured by someone other than the dreamer. Every detail is symbolic, being characterized by the dreamer himself, and deals with issues which cannot be dealt with in the conscious state. Caution is needed in the interpretation of these dreams because they may deal with parts of the dreamer that he does not want to – or indeed cannot – deal with and therefore could reveal hidden demons.

All these dreams deal with conflicts in the dreamer's life, male/female, right/wrong, inner self/outer self – or, put another way, the conflicts and choices that need to be met in both the waking and the sleeping state. Dreams use different standards to gauge what the dreamer should do compared to the waking state and can often provide a truer answer. This is because we are able to ask ourselves questions in the unconscious state that we are too afraid to confront in the conscious state. When the truer inner state senses that the conscious state has strayed wildly from the inner there is physical difficulty and illness.

Prophetic dreams are called *ruhi* and are more comprehensive than *kalbi*. In this state, the dreamer senses rather more of the whole 'message' somewhat more objectively. *Ilhami* are divine messages shown to men where an angel or spiritual being can often be heard. Both *ruhi* and *ilhami* are more highly evolved dreams than most of us can imagine, and take on the nature of mystical experiences.

Before we are able to have such mystical experiences as a matter of course, we probably need to spend some time in developing the Spiritual Self.

DEVELOPING YOUR SPIRITUAL SELF

We have already seen how dreams can put you in touch with your inner selves, the part that is not easily revealed consciously in everyday life. Revealing this part will enrich and enhance your creativity and your ability to be the person you want to be. There is, however, a further step into the unknown which you can take if you are brave enough. It can completely alter your viewpoint, and ensure that your life will never be the same again – probably neither will the people with whom you come into contact. Through your dreams, you can develop a relationship with what some call Source, others the Ultimate, some the Centre, and yet others God.

This is the energy which has already been referred to above and is the Light of true understanding. This is not a journey which is undertaken lightly, since it requires discipline and commitment, but it is one which will delight and intrigue you. In essence, it means that you will come to accept that there is a force beyond yourself which permeates everything and allows you to be who you are – a Life Force, if you like. We have seen how creative dreaming can remove the obstacles to progress on many levels of awareness, and this final stage is about clearing away previously held concepts and beliefs which dictate that we are separate from this energy and do not have the right of access to it.

To be comfortable with this idea we must go through several stages:

• Create a new consciousness
• Develop insight from working with our dreams
• Use this to develop the Spiritual Self
• Use 'Great Dreams' to help with this process
• Develop a meaningful relationship with the Ultimate.

In the first stage there are several things that need to be accomplished in order to give us the security and stability to move to the next step. We need to use our dreamwork to clear the mind and develop an increased awareness of a source other than our own ego. In ordinary dreamwork or consideration of our dreams this means accepting the idea that beyond ourselves there is a vast depository of information available to us – a library of all that is, was or ever shall be. This occasionally visits our dreaming self and makes some of that information available to us. The more we work with dreams, the more that information becomes available. Lucid dreaming takes us one stage further in this process and allows us deliberately to seek information.

A simple technique to take us further is to use a statement of intent when preparing to have a lucid dream, such as 'I wish to access the information I require'. Such a simple statement means that the knowledge then becomes available to you either through lucid dreaming or in other ways – such as apparently by chance finding a book which tells you what you need to know, or perhaps overhearing a conversation. If you wish the information to come to you through creative dreaming, then your statement must reflect this: 'I wish to access the information I require through lucid dreaming'. It is perhaps more satisfying to keep your parameters as wide as possible, however.

As part and parcel of taking responsibility for your new consciousness, you probably need to look at some of your old attitudes and concepts and be prepared to let them go. This may include learning to manipulate your dreams. One of those manipulations may be to change the setting or scenario of your dream.

Many people do not feel that it is right to try to create new settings in their dreams. They feel that their minds already have the right information to create the correct scenario for whatever it is that they are trying to achieve. For them, trying to tamper with the basic components of a dream is tantamount to manipulating the very fabric of life. However, for those who are prepared to take responsibility for themselves you can use the technique of 'spinning' to change the dreamscene.

When you first master the art of lucid dreaming, you will have enough to do in remembering to prepare for lucid dreaming, forming the intention and deciding on the subject. Once you become more proficient at doing these things, however, you can turn your attention to other aspects of the dream and begin to manipulate those. The questions you should ask yourself are:

Should I give myself permission to change the scenario?
Do I believe I *can* change it?

Expectations play such a huge part in this aspect of lucid dreaming that, quite frankly, if the smallest part of you is apprehensive or anxious, the procedure will not work. It is that negativity that acts like a 'spanner in the works' and will not allow the scenes to change. You can deal with the negative thoughts by visualizing them as a dark cloud which can be absorbed into the light. Then you can operate your sense of integrity and allow yourself to become aware of the opportunities you have.

When you realize how easy it is to create an illusory scene, it will help you to be more creative in your other pursuits. You will then be able to set the scene to empower yourself to be in charge of your environment within your daily life.

In creating a new consciousness, we can also use dreaming to develop new attitudes, as well as increasing our commitment and experience of manifesting our own connection with the Ultimate. The closer we get to our own understanding of this energy, the less the pettiness of everyday concerns will bother us. A warning has been given not to lose touch with the reality of the everyday, yet at the same time we do need to appreciate that we have the ability to create our own world. As we become more proficient at creative dreaming, we are more able to try out new ways of relating to others, new ways of making what we have learnt and experienced available and even simply new ways of being before we inflict these on others.

All too often, when we make changes, others do not understand, and we may be accused of madness, instability, wackiness and so on. Some might even accuse us of being mentally ill. Certainly as we venture further into this new way of being, we need to find a new inner stability, and again lucid dreaming can assist in this process. The statement of intent needs to be as simple as possible. 'I wish to find my own inner core' or 'I wish to experience my own inner stability' will suffice.

In the next stage, it is possible to face in depth some of the key questions about ourselves and the world in which we live. From the question 'Who am I?' arises a number of other thoughts which are questions more properly dealt with in the section below on Insights. A start can now be made, however, by asking for clarity in your search, so rather than asking the straight question, you may find that it is easier to make a statement and a request. This might be, 'I wish to know who I am and therefore request clarity on this matter'. Put more simply, it might be, 'I wish to be clear on who I am'. Other philosophical questions, such as exploring Man's inhumanity to Man, could also be simplified to a statement of desire, prefacing any statement with the phrase, 'I wish to understand'. As always, a fair degree of patience with yourself (and with the universe) is required, since these are not concepts which can be absorbed in one sitting. Interestingly, meditation and creative dreaming will only give you as much information as you can handle at any one time, so you will learn to take your time anyway.

You are now in a position to be able to monitor your dreams for spiritual symbols, statements of wisdom, visitations from guiding figures and so on. Almost inevitably, to begin with, you will think you are imagining things because such appearances are fleeting and often scarcely noticeable. As you become more proficient, however, you will find they appear more frequently. A little bit like learning to read, the 'words' become easier as you go on. With lucid dreaming, you will be able to focus on such impressions and assimilate more and more information. Your affirmation of intent might be something along the lines of, 'I wish to make contact with the one who guides me' or 'I wish to deepen my understanding of the sacred meaning of numbers'. In Section 6 there is information on the meaning of totem animals and the meaning of numbers, so this is a good time to experiment and develop your own understanding.

Now is also the time to experience and undertake your own spiritual journey. The shamanic journey has been practised for many years. The seeker on the spiritual path understands the need to enter a different dimension from our own in order to gain a deep understanding of the meaning of life. Spiritualists and practitioners of Eastern religions are well used to the idea of such a journey. You can now develop your own idea of your personal journey. An easy way of doing this is by a mixture of visualization and lucid dreaming:

1. Visualize a path in front of you which stretches into the distance. As you see it it may be fairly straightforward,

winding or perhaps not easily discernible from its surroundings. Remember that this is your construct, so how it presents itself to you will have meaning should you care to think about it. A winding path might, for instance, represent the fact that you generally choose not to accept straightforward solutions in your life. The path that is not easily seen may mean that you do not find it easy to make decisions. The interpretation is yours.

2. Now visualize yourself walking along the path and coming to a fork in the road. You must decide whether to go right or left – one way being relatively easy, the other more difficult; again it is your choice which way to go. At this point, you could choose to have a lucid dream to help you to decide.

3. Remember to record and interpret your dream, this time looking for spiritual symbols and clues that can help you to conduct your life in a more spiritual way. Perhaps you will find that you wish to control your anger, monitor your behaviour towards others or perform better within the work situation. These are, of course, only examples and you will find that your own ideas make themselves felt.

4. The next step can be either a continuation of the process in the same night or at a later date. You continue to visualize yourself on the path – this time a little further along the way. Ahead of you the road goes straight forward but also has turnings to right and left where you must again choose your route. You might use either meditation or lucid dreaming to progress further on your journey.

5. Repeat steps 3 and 4 as often as you feel comfortable.

6. During this time, you may like to attempt to gain some insight

into yourself and the way you function. A question from the list below could be posed at each change in the road:

What am I hiding from myself or not facing?
What are my talents? What are those things I do well?
What are those things which have meaning for me?
What are my constraints? What takes me away from my comfort zone?
What are my expectations of life?
What are my desires in life?
What keeps me focused?

As you can see, you are now beginning to use dreams and dreamwork deliberately to develop your spiritual life. You may find that your dreams become more vivid and meaningful. At this point, we suggest that you step back and take stock how you wish to proceed. Hopefully the world around you is also becoming a nicer and brighter place, and you may wish to take time out to explore beautiful things such as fine art, sculpture, well written words or whatever takes your fancy. You will often be able to use creative dreaming to help you to understand the artist or author. This may give you an insight into your own creative process and the courage to experiment.

Another way in which you might wish to enhance your knowledge is by deliberately studying a religion or system of knowledge and finding out if it has meaning for you. Again, as well as reading and studying, you can use meditation and lucid dreaming to round out your study. In that way, you will find that you develop a system which has personal meaning rather than following the crowd. The Archetypes, Myths and Tarot images are all good places to start. Remember to take things calmly and gently and not to experience frustration – unless this is part of your learning process!

Now you may find that you are developing the ability to experience what have been called Great Dreams. The principle of Great Dreams is well known to followers of C. G. Jung, but less well known to others. Great Dreams are those which have a deeper meaning than ordinary dreams and which stay with us, requiring further interpretation and elucidation. We have seen how in primitive cultures there were certain dreams which were meant to be shared with the community, and this is what great dreams are in essence. They are dreams which give us direction, reveal a truth or clarify an issue from a spiritual viewpoint – that is, from a wider perspective than just our own petty concerns. Through such dreams, we may gain a greater grasp of spiritual meaning. There does not seem to be any empirical evidence that lucid dreaming enhances the occurrence of Great Dreams, though my own personal experience would seem to show that it does.

Now it may be time to use dreamwork to transform your personality and life into a meaningful whole. Hopefully, you will now be relatively adept at making minor changes to your behaviour and the way that you relate to other people. Now you may choose to make further adjustments to take into account your new learning. This, depending on your personality, may be easy or difficult, but your practice in changing the scenarios in creative dreaming can help you to make small – rather than large – changes.

As you learn to follow philosophical arguments, you may find yourself spontaneously tuning in to a greater power and becoming aware of the many opportunities open to you both to change your life and the lives of those around you. Remember that you are a unique individual with your own abilities and talents, and can now make a commitment to the person you truly are and to that part of the life force which is singularly yours.

As you progress, each part of your life will take on new meaning and significance. It is more than likely that you will begin to feel that you are much more part of a greater whole. Coupled with this feeling is the realization that the aforementioned 'whole' is very large and that you are but a very small cog in the wheel. Life tends to take on greater meaning, however, and you will wish to perceive some spiritual significance in everything that you do and everything that you are. Lucid dreaming is a way to help you to test your commitment to yourself as well as acclimatize yourself to the new feelings which are perfectly natural at this time.

Another way in which you may choose to use the art of lucid dreaming is to develop rituals and meditations from dreams and dreamwork. The ritual of setting out your dream journal and of preparing yourself for lucid dreaming is a way of focusing your mind on the task in hand. Remembering and recording your dreams is a way of clearing your mind so that you can pay attention to the coming day.

You may like to use one of the symbols from your dreams to set the tone for your day in order to enjoy it to the full. This may give the ability to create circumstances around yourself which give rise to an advance in spiritual progress. It may be found that during the day you will recognize the need to make further adjustments in order to maximize your own potential. These can then be carried forward into lucid dreaming.

One of the best outcomes of working with dreams is that it enables us to link with a huge stream of healing energies which allows us to help ourselves and others. Those symbols and flashes of light which we saw at the beginning of our experiments with creative dreaming now take on a different meaning and can be recognized as indications of healing power. We can begin to use these symbols in everyday life to help us to focus within in order to help us to work with others. A circle, for instance, can be a symbol for wholeness, or indeed an arrow can suggest the correct direction. The more we work on our dreams, the greater we develop our own personal dictionary of symbols.

Dream symbols appear from the unconscious, so, having been brought into focus, they need to be assimilated in such a way that they become an integral part of our everyday life. They need to be contemplated perhaps with the help of lucid dreaming from a state of dynamic awareness (a clear, functioning mind) and for this you need to be completely relaxed. Any relaxation techniques that work for you can be used and a simple one is given elsewhere in the book.

There are three ways in which you can work with any symbol in your dreams.

1. The first is to allow it to come 'alive' for you, that is, to move from being simply an image in your dream to something that you give relevance to in your ordinary everyday life – the guide or 'wise old man' is one such figure.

2. The second way is to allow the symbol to develop further – to observe it and to watch what happens. Let us suppose that a violent storm has been experienced in the dream. Symbolically this can represent an upcoming problem, our own suppressed passion or even, for some people, the intensity of their spiritual belief. Only by being prepared to watch and wait can we be certain of its real meaning for us. Given the opportunity, the symbol will clarify exactly what is intended.

3. The third way is to allow the symbol to devolve – that is, to

go back to basics. For those other than experienced meditators or lucid dreamers this is a little more difficult to accomplish, although the technique of watching and waiting with your purpose in mind usually works. To dream of a pool of water, for instance, might by association take us to a contemplation of water, of rain, clouds and of the complexity of your own emotional makeup.

Having come this far in your exploration of creative dreaming and how it can affect your life, you are ready to develop your own personal action plan. However, before you do this, we have gathered together in one section exercises, tips and techniques to help smooth your path.

SECTION

8

YOUR
WORKBOOK

In this section, we gather together all of the exercises and the tried and tested techniques which enable you to develop the art of dreaming creatively. To have the courage to transcend the fears, doubts and barriers that we all have in becoming creative, we need to be in touch with our own inner being and the creative urge that is ours by right. We must move from feeling that we are prevented by circumstances from being the person we know we can be to taking control of our lives and being able to link to that stream of knowledge and awareness that enables us to create our future.

To do this we have to be intensely practical. To that end, this section contains the exercises, tips and techniques which will help you to develop creative dreaming. You may notice that some exercises have been repeated from earlier in the book. They have been repeated in this section so that they may be more easily photocopied. You may do this with the full permission of the publisher and author. Of course, you do not need to follow the order given, though this is the one that is probably the simplest, because it takes you from when you first remember and record your dreams to using them with full awareness.

Hopefully, you will be able to progress from the simpler ones to the more difficult, and to experiment with all of them before undertaking to develop your own personal action plan.

WORKPLAN

Dreamwork, for the purposes of this book, can be defined as any activity we choose to carry out once we have had a dream. It entails working initially only with the content of that particular dream. Later the dream can be investigated along with other dreams, to see whether it is part of a series or perhaps clarifies other previous dreams. The dream can be looked at in several different ways. You should be able to:

1. List all various components of the dream.

2. Explore the symbols of the dream with all their various meanings.

3. Widen the perspectives and components of the dream.

4. Work with the dream in as many different ways as possible to complete unfinished business.

5. Work with the spiritual significances within the dream.

6. Bring the message through to everyday life to make necessary choices and changes.

We will now look at these points in more detail.

1. The components

The components of a dream are all of the various parts of the dream: the scenario, the people, the action, the feelings and emotions. Each has its part to play in your interpretation and it is only when you consider the dream really carefully that you will be able to appreciate some of the more subtle meanings of the dream. In lucid dreaming, as we have already seen, it is feasible to make changes to any or all of these things, though not necessarily all at once.

The more adept you become at recognizing your own individual way of creating your dreams, the easier your own interpretation will be. Making a simple list will help you to do this.

The following dream was submitted via the Internet by a 19-year-old woman and illustrates perfectly the availability of dreamwork material. Our italics show the important components of the dream.

It was an *underwater* dream. I was in a *very large bubble* and there were *turtles* all around me.

As far as I could see, *nothing but turtles*. They were all *different sizes*. I remember *steps leading down* into the water; it was kind of like a *swimming pool*.

I could see the sides and I was very close to the steps. I remember looking around and seeing *all kinds of plants* and turtles and thinking, "Why are there so many turtles in the pool?"

I also remember that the only colours I saw were *blue and green* in varying shades. The underneaths of the *turtles* were a *pale yellow/green colour*. It was very *beautiful*.

I can also remember *wanting* to get out of the *bubble* somehow, but I was *scared* that if I did, the *turtles would kill me*.

In this dream, the lady could have decided to become lucid when she asked the question 'Why are there so many turtles in the pool?' Many dream researchers do not feel that lucid dreams should be interpreted. If you remember, however, that dreams are always multi-level and may have different interpretations according to the needs of the dreamer, even creative dreams are capable of meaning.

Calvin Hall and Robert van de Castle, in an effort to be scientific, developed the method of quantitative coding which is still used nowadays in dream research. This led to the cognitive theory of dreams, which meant that dream content was divided into several categories. There were characters, emotions, interactions, misfortunes, objects and settings. By dividing dreams up in this way, they recognized that dreams expressed perceptions of family members, friends, social environment and self. Dreams reflected waking concerns, interests and emotional focus. Just as a matter of interest, when carrying out their research they discovered that there were strong similarities in dreams from people all over the world.

In your own work with dreams, you may like to record the number of times over a given period of, say, a month how many times – and it what form – these perceptions and concerns appear. For this you will, of course, have regularly remembered your dreams and taken care to record them, whether lucid or otherwise, as fully as possible in your dream journal.

2. The symbols

When the mind has a message to impart, it will often present the information in symbolic form. It is important, therefore, for you to understand the symbolism of your dreams. You will, over time, develop your own symbolism: certain things in dreams, which have relevant meaning for you. The conventional symbolism of dreams is very rich in imagery. Though many exponents of creative dreaming do not attempt to interpret dreams in this way, it is always worthwhile taking a good look at your dreams, so that if they have symbols within them they can be properly interpreted. Any good dream interpretation book will act as a starting point. With any of your dreams, it is worthwhile making an alphabetical list of your dream content and then deciding whether it can be interpreted symbolically rather than literally.

3. The perspectives

Perhaps the most satisfactory work which can be done with dreams is to deliberately widen the perspective within the dream and to consciously push the dream further. Thus you might like to see what would happen next to one of the characters. For example:

What would happen if the action that was being carried out were continued?
How would the other characters react?

How would this change the dream?

If a particular character acted in a different manner would the whole dream change, or only parts of it?

How much would you want characters to support you or leave you alone?

You can see that these considerations are the beginning of you taking control within your dream, and you are therefore moving more authoritatively into lucid dreaming. Another way in which you can change perspective is to look at your dream as if you were one of the characters. If this were so, would you 'direct' the dream differently? Would there be a different outcome? Working with your dream in this way enables you to become more aware of the effect on various parts of your personality (the characters in your dream).

4. Working with your dreams

You can use any method you are comfortable with to look at issues connected with your dreams. You might like to use either the Jungian or the Gestalt method of working which is shown below. The Gestalt method is a way of confronting or making friends with various parts of your personality, which tend to show themselves as characters or aspects of your dream.

You may like to look at some of the even earlier methods of interpretation. You might try to decide whether your dreams are messages from the unconscious (or from God) – which used to be called *oracula* – or are simply images known as 'visions'.

5. Working with the spiritual significances

From the idea that God, as seen in primitive societies, gives dreams, we would speak nowadays more of a recognition of spiritual influences. This is when your truly altruistic and selfless side recognizes that you must make adjustments to your everyday behaviour if you are to live your life as fully as possible. That part of you which 'knows best' attempts to inform you not only of the changes that need to be made, but also how to make them.

By and large, the spiritual significance of a dream has much to do with your sense of responsibility to the rest of your community or the world in which you live. Not everybody is able or willing to consider the greater good, but if a dream does allow itself to be interpreted in any other way, you may wish to look at it from this point of view. The three things to look for here are right thought, right speech and right action. The questions you might ask yourself are:

How does this dream help me to be a better person?
What information does it give me to help others?
What fresh understanding does this dream bring me?

6. Bringing the message through

Once you have explored the dream in every way possible, you will be able to apply the things that you have learnt in your everyday life. You will need to practise new patterns of behaviour, think in new ways, change some attitudes and create a new way of being. This is indeed where lucid dreaming can help you tremendously.

* * *

You will see various other techniques throughout this section for doing all of these things and will be able to practise your mode of behaviour carefully before actually making radical changes in your everyday life. Let us suppose, for instance, that you have concluded that you must become more proficient at handling difficult relationships. Using lucid dreaming to assist you, you can both practise the new way of behaving and get a fair idea of what effect your behaviour will have on other people in your life. You will be able to judge whether that behaviour will be welcome or otherwise. When using creative dreaming in this way, try to be patient both with yourself and others.

GESTALT METHOD

The Dream

If all parts of the dream are reflections or aspects of me then the part I choose to communicate with is the person/thing in my dream represented by...?

(If you find it easier, place two chairs opposite one another and play each part in turn or use your own image in a mirror to signify the dream character.)

What I want to know is...

Result

QUESTIONING YOUR DREAM CHARACTERS

There are certain questions which can be asked during the course of a dream, even a lucid one. The first is, 'Who or what are you?' In recognizing that you are dreaming, this question can do one of two things. It can confirm lucidity for you, in that you recognize that the being or entity that you are speaking to is in fact a dream image, or in becoming aware of the image you realize that you are dreaming and instinctively wake up. Identifying the image allows you to work with it, to make sense of it and to make use of it – thus laying the foundation for further elucidation.

The second question that can be asked from the lucid state is, 'Why are you in my dream?' Such a question is probably more correct in dealing with bad dreams and nightmares, in that it initiates the process of confronting your negatives. Working from a positive viewpoint and remembering that your inner self is the one that produces the images, the question highlights the motive *behind* the image rather than what the image represents. This means accepting that you yourself have been responsible for the presence of the image, rather than that the image is attempting to tell you something. As time goes on you may find that with greater understanding the question becomes, 'Why is this in my dream?'

The next question to be asked is, 'What have you to tell me?' Some dreamers are able to set up a dialogue with their images. This is very similar to the Gestalt technique shown in this section. For those who prefer to adhere to a clearer focus, the question may be better phrased as, 'What information can I gain from you?' This requires a careful appraisal of all aspects of the image. This includes the way it is placed, how it holds itself, what part it plays in the overall scenario of the dream, what it does and so on. For those who are less practised at lucid dreaming this question can be asked in the waking state after remembering the dream, but the more accomplished should be able to seek answers from a state of lucidity.

A further way in which the dream image can be questioned is to ask, 'Why is this happening in this way?' or 'What is the purpose of this image's action or non-action?' In this way you will discover whether the image's purpose is solely to facilitate the other actions within the dream, or to impart further information. Thus, to be inside a large building might be to impress upon you its importance, the large empty space or its use as a public meeting place. If you wish to follow the Gestalt method of interpretation, you will be able to accept that each thing in the dream is an aspect of yourself. Therefore in the previous example you would question yourself as to which part of you is important, which part is empty space and which part is publicly on show.

'What do you want from me?' is a question which can take one in many different directions. The first thing to look at is what the dream itself requires. The dream as a complete entity contains a 'message' or information which often needs to be unravelled even if the dream is lucid. Equally, as we have already seen, each part of the dream contains its own information. So it often helps in the waking state to make a list of what is relevant to a successful completion of the dream. As you become more competent at lucid dreaming, you are capable of making lists in your head of what you have discovered. It is worthwhile remembering to record such findings as quickly as possible after the dream has ended.

Frequently, once you have woken up, you will need to find out how the dream relates to your waking life and the situations in which you find yourself. This often requires you to look at the content of the dream for clues in order to discover information which helps you to handle the main issue in your life. You can then review it for help in particular circumstances, perhaps at work or in your personal life. Be sure also to look for ways of expanding your ability to lucid dream by taking a specific aspect of the dream. Choosing to work lucidly with the specific enables you to delve even deeper into the hidden aspects of your psyche. This is where working with the symbols of the dream on an individual basis can help you to become extremely creative.

DAILY AUDIT PLAN

If you are to use your dreams to help you to deal effectively with your everyday life, there are certain techniques that you must practise first in order to clear your mind successfully so that you can learn the art of creative dreaming. We show these, wherever practicable, on separate pages.

As part of your nightly routine to clear your mind ready for lucid dreaming, it is wise to do what we call a daily audit. This consists of doing a review of your day and balancing the good with the bad. You might like to concentrate on your behaviour and decide whether you have acted appropriately or not, or simply to decide which parts and actions of the day have been productive and which not. Your audit will be of the issues which concern you most at that particular time. Your starting point should be the hour immediately preceding bedtime – you should then work backwards throughout the day until you reach your time of awakening.

1. Taking a sheet of paper divide it into two columns. On one side list actions and types of behaviour you consider 'good' and on the other those you consider 'bad' or 'indifferent'.

2. Looking at the bad side first, review where your behaviour or action could be improved and resolve to do better in the future. You may like to develop a ritual for yourself which represents your rejection of the disliked patterns of behaviour. This can be as simple as writing down the behaviour and discarding the paper on which it is written.

3. Now look at the good side and give yourself approval and encouragement for having done well. Resolve to have more of the good behaviour and, if you wish, form an affirmation which indicates this. You might take this affirmation into lucid dreaming.

4. Where your behaviour has been indifferent, again resolve to do better and to give yourself more positive feedback for having made the effort.

5. Forgive yourself for not having achieved a best result and praise yourself for doing your best. This is the aspect of 'balancing your books'. Now let your day go, do not dwell on the negatives and go peacefully to sleep.

This exercise helps in the process of keeping you spiritually strong.

INCUBATING THE DREAM YOU WANT (CARDS METHOD)

The next action that you will wish to undertake is that of incubating the dream you want. This technique works well, as discussed earlier in the book, for incubating any dream but also as a preliminary to learning the art of lucid dreaming itself. The stages are:

Clarify the issue under consideration and write it down.

Ask the question. State it as positively as possible and, to commit it to memory, write it down.

Repeat the question and then turn it into a statement (e.g. from 'What is...?' to 'I want to know about...'). If you wish, write it down in the form of a statement and place it under your pillow, since this seems to focus the mind.

Dream the dream and document it. Answers can take longer than just one night to appear. Keep a note of how long it takes.

Study the dream in detail and look for further clues. Decide if the dream has been helpful or whether more work is needed. Record your reaction to the dream.

REMEMBERING YOUR DREAMS

To be able to remember your dreams you need to train yourself to do so. Good-quality sleep is the first prerequisite since, while you are learning, you may well be waking yourself up fairly frequently. What we mean here is remembering all of your dreams. Later you will remember lucid dreams particularly, but first of all you must get into the habit of a particular routine.

1. Decide which sleep periods you are going to monitor. A good idea is to give yourself an approximate four-hour period to have a proper sleep, then to monitor everything after that in chunks of waking yourself up every hour or so.

2. If you have an illness or are taking medication, please check with your doctor or medical practitioner before undertaking this exercise.

3. Set your alarm or wake-up device – soft light or soothing music – for the time you wish to wake. Under no circumstances allow yourself to be 'shocked' into wakefulness, for example, by very loud music. It is counter-productive because it is most likely to chase away the dream.

4. When you have woken up, lie perfectly still. Do not move until you have recalled your dream with as much detail as you can remember.

5. Write down your dream, including as much information as you can, and analyze it when you are ready to do so. If it was a lucid dream record it as such. If not, then interpret it in your usual way.

6. It is here that your dream journal will come in useful, because in it you will also be able to record fragments of dreams which at the time may not seem to have relevance but, later on, may do so.

7. Dreams are remembered best from periods of REM sleep, so with practice, you should begin to discover when these periods are. Don't be too worried if at first your dream recall is deficient. You will get better with practice.

8. Try not to let the affairs of the day get in the way when you first wake up. You can begin to consider them when you have paid attention to your mind's nighttime activity.

KEEPING A DREAM JOURNAL

Here we repeat the instructions given earlier in the book on keeping a dream journal so that you develop good practice before you attempt creative dreaming.

1. Any paper and writing implements can be used – whatever is most pleasing to you.

2. Always keep your recording implements at hand.

3. Write the account of the dream as soon as possible after waking.

4. Use as much detail as possible.

5. Note at which point in your dream you consider you 'went lucid'.

Be consistent in the way that you record your dreams. One simple scheme is given next.

RECORDING YOUR DREAM

This exercise gives an easy format for you to record your dream. Obviously the first three parts only need to be recorded if you intend to submit your dream to an external scrutiny. If you intend to keep your dream journal private, this method gives you the opportunity to look carefully at each of your dreams and return to them at a later date if necessary, perhaps to compare content, scenarios or other aspects. It can also allow you to quantify your own progress both in the process of developing lucid dreaming and in that of self-development.

Name

Age

Gender

Date of dream

Where were you when you recalled the dream?

State the content of your dream.

Write down anything odd about the dream (e.g. animals, bizarre situations, dream signs, etc.).

What were your feelings in/about the dream?

HOW TO HAVE A CREATIVE DREAM

This technique is extremely simple and is used as a preparatory exercise to the MILD Technique shown afterwards.

1. Prepare yourself for sleep

As you prepare yourself for sleep give yourself the instruction that tonight you will have a lucid dream. Form an affirmation of intent along the lines of a very simple statement such as, 'Tonight my dream will be lucid.' Keep the statement that simple because you are simply learning to 'go lucid' initially. The content of the dream does not actually matter at this point.

2. Repeat your affirmation

Repeat your affirmation either out loud or to yourself as many times as you need to in order to fix it in your own mind. This in itself is helpful, since it is teaching you how to focus your mind on one thing at a time. An affirmation is a simple, positive statement encapsulating as succinctly as possible what you intend to happen.

3. Hold your intent in mind

Keep your mind on your intention, and then allow yourself to drift off into sleep.

4. Note the degree of lucidity you have achieved

When you wake up, note the time and whether you remember having been lucid. Also note how long you think you were in a state of lucidity. Your estimation will probably not be very accurate to begin with, but this does not matter since you will become more proficient as time goes on.

REALITY CHECK

As the periods of lucidity become longer, you will find that there is a need to check whether you are truly dreaming or not. Probably the best way of doing this is to look at the ground, or at your own hands and feet, to see if they are as they should be.

1. Ask yourself a question

The most sensible question to ask is, of course, 'Am I dreaming?' The simple asking of the question may initially be sufficient to chase away the dream, and you may well wake up. In time you will be able to apply other techniques to allow you to stay within the dream.

2. Look at your hands and feet

Checking your hands and feet for size and normality helps to stabilize the dream. If they seem larger or smaller than normal, then you are probably dreaming. In your dream, try to move them and watch what happens.

3. Carry out an action that you know is impossible in real life

This could be anything from jumping into the air for a huge distance, to rolling up a hill. The important thing is that it is an action which goes against the normal parameters of everyday life. If you perform the action, you are dreaming.

4. Look at the ground or the dream scenario

If there are bizarre elements in either of these, you are probably dreaming. If you do not believe that what you are perceiving is real, then you are probably dreaming. You might ask yourself the question, 'Is this real?'

5. Remind yourself that you are or have been dreaming

If you can, during the dream remind yourself that 'This is a dream'. Also when you wake up tell yourself, 'That was a dream.' Gradually you will come to recognize very quickly what is dream and what is not.

This reality check is also good to do even when you know you are awake, and helps to remind you that we live in a state of illusion anyway – that life itself is an illusion.

INCUBATING A SPECIFIC CREATIVE DREAM

When you have had some success with incubating the type of dream that you want, you can then progress to developing a specific lucid dream. We remind you to be patient with yourself, because you may not at first find that your incubation gives you the exact environment or content that you have requested. Gradually, however, you will find you are 'hitting target' more and more often.

1. Prepare the focus of your dream

Before you go to bed take the time to formulate a single idea or query which states clearly the subject of your dream. Write the phrase down and use a visual image, such as a picture or appropriate symbol, to fix the idea. Memorize the phrase and your representation of the scene. Create your dream scene or event verbally now. Remind yourself that when you dream of that particular event you will know that you are dreaming. Repeat to yourself at least three times, 'When I dream of [whatever you have decided], I will remember that I am dreaming.'

2. Go to bed

It is important not to let anything else intrude on your concentration. So, without further ado, go to bed and make yourself comfortable.

3. Keep the phrase or image in your mind

Concentrate on your phrase and aim to become lucid. Imagine yourself dreaming about the issue and progressing into lucidity. If there is something you want to try in the dream, such as flying, concentrate on the idea of doing it once you are lucid.

4. Meditate on the phrase

Keep your objective to become lucid in focus until you fall asleep. If at all possible don't let any other thoughts come between thinking about your issue and falling asleep. If your thoughts wander, just revert to thinking about your phrase and becoming lucid.

5. Follow your focus in the creative dream

When you feel have achieved lucidity and are satisfied that you are considering your issue, carry out your aim (e.g. ask whatever question you wish to have answered, request ways to represent yourself, try your new responses or contemplate your position). Note your impressions and be aware of all contents of the dream.

6. Keep the dream active and sustain it if you can

To sustain the dream, learn to use the techniques in the exercise below. Initially, lucidity will only occur in short flashes.

7. Come out of lucidity

When you acquire a good enough answer in the dream, come out of lucidity and make a point of rousing yourself into full consciousness. Before everything disappears, lie quite still thinking about what you have achieved.

8. Record the dream

Record the dream (see page 333), deciding exactly how it has answered your question or intent.

THE MILD TECHNIQUE

By now, your own dreams will be beginning to intrigue you and hopefully you will be wishing to practise the technique of lucid dreaming for yourself. To make it easy for you we repeat here the technique developed by other dream researchers.

1. Set up dream recall

Learn to wake up from dreams and to recall them. Initially you may need to use an alarm clock, soft music or diffused light. Eventually you will be able to wake up at will by giving yourself the instruction to do so. When you do wake from a dream, try to recall it as fully as possible and, if necessary, write it down.

2. Focus your intent

As you go back to sleep, concentrate intensely on the fact that you intend to recognize that you are dreaming. Use an expression to fix this idea in your mind, such as 'Next time I'm dreaming, I intend to remember I'm dreaming.' Keep focused on this idea alone and don't allow yourself to be distracted by stray thoughts.

3. See yourself become lucid

Using your imagination, perceive that you are back in a dream you have had, whether it is the last one or another one that you clearly remember. Tell yourself you recognize it as a dream. Look for something odd or out of place that demonstrates plainly that it is a dream. Tell yourself 'I'm dreaming', and knowing what it feels like to be dreaming, continue to remember your chosen dream.

Next, imagine what your next lucid dream will feel like. See yourself carrying out your chosen plan. For example, note when you would 'realize' you are dreaming. See yourself carrying out a dream action, such as flying or spinning around.

4. Repeat until your intention is fixed

Repeat steps 2 and 3 until your intention is fixed; then drift off into sleep. Sometimes while falling asleep your mind may wander. If so, repeat the steps, so that the last thing in your mind before falling asleep is the thought that you will remember to appreciate the next time you are dreaming.

Keep a record of how proficient you become.

PROLONGING A CREATIVE DREAM

All of these methods have been found to be useful in prolonging the lucid dreaming state. More extensive explanations of the techniques and their relevance are given earlier in the book.

1. Spinning

As your original dream begins to fade, but before you become properly awake, try spinning on the spot. You should do this as rapidly as possible and begin from an upright position. You should find that you either re-enter your own dream or spin to a new scenario.

2. Continuing an activity

When you find yourself in the middle of a lucid dream and it is beginning to fade, carry on with what you were doing in the dream but ignore the fact that the dream is losing clarity. As you continue with your activity, repeat over and over again to yourself 'The next scene will be a dream.'

3. Rub your (dream) hands together

When you become aware that you are dreaming lucidly and the dream begins to fade, try rubbing your hands together very hard – you should experience the movement and friction. Keep rubbing your hands together until you wake up or the dream scenario shifts. Keep repeating a phrase which ensures you stay with the dream such as 'I am continuing to dream'.

4. Flying

Flying has much in common with spinning. You are inhibited only by your imagination. Experiment with flying in your own way, according to what you find most comfortable.

5. Sensory manipulation

Use the senses to help you to stay with the dream. Concentrate on each of the senses in turn and expand your awareness of each one.

Listen, for instance, to your own breathing and then become aware of other inner sounds and voices. Try holding a conversation with one of your dream characters.

It is quite important that you develop your own way of prolonging your dreams. You will find that you are more comfortable with one particular way, but you could try experimenting with the others just to see what happens.

Note below how successful you were.

ANALYZING YOUR DREAM

Whether your dream has been lucid or not, you will want to get into the habit of analyzing its content more fully. It is suggested that you divide it into segments so that you can consider each part of the dream and whether that segment was perhaps either lucid, or approaching lucidity. You will also be able to pick up the theme of the dream by doing this.

The Dream

The Dream Segments

The differences/similarities in the segments

The main theme of the dream

ADVANCED TECHNIQUES

Now having practised all of the basic techniques for lucid dreaming, you are ready to move on to the more advanced methods of dreaming. Actually, before you do that, we suggest that you take time to consolidate what you have learnt. Think carefully about what you have been doing and consider whether you are satisfied with the results.

Is there anything that you could do to improve your methods?
Do you want to try anything else?
What do you now want to happen?
How do you want to use lucid dreaming in the future?
Do you need to do further research into the subject?
Do you want to put yourself in touch with other people who are practising lucid dreaming?

The more advanced techniques help you to focus on your objectives, and to decide whether you are more interested in researching the actual technique or whether you want to be creative and help to make things happen.

It often helps to alter the way you express yourself to accommodate the creativity of dreams. If your day-to-day way of self-expression is through words, then experiment with colour or with form. If you enjoy music, try to find a particular piece which expresses the mood of your dream. If you are a sedentary sort of person, then express elements of the dream through movement such as dance or Eastern disciplines of *t'ai chi* or *qi gung*. The basic idea is that you can use your dreams to enhance your creativity in everyday life. They can act as starting points for projects or they can be used to explore other modes of self-expression.

Virtual reality for dreaming

As part of your advanced procedure for lucid dreaming, you should be able to start building your own virtual dream reality. Start from a waking state and focus your mind so that you will recall what you have done. A word of caution is needed here, however – not everyone can achieve the necessary measure of control to carry out the following exercise. It is an excellent exercise to practise in the development of lucid dreaming but can seem too much like hard work.

As soon as you are aware that you have 'gone lucid', form a huge screen in front of you. This is your personal screen, of which you have total control, which you may think of as a television set, a cinema screen or a kind of projection created from the mind itself. Onto this screen you will project your images and learn to command how this projection operates. You work with the colour, tone, brightness or anything else you may require. Initially you may wish to think of having control of the switches, though later you will probably find that you only need mind control – that is, to think of the changes and they will happen. This screen allows you to be objective about your attempts in the first place and to use it later to surround yourself with your creations. You may then find it easier to think of it like a night sky, on which to project your images. For some, this gives a greater sense of the connection with the cosmos.

One aspect of creative dreaming is that you can make use of all the senses in much the same way as you can in waking life. So try them all out, first attempting 'normal' changes, such as hearing a new sound or experiencing a different smell. Then, making use of the mind's ability in creative dreaming to invent the bizarre, create the wrong colour for something – perhaps a green cow, for instance. Your rational mind will probably try to wake you up at this point. This is overcome by reminding yourself that you are dreaming. Take time and have fun, because you are learning how to remove the restrictions of perception that belong to the normal everyday world. You are also learning how to make your mind act as your servant rather than control you. Try to get a sense of what is happening within you as you make the changes, since it is this faculty that will eventually help you create your own reality in the everyday world.

REFINING THE SPINNING TECHNIQUE

We have already spoken of the spinning technique as a way of stabilizing dreams. We give a refined technique below. The steps to begin with are similar:

1. Take note of when the dream starts to fade and as soon as this happens begin to spin. At this point, you will still be conscious of your dream body; the action of spinning should be begun before you come too far into waking consciousness. It is important that you actually feel yourself spinning – you should try to use an image which enhances your reaction. So, if spinning like a ballet dancer feels inappropriate to you, it will not work. As you can see, some groundwork is essential in the conscious state so that you begin to switch automatically into whatever your 'control state' – that is, a state that you identify as dreaming – might be, even if you are dreaming. While awake, you can picture what spinning feels like, but in the dream state you must actually 'feel' the spinning.

2. Keep in mind whilst spinning that the next state you encounter will most likely be a dream. Taking each of the senses in turn, remind yourself that you will be dreaming. Whatever you see, hear, touch, feel or smell is more than likely to be a dream occurrence.

3. Always do a 'reality test' wherever you end up. When you come to stillness after spinning you may either still be dreaming or have woken up. If you are still dreaming, you may have transferred into a new dream state or you may have re-established your former dream scene, but it will be more vivid and stable. If you have woken up, then do test reality by observing the time or by recognizing the flawlessness of your bedroom – that is, that everything is as it should be in real life – there being no grotesque elements in your environment.

4. It is recommended that you constantly remind yourself that you are

dreaming or are in the middle of a dream during any transformation which takes place while you are spinning. Hopefully, you will continue to be lucid in the new dream, though you may make the mistake of thinking that this new dream is real and actually happening.

5. It is now time to determine how you wish to proceed with your routine. You may simply wish to test the art of creative dreaming itself, in which case you will play with the act of becoming lucid and leaving the lucid state. You could, if you wish, practise altering the scenario of the dream or giving yourself orders which provide the means for you to astral travel, fashion new realities or complete different levels of being. If you believe in such things, you might also find yourself visiting other worlds; these techniques are shown elsewhere in this section.

CREATING A NEW DREAM SCENARIO

You might use this technique to produce a dream scenario, whether new or otherwise. The technique is very simple.

1. Select an objective

Before going to sleep decide on a person or place you would like to 'visit' in your lucid dream. Choose initially something you are fairly confident of achieving – perhaps a visit to a close friend or relative. Often you may be able to check whether that person has been aware of you either in dreams or while awake. You could also choose a historical character or even an imaginary one. The choice is yours and the possibilities are endless. When you feel confident enough to do so, you could also choose a different time and place.

2. Develop a steadfast intention of achieving your objective

Having decided on your goal, write down your intent, using simple words to which you can relate, then strongly visualize yourself meeting your objective. State your firm intention to do so in your next dream.

3. Spin to your target in your lucid dream

It is possible that, purely by chance, you find yourself in a non-lucid dream with your target; in which case, do your best to become lucid within the dream. You could also try it the other way round and become lucid first, then visit. If you can, practise both ways and then decide which one – if either – you are more comfortable with. As soon as the dream begins to fade and you perceive you are about to wake up, put yourself into another spin. Repeat your chosen phrase until you find yourself in a new vivid dream scene – one hopes with a sense of achievement at having been successful in the task you set yourself.

DIRECTING YOUR DREAMS

This exercise is a way of achieving changes of a mystical kind. It is different from the movement involved in spinning and flying and is more a matter of actually changing the environment in which your dream takes place. Remember that you can do anything you please in the dream state. You can either use the idea of the 'big screen' or of a stage production.

1. Decide that instead of moving yourself to a new location you will draw the location to you.

2. Start by changing something small in your dream surroundings and gradually work up to bigger changes.

3. Do everything at different speeds and play with what you are creating, much as you did in the virtual reality exercise.

4. You might then like to think of yourself as the director and producer of your own play. You can use any props you like and can experiment to achieve the right atmosphere.

5. Follow this up by creating a stage set for your next learning experience.

THE IFE TECHNIQUE

Life teaches us that we have to have restrictions. From an early age, we learn what is acceptable behaviour and what is not. We are taught that to be spontaneous is dangerous and that we must be 'sensible'. Within the framework of lucid dreams, however, we have the freedom to be totally eccentric and to use patterns of behaviour which re-educate us in the art of personal freedom.

Most creative people have a very highly developed ability to create fantasies. If you dare to practise lucid dreaming, you will find that you are capable of doing and being things that are not possible except in an altered state of consciousness. One yoga exercise that is practised to give a sense of the meaning of life is to try to discover what it is like to be a tree or flower or other sentient (aware) being. This exercise consists of three stages, which we will call the IFE technique.

- First *Imagine* what it would be like to be your chosen object.
- Then *Feel* how the object feels.
- Finally *Experience* being that object.

Because the rational aspects of everyday life are suspended during lucid dreams, you should be able very quickly to reach a state of awareness where it is easy to do all of these things. You could practise being the opposite sex, being an animal – domestic or otherwise – or, if you are feeling brave, being something like a rock or the sea.

Initially, you will probably not be able to hold this state for very long, but with practice you will find that it becomes easier and that you can widen your perception to encompass other states of being as well. You might, for instance, try to experience what it would be like to be suspended in space or time, to belong to other worlds or to sense what you will be like in twenty years' time.

RELAXATION TECHNIQUE

There are many relaxation aids on the market, and it is perfectly right that you use the one which works best for you. Shown below is a simple one which can be done with or without the help of relaxing music, according to preference. The technique is a good beginning to the exploration of meditative techniques and other altered states of consciousness.

1. Find a quiet spot where you will not be interrupted.

2. If you choose to lie down, ensure that you will not fall asleep. For the purposes of this exercise, you need to remain awake and aware.

3. Start with your feet and begin to tighten them as much as is possible, then relax them.

4. Then work progressively up your body, tightening and then relaxing each set of muscles in turn. Firstly, your calves, then your thighs, your buttocks and so on, until you reach your head.

5. Repeat this three times in all, in order to sense what relaxation is really like.

6. Finally, in one go, tighten all the muscles you have previously relaxed and let go.

You may choose now to use a deep breathing technique, a creative visualization or a meditation to help you in your process of creative dreaming. All of these methods are useful in dealing with stress.

CONTEMPLATION AND MEDITATION

When you are suitably relaxed, it is possible to use other techniques to help you in the art of creative dreaming.

1. A simple way of preparing for creative dreaming is to use contemplation. In this, as a precursor to meditation, you give yourself a visual image of the subject in hand.

2. You might, for instance, think of the words 'lucid dreaming' as being carved out of a block of wood. Holding this image in your mind, let it develop in its own way and just watch what happens.

3. You might wish to consider the idea of a visit to Egypt or some other far-flung country, so again, you hold the idea in your mind and contemplate it.

4. When you have become proficient at contemplation, you can then attempt meditation, which is a further stage of allowing the image or thought to develop spontaneously of its own accord. You may then wish to take the results of your meditation into lucid dreaming.

DEALING WITH NIGHTMARES

When in dreams you come up against a character or a situation which is threatening or has the quality of a nightmare, there are certain techniques that you can use in creative dreaming which help to remove the anxiety. One such exercise is shown below. It should be said that the more you are able to relax and use contemplation and meditation, the less likely you are to suffer from nightmares.

The RISC technique

A full explanation of the RISC technique is given in Section 2. This is a very simple technique which was and is used therapeutically to help people to face bad dreams. It is, in many ways, the precursor of other lucid-dreaming techniques.

1. **Recognition.** When you are having a dream which you feel is a bad one, recognize that you do not need the feelings that it leaves you with, whether that is anger, fear, guilt or any other negative feeling.

2. **Identification.** You need to be able to identify what it is about the dream that makes you feel bad. Look at the dream carefully and find out exactly what it is that disturbs you.

3. **Stopping a bad dream.** You must always remember that you are in charge. You do not have to let a bad dream continue. You can either wake up or, recognizing that you are dreaming, become lucid.

4. **Changing.** Each negativity in your dream can be changed for the positive. Initially, you may have to wake yourself up to work out a better conclusion, but eventually, you will be able to do it while you are still asleep.

CONVERSATIONS WITH DREAM CHARACTERS

This technique is useful for dealing with dreams where you come up against a figure which frightens you or is one which you do not understand. It can also help in moving your understanding forward so that you can begin to integrate what you have already learned. When you have had an unpleasant dream, or perhaps when a lucid dream has not gone as you expected it to, it is useful to work with it as soon as possible afterwards.

1. Taking the dream forward

You can do this by having imaginary conversations while you are awake. Get a pen and either your dream journal or a piece of paper, so that you can make notes of what happens. Visualize a dream character in front of you, one with which you have had some difficulty in a recent dream. Initiate a conversation with this character. You will probably have to suspend disbelief until you get used to the technique. You may feel a little foolish to begin with but please do persevere, since the benefits are tremendous. Decide that you will have a conversation with this character that will give you a resolution to your difficulty. Imagine yourself really talking to the dream character, remembering that it is better for you to begin the conversation. Sometimes it is easier to start with questions such as, 'What are you doing in my dream? Why are you pursuing me?' or other relevant questions. Spend some time to begin with working out what questions you wish to ask your dream character and write them down, but equally try to be as spontaneous as possible. It is more than possible that your questions may change as you become further involved with your character, but it is wise to give yourself a starting place. You may wish to choose a question from the list below or substitute questions which are relevant for you.

Why are you in my dream?
Who are you?
Why are you acting the way you are?

What are you trying to do?
What are you trying to tell me?
What do you want to know?
What do you want me to do?
What do you want me to be?
What part of me do you represent?
Why is this happening in this dream?
What do I need to know?
How can I help you?
How can you help me?

Write down your questions, and brief notes of the answers you get from the character. These may pop up and seem more like thoughts rather than speech, but record them all the same. You may well wonder if it is all your imagination but that is fine. Trust your own intuition and continue with the work because, as you become less critical of the process, you will find that it flows more easily. Don't try to evaluate what is happening while you are doing this – save that for later. Bring the conversation to an end when it seems to be running out of steam, going round in circles or has reached some kind of resolution.

Then evaluate what you have just done and ask yourself whether you are satisfied with the result or if there is something you would do differently next time. You are now well on the way to developing your own technique for dealing with nightmares and can try the same exercise on another dream.

2. Setting your dream purpose
Now that you have a technique for dealing with dream content and one for lucid dreaming, you should be able to combine the two. Tell yourself that the next time you have a difficult or frightening encounter with a dream character, you will become lucid and have a conversation with that character.

3. Conversing with dream figures

When you come across any character within a dream which is problematical, whether there is a conflict or not, try to establish if you are dreaming by asking yourself if you are. If you discover that you are in the middle of a dream, continue in the following way: turn and face the character and, using the technique above that you have practised, begin a dialogue using one of the questions from the list. Listen to the character's responses and try to get to the bottom of problems on its behalf – for instance, ascertain why it feels it has a right to harass you – as well as your own. Try to reach an agreement or resolution and, if at all possible, try to befriend the character. Continue with the dialogue until you reach a reasonable conclusion. Then, bring yourself to full wakefulness and write the conversation down while you still remember it.

4. Evaluating the conversation

Try to decide if you have achieved the best possible result. If you are dissatisfied, think about how you might improve your results next time. For the time being, go back to step one and work consciously with the dream, using more of the questions to get a better result. You might also use the technique of Carrying the Dream Forward shown elsewhere in this section.

ADDRESSING RECURRENT NIGHTMARES

If you are subject to recurrent nightmares you can use an extension of the RISC technique to help resolve the problem.

1. Recalling and recording the nightmare

Recall the nightmare, including as much detail as possible, and write it down. Sometimes just writing it down is enough to take a great deal of the fear out of the situation. Examine the dream for various points where you could influence the turn of events by doing something differently.

2. Choosing a point of influence and a new action

Choose a specific point in the dream where you felt that you were most in control, just before you now wish to change the dream. Choose a different course of action which you feel will alter the dream. By starting from a position of control, you will be more likely to be able to change things for the better.

3. Relaxing

Now you need to get into a frame of mind where you are completely relaxed and can work with your dream. Find a time and place where you can be uninterrupted for about half an hour. Close your eyes and using your favourite relaxation method let go completely.

4. Re-running the nightmare

Beginning at the entry point you chose in Step 2, visualize yourself back in the dream. See it happening as it did before until it feels right to practise your new action and let the dream continue until you find out what happens and whether the action has the desired result.

5. Considering your reworked result

Return to normality when the imagined dream has ended. Treat the imagined dream as though it were a real one and document it. Be aware of your reaction to the new ending. If you still do not feel the ending is satisfactory, then feel free to rework it until you do. It is possible that working with the dream in this way is enough to stop it from recurring. It is as though the dream loses its power.

6. Dealing with the recurrent dream

If the dream occurs again, having taken yourself to lucidity follow the new plan of action. Having prepared your new mode of behaviour, carry it out to the best of your ability, and be clear as to the results you expect. Remember that the dream will never be able to harm you and that you choose to be in control.

CARRYING THE DREAM FORWARD

By the time you have experimented with your dreams sufficiently to be able to recognize lucidity and to wake yourself at will from a bad dream, you are in a position to manipulate your dreams even further. Almost inevitably we come up against the question of whether the technique about to be described is lucid dreaming or not. To be frank, it really does not matter what name you choose to give it, but to save argument let us call it Focused Reverie. Here, the technique is to remember the dream up to the time you woke up, then choose to take the dream forward as a whole.

We have already suggested that you might work with characters and objects in your dream and ask yourself what happens next with each of them. Now that can be extended to include the whole dream. This is not the same as spinning yourself into a new environment, nor is it taking conscious control – it is simply to allow the dream to continue in its own way. The steps are quite simple:

1. Remembering the dream as it was, make contact with each part of the dream as though it was still happening to you.

2. Now put yourself in the position of observer and allow the dream to unfold around you.

3. Do not attempt to influence the dream at all. Just allow it to happen.

4. If the action or characters get stuck, then assume that that is the point at which you would have woken up.

5. Think about why the dream will not go any further. Resolve to deal with any issues that might arise.

6. You might choose the subject for your next lucid dream from these issues.

RESOLVING YOUR DREAM

For the purposes of this exercise we suggest that you take one aspect of your dream, perhaps the main storyline, and become creative with it. As we have said previously, it does not matter what sort of quality you achieve in your creative projects: it is more important to recognize your own creativity. Here you are thinking about the dream itself and how to make it work for you. These are some questions you might ask yourself:

What will happen next to me as the main character?
What do I want to say?
What response do I need from the different parts of my dream?
What will happen next now that I am in control of my dream?
Do I want any of the characters, objects or aspects of the dream to act differently?
Who or what is acting out of character in my dream?
Does it help in the resolution of my dream to have them continue to act out of character? Should I impose some kind of further control?

By working with your dream in this way you are learning not only to gain some control over the dream itself but also to work towards a resolution of the dream – that is, to work out what the dream is trying to put across. You are able to decide whether there is more or less control needed in your life. This means that you can either choose to be totally spontaneous or to focus more clearly on your aims and objectives.

TOOLS FOR CREATIVE DREAMING

Crystals

Many people believe that working with crystals can enhance dreaming, both lucid and otherwise, and help one to ground the wisdom that is available for each of us through these natural objects. It is as though the subtle energies act as both receivers and transmitters and give the ability to tune into those aspects of knowledge both of ourselves and of the world in which we live.

Below is a table of some crystals and their particular relevance to sleep and dreaming.

CRYSTAL	FUNCTION
Beta quartz	Helps in decoding dreams.
Chinese Writing rock is porphyric with patterns resembling Chinese script.	Good for assisting one into the dream state and directing dreams towards an intended subject.
Diaspor	Gives clarity of dream recall.
Green Sapphire	Encourages the remembering of dreams.
Jade	Known as the 'dream stone', it assists in solving dream interpretation and in the release of emotions. Placing it under your pillow will encourage successful dreaming.
Jasper (red)	Allows one to recall dreams as though one were watching a video. It is good for the technique of carrying the dream forward.
Kyanite	Calms and clears the mind and gives good recall and dream interpretation.
Lapis	Gives insight and makes possible a deeper connection with the Higher Self.
Manganosite	Enhances the dream state and helps the memory both during and after the dream.

Opal	The 'happy dream' stone, gives understanding of the dreamer's potential.
Rhonite	Stimulates the vividness of dreams, and allows one to 'hold on' to the dream while it is recorded for later consideration.
Ruby	Protects against nightmares and distressing dreams.
Star garnet	Helps the dreamer to remember dreams, particularly those which clear a state of mental chaos.
Tunnellite	Stimulates beta waves, promotes creativity and the achievement of one's ambitions.

Most good crystal or New Age shops will have a good selection of stones.

Programming a crystal

It is a simple matter to programme your crystals in order to help you in your dreamwork whilst remembering their inherent qualities.

1. You should choose your crystal or crystals for working with dreams very carefully. If you wish, you may also have a small bag, made of any material which appeals to you personally, in which to keep them safe – this way, they could be hung at the head of the bed or placed under your pillow while you sleep. Choose the best you can afford, and the nicest example you can find. Don't worry too much about minor imperfections, just let your intuition guide you to the right stones for you. Often as you choose your crystal, you will feel a slight tingling in your hand or fingers as you do. This tells you which stone is the one for you. You can use each crystal for a specific purpose or programme the crystals as a group to enhance your dreaming. For creative dreaming, you might try red jasper or rhonite. Clear quartz is also a good crystal to use for clarity. It does not matter whether the stone is polished or rough-cut: it is your preference.

2. Thoroughly cleanse and clear your crystal. You can do this by standing it in the sunshine for as long as possible, by leaving it outside on a bright moonlit night, or leaving it in salt (preferably sea salt) water for a period of 24 hours. This will remove any previous programming and adverse or negative influences.

3. It is better to use and programme these particular crystals only for working with dreams. Let us suppose that you wish to programme the crystals to help you with lucid dreams. Programme each crystal for at least a period of three nights and a maximum of ten. (Three nights cover all aspects of the physical, mental and spiritual and ten is numerologically a representation of all knowledge.) Programme your crystal every night before you go to sleep by using an affirmation or question of intent as follows: 'My dreams will be lucid and reveal inner knowledge' or 'What knowledge do I need to understand lucid dreaming in relation to myself?'

   Remember that at this stage not only are you programming your crystals, but you are also learning to focus your mind. You can do this before you give yourself the instruction to remember your dreams. This specific programme will help you lay your foundation for working with dreams. Understanding yourself will ultimately help you to achieve lucid dreams. Obviously if there is no true desire or need either to understand yourself or to achieve lucid dreaming behind the statements, your results (or non-results) will reflect your lack of commitment. All of your programming should be what you really desire, or want to know.

4. Do remember that whatever your mind can conceive can be incorporated into a programme for your time of dreaming, not just

creative dreaming. Your programming should be very clear and as creative as you wish to make it. Holding your crystal, either in both hands or in the hand that you feel to be more powerful, gather your full attention, then begin to formulate your thoughts clearly and simply. If it feels right, then you might like to write them down, so that you can commit them properly to memory. Then sit quietly with your crystal until you sense the rightness of it.

This method works to bring concepts into reality, both on a physical and spiritual level. By programming the crystal, you are allowing the use of very subtle but powerful energies to be channelled into existence and perception.

5. Concentrate on your crystal and allow your energy and intent to flow into it. Repeat this at least three times. Try not to let your attention wander during this period. If it does, just start again. The more you do it, the easier it becomes. Repeat this action for each crystal.

6. Programme your crystal shortly before going to bed and put it in your chosen place. Bring your desires or wants to the forefront of your mind, thinking of them as already fulfilled. (In the case of lucid dreaming, you would try to sense what it would be like to have had a lucid dream.) Now completely let your mind go free and then relax. Do this three times and then go straight to sleep. Your last thought should be your programming of the crystal and the feeling of your wish already having been fulfilled.

Programming your crystal is just one way of having you concentrate fully on making your dreams work for you. For too long it has been thought that the dreaming self is entirely separate from the conscious self. We are now finding that we can build pathways between the two; this crystal gateway is one that can be used by both believers and non-believers alike. At the very least, the crystal acts like worry beads and helps us to focus our intent, while at best the very subtle energies open up new vistas of awareness which give us access to the rich sources of knowledge of ourselves and mankind.

Archetypal Images

The methods of preparation for working with archetypal images as triggers for both creative and lucid dreaming are similar.

In the case of the Tarot, you use the cards as a mental and visual starting point to help you to make sense of them and the feelings they evoke in you. There are eight steps to this process:

1. Sit quietly where you will not be interrupted.

2. Holding the card you have chosen from your own pack, look at it in detail. What comes to mind as you do so?

3. Think about your own life at this moment and how the card you have chosen applies to you. How can you apply your knowledge of the meanings of the card in the situations in which you find yourself?

4. Contemplate the card and allow yourself to internalize its power.

5. Now close your eyes and try to visualize yourself as part of the action of the card. How does it feel to be the main character? How do you interact with the other aspects of the card?

6. Decide to have a dream about this card and choose whether it will be lucid or not.

7. Note in your journal which card you have chosen and go to sleep with it in mind.

8. When you wake up, follow the usual routine for recording your dreams.

Myths, Astrological Planets, Numbers, etc.
These should be treated in the same way:

1. Choose a particular trigger – a myth, planet or number, and think about how the story or the qualities might apply to your life at this moment.

2. Contemplate the story and feel how powerful it is.

3. Put yourself in the position you wish to be in, that is, as a character in the myth, on a planet or expressing its qualities. Imagine what it would be like to be part of that scenario. If working with numbers, think of the qualities of the number you have chosen and sense them within you.

4. In the case of sacred geometry, think of the shape – a square, a pentagram and so on – and try to get a sense of what it feels like to be in that shape. Gradually you should be able to become aware of the qualities of each figure and can progress to a more solid shape.

5. Try testing the boundaries of that shape and move the figure to be larger or smaller. Play with the shape in any way you like. Make it into a solid object and try to find out what it would be like to be inside such an object.

6. Allow yourself to go to sleep, and remember that in creative dreaming, you can do anything you choose to. It is simply a matter of telling yourself you can. Have fun but at the same time remember that you are training yourself to control your environment.

MEETING WITH SPIRIT

When you feel ready to meet your totem animals, your own concept of your Higher Self, your Spirit Guide or any other aspect of Spirit such as your personal representation of healing energy – perhaps the *caduceus* – you might like to try the following:

1. Decide what will be the focus of this particular meeting and form a statement of intent such as 'I wish to meet my personal totem animal' or 'I wish to meet my Spirit Guide'.

2. Think very carefully about how your life might be changed by this meeting, but try not to have too many expectations.

3. Visualize a scenario where it would be possible for you to meet the entity you have chosen. The path you visualized for your personal journey (in Section 7) might be suitable. Imagine how you would feel were you able to have such a meeting.

4. Allow yourself to drift gently off into sleep, knowing that in due course, whether it be this night or another, that meeting will take place.

CREATIVE PROJECTS

Lucid dreaming is a rich source of information for creative projects that you might like to try. Such projects help to ground the energy developed in dreaming and mean that you have a tangible result.

1. Choose a dream which is best suited to the project in hand. This project could be a story, play or dance. Make a note of it in your dream journal.

2. Write down the titles of pieces of music which appeal and fit the theme, words you might use or shapes that interest you. Spend some time thinking about your project and enjoy the research entailed.

3. Make as many notes as you like and see whether any other of your recorded dreams can be made use of in developing the project. You will often find that you go through a particularly productive period, though sometimes you may feel very stuck.

4. Make a note of any problems and negativities that arise in creating the project. These can be resolved through lucid dreaming.

5. It is worthwhile carrying a notebook or tape recorder with you at all times, so that you can note down any inspirations which occur. This may also give you further material for lucid dreaming.

6. You may find you run out of enough energy to complete the project. This is another way in which lucid dreaming could be used to help to give you the impetus to finish off what you have started.

You will note that there are several instances where lucid dreaming can help in the process of creativity. This is perhaps one of the best outcomes of the art of lucid dreaming: to realize that you have within you a huge store of previously untapped energy which is now accessible.

SECTION

9

LIVING
WITH CREATIVE
DREAMS

Perhaps the best way to finish a book on lucid dreaming is to briefly draw together all the various strands to help the reader to define what he or she means by creative dreaming and what they expect from their newfound skill. It is also perhaps wise to lay down a partial schema for using the skill in everyday life.

Lucid dreaming might be defined as dreaming with awareness. Simply to be aware that one is dreaming is only the first step and holds the door open between the conscious and the unconscious self. This allows a free flow of information and energy between the two states which can then be utilized to full effect.

Dreaming is often likened to entering a hidden room in an effort to find out what the room contains. Lucid dreaming is much more akin to starting out from a small room (which we know) very well and exploring the rest of the house (which we do not know). As we enter each new room, there are new things to be appreciated, possessions we did not know we had to be discovered and also further old assets we have forgotten about. We do, however, need a plan of campaign to help us to accomplish our task, accompanied by a 'box of tricks' to make life easier. Hopefully this book will be your box of tricks and campaign map.

Your first assignment should be, purely for the sake of convenience, to set yourself some kind of time target for each task. In fact, it is almost a foregone conclusion that you will not stick to this; it is simply designed to give you a structure while you need it. You also should instigate some kind of discipline in your practice, so that you are using your sleeping time wisely and well.

You next need to learn to remember and record all of your dreams, whether lucid or otherwise. For this you will need to train your memory and to keep a dream journal. Suggestions for doing these things are found in Sections 2 and 8.

Having learnt to record your dream, you should next train yourself to control your waking and dreaming. Creative dreaming develops best within the dozing periods after a time of proper sleep, and you will need to experiment with what suits you best. This will take time, so do not be too disappointed if you are not able to achieve lucid dreaming very quickly. When it does happen it will probably happen quite spontaneously and surprise you with its intensity.

Initially, you will probably find that lucid dreaming does not happen very often. However, as you become more competent at recognizing that you are dreaming, you will be able to hold the state more often and for longer. This is when you can begin to use it to explore the hitherto hidden aspects of your personality and elements of universal knowledge which will help you to live your life more successfully. You should be able to access those things which have been available to the so-called primitive cultures through shamanistic and priestly knowledge – that which Jung called the Collective Unconscious.

If you subscribe to the belief that you are in charge of your own existence – that things happen because of you, not to you – creative dreaming can help you to adjust that existence. You can make things happen in such a way that you maximize your potential in life. Even if you believe that you are at the mercy of circumstances – that things happen despite you – you will be able to use lucid and creative dreaming to help you understand what is happening to you and those around you.

As a game, learning how to fly, spin and shift space is great fun to do and can be a welcome relief from the problems and difficulties of waking life. This is the next stage of learning that you will experience. Creative dreaming and its techniques, however, should never be used purely to escape from the reality of the everyday world, but only to enhance it. The adjustments that you can make will intrigue and surprise you, but you should use this new skill wisely and well. It will depend on you and your personality whether you will be able to achieve results quickly or slowly or in small steps or large leaps.

As with all newly acquired skills, you will by now be developing your own versions of the various techniques suggested in this book. This is where you are becoming truly creative and hopefully will feel that you can experiment with your chosen path in the use of lucid dreaming. Some will wish to use lucid and creative dreaming as a learning tool, some will wish to use it in the service of healing – both of themselves and others. If you wish to use lucid dreaming to assist your spiritual progression, you will be able to do this, too. The choice is yours and the opportunities are endless. Finally as an encouragement we would like to offer one person's experience of the path to lucid dreaming.

AN INSIDER'S VIEW

I have no idea what other people believe lucid dreaming to be, or how much it differs from their normal dream state. What I can say is that I have been experiencing powerful dream sensations ever since I can remember.

My parents sometimes like to embarrass me (well, they always like to embarrass me actually, but that's another story) by telling dinner guests about how, when I was very young, they first realized that I was aware of dream sleep.

One evening when I was around three years old, I curtailed my usual play, fighting with my dad, by saying I wanted to 'see the pictures in my pillow'. Even then I was aware that dreams have always affected my daytime mood and been part of my day-to-day life. I cannot remember a time when I have woken up and not been aware that I was in dream sleep before I awoke.

Although I have no proof – and have not made any sort of detailed study of this subject – I would suggest that during my dream cycle I dream far more than an average person and have therefore learnt to 'use' my dreams in a manner that is not necessarily 'the norm'. I am also one of those people who need at least eight hours' sleep per night and this need for sleep, coupled with my seemingly continual dream state whilst asleep, has no doubt meant that my experience of different types of dream sleep is also above average.

In the past year or so I have started having more dreams. Not only are they remarkably vivid – I presume that many, if not all, people have vivid dreams – but in them I have an element of control. This control is not just over my movements in my dream world but also over the dream world that surrounds me. In this state I am actually far more in control and conscious or aware than I ever am during my waking hours!

I imagine that many people reading this passage have had the feeling in a dream of suddenly become aware that – possibly due to the ridiculous nature of their surroundings – they are asleep. From what I have been told by friends, this usually means that they are just about to wake up. I have learnt to programme myself the night before, so that when I experience this feeling of knowing or suspecting I am in a dream, I can take control from that moment.

Firstly I concentrate on maintaining that dream feeling or state. I have found that unless you concentrate on some aspect of the dream – either a particular part of your surroundings or an aspect of yourself – you very quickly begin to wake up. It helps if you can let your fascination with the dreamscape hold your dream together.

When this was a relatively new experience to me, I used to spend what seemed like a long time checking on the level of detail that actually existed in my dreams. In many of these dreams, I would inspect a normally boring object with sheer fascination. I remember in one of these dreams approaching an average looking wall. I was almost challenging myself, in my dream, to have constructed a wall that under close scrutiny would bear close resemblance to the sort of wall that you would see on a daily basis in normal waking life.

Needless to say, it was as detailed as any wall I have ever seen whilst awake – with different shades of colour, scars from wear and tear and similarly rough to the touch. This sort of fascination with detailed inspection soon wears thin once you start to play with the possibilities in a completely lucid dream. After I had convinced myself that my dream world environment was just as hard and 'real' as my daytime world, I began to think more deeply about the possibilities within this completely self-created universe. All the time I concentrated on keeping the dream feeling to inhibit my natural tendency to wake up.

During the waking hours, I had thought that anything was possible in a dream and that I could create completely different universes and completely alter the 'me' that was travelling within them. I am afraid that this is not necessarily true – or not true for me so far. It seems that there are certain rules even in the dream world. Yes, I can fly at will and am pretty much indestructible – although some dream events can still wake me – but I lapse in and out of control of my environment and cannot logically work through problems and challenges in the same way that I might during the day. I can also be moved much more quickly and on a far deeper level by emotion than during the waking hours; lust, fear, hatred and love are all felt but at heightened levels and can affect my rationality and destroy a consciously created dream 'story'.

In the past few months, I have been challenged on a couple of occasions by work colleagues to use these lucid dreams for something tangible – in one particular instance to effectively 'remote view' some numbers left in an envelope on my boss's desk. The idea behind this was to establish whether what I was doing in my dreams had a practical and indeed financial angle – ultimately whether it could be used for profit.

For a few nights after this challenge was thrown down, I did not lucid dream. Of course, I dreamt, but not with the clarity or conscious level of awareness that has become normal to me. Then one night I realized that I was in a dream – I could see my hands in front of me and I looked at them, examining them for a while.

This is a technique that I use to gain control in my dreams and for some reason it helps.

I looked around myself in the dream and realized that I was in London – not very far away from my office. All I had to do was prevent myself from waking up and I would be in my office checking the numbers in a matter of seconds. I tend to get around by flying Superman-style – none of these big leaps or erratic uncontrollable flying situations for me! I realized very quickly that I was going to be at my offices within moments and the only real barrier to me was the River Thames. All I had to do was fly over the water, pass through the walls of the building – this can be quite uncomfortable but is not usually very difficult – and read the numbers.

Even in the dream I was very excited. I was slightly worried that time, in its many guises, is not the same in even the most contrived dream world and that I might be arriving at my office long before or long after the time when the envelope had been left for me to view.

Then the most annoying thing happened. As I crossed the river, and I caught sight of my office, I realized that I had crossed into the previous century. There were men and boys in flat-caps, wearing very brown and dull clothing. There were also horses pulling carts. I can remember thinking in my dream that I had been cheated – I had controlled all the other variables almost perfectly but had been outwitted by time.

This young man's account is truly fascinating, in that it contains all of the elements that most intrigue. There is no evidence to corroborate that creative dreamers are better at dreaming than anyone else, yet he testifies that he has always been a prolific dreamer. He highlights the element of control that he feels he has over his dreams and also the potential for the bizarre ('due to the ridiculous nature of their surroundings'). He also speaks of the necessary programming the night before and the need to concentrate on maintaining the dream feeling or state, lest he wake up.

He has used 'checking on the level of detail' as his way of reality checking and also later speaks of examining his dream hands – a technique he seems to have taught himself. We have already mentioned this elsewhere.

He speaks of his belief that 'anything can happen in a dream' but also notes that for him there appear to be certain rules that apply within his dream world. Logic does not operate and emotion is considerably heightened in the lucid state, sometimes interfering with his rationality.

When challenged to use the ability for profit rather than pleasure, he temporarily loses the ability to lucid dream, and indeed loses clarity even in ordinary dreams. He flies 'Superman-style', which is presumably for him aerodynamically correct, but his control is disturbed by his own thoughts on the meaning of time. Interestingly, his perception is distorted to the point where there is a time slip, and though he has obviously remained lucid, he can do little to succeed in his original task.

This young man has developed his own techniques over the years without the help of a manual for creative dreaming. He instinctively has used methods which have suited his own personality, but also has an almost 'textbook' approach in his development. People who have experimented with all sorts of altered states of consciousness are agreed that lucid dreaming is but one of many states that requires a learning process of adaptation and adjustment.

Hopefully this book will act as a textbook for you, the reader, and give you not only the basic methods but also the ability to adapt and adjust your dreaming and your whole lives. We wish you successful lucidity.

NOTEBOOK

MY DREAM

THE INTERPRETATION

MY DREAM

THE INTERPRETATION

MY DREAM

THE INTERPRETATION

MY DREAM

THE INTERPRETATION

BIBLIOGRAPHY

Antrobus, J. S., Dement, W. & Fisher, C. 'Patterns of Dreaming and Dream Recall: An EEG Study'. *Journal of Abnormal and Social Psychology*, 69, 244-252. 1964

Arnold-Foster M. *Studies in Dreams*. Allen and Unwin, London, 1921

Aserinsky, E. & Kleitman, N. 'Regularly Occurring Periods of Eye Motility and Concomitant Phenomena During Sleep'. *Science*, 118, 273-274. 1953

Blackmore, S. J. *Beyond the Body: An Investigation of Out-of-the-Body Experiences*. Heinemann, London, 1983

Fenwick, P., Schatzman, M., Worsley, A., Adams, J., Stone, S. & Baker, A. 'Lucid Dreaming: Correspondence between Dreamed and Actual Events in One Subject During REM Sleep'. *Biological Psychology*, 18, 243-252. 1984

Foulkes, D. *Dreaming: A Cognitive-Psychological Analysis*. Lawrence Erlbaum Associates, Hillsdale, New Jersey, 1985

Gackenbach, J. & LaBerge, S. (Eds) *Conscious Mind, Sleeping Brain: Perspectives On Lucid Dreaming*. Plenum, New York, 1988

Garfield, P. *Creative Dreaming*. Ballantine Books, New York, 1974

Garfield, P. *Pathway to Ecstasy*. Holt, Rhinehart, & Winston, New York, 1979

Green, C. *Lucid Dreams*. Hamish Hamilton, London, 1968

Green, C. *Out of the Body Experiences*. Hamish Hamilton, London, 1968

Green, C. & McCreery, C. *Apparitions*. Hamish Hamilton, London, 1975

Hall, C. S. & Van de Castle, R. L. *The Content Analysis of Dreams*. Appleton-Century-Crofts, New York, 1966

Hearne K. M. T. *The Dream Machine: Lucid Dreams and How to Control Them*. The Aquarian Press, Wellingborough Northamptonshire, 1990

LaBerge, S. *Lucid Dreaming*. Ballantine, New York, 1985

Piaget, J. *The Child's Conception of the World*. Harcourt, Brace & Co, New York, 1926.

Springer, S. P. & Deutsch, G. *Left Brain, Right Brain*. W. H. Freeman & Co, New York, 1981

Van Eeden, F. *A Study of Dreams*. Proceedings of the Society for Psychical Research, 26, 431-461. 1913

Whiteman, J. H. M. *The Mystical Life*. Faber & Faber, London, 1961.